MW01253168

CANADIAN TELEVISION POLICY AND THE

BOARD OF BROADCAST GOVERNORS, 1958–1968

The Board of Broadcast Governors with Hon. George Nowlan, at its inaugural meeting in Ottawa, November, 1958. From left to right, front row: Irene J. Gilbridge, Roger Duhamel, Vice-Chairman, Dr. Andrew Stewart, Chairman, Carlyle Allison, Dr. Mabel G. Connell; back row: Ivan Sabourin, Lieut.-Colonel J. David Stewart, Edward A. Dunlop, Hon. George Nowlan, Minister of National Revenue, Robert S. Furlong, Dr. Eugene Forsey, Guy Hudon, Joseph F. Brown, Dr. Emlyn Davies, and Roy Duchemin. Missing from the picture is Colin B. Mackay. *Photograph courtesy of the City of Ottawa Archives, Andrews-Newton Collection, 60832 #1*

CANADIAN TELEVISION POLICY

AND THE BOARD OF

BROADCAST GOVERNORS,

1958–1968

Andrew Stewart
William H.N. Hull

The University of Alberta Press

First published by
The University of Alberta Press
Athabasca Hall
Edmonton, Alberta, Canada T6G 2E8

Copyright © The University of Alberta Press 1994

ISBN 0–88864–256–3

Canadian Cataloguing in Publication Data

Stewart, Andrew, 1904–1990.

　　　Canadian television policy and the Board of Broadcast Governors,
1958–1968

　　　Includes bibliographical references and index.
　　　ISBN 0–88864–256–3

　　　1. Television broadcasting policy—Canada—History. 2. Canada. Board of
Broadcast Governors. I. Hull, William H.N. (William Henry Nelles), 1929　II. Title.
HE8700.9.C2S84 1994　　384.55'4'0971　　C93–091823–1

Printed on acid-free paper. ∞
Printed and bound in Canada by Quality Color Press Inc.,
Edmonton, Alberta, Canada.

The University of Alberta Press acknowledges the Alberta Foundation for the Arts, a
beneficiary of the Lottery Fund of the Government of Alberta, for their financial support in the publication of this book.

COMMITTED TO THE DEVELOPMENT OF CULTURE AND THE ARTS

IN MEMORIAM

Andrew Stewart
1904–1990

CONTENTS

Preface   ix
Acknowledgements   xii

I   THE BEGINNINGS

1   The Evolution of Canadian Television Policy   3
2   The Board of Broadcast Governors: Constitution
     and Functions   9

II   POLICY ISSUES

3   Canadian Content   29
4   The Initial Second Station Applications   45
5   The Toronto Station and Involvement of ABC   67
6   The CTV Network   75
7   The Grey Cup Game, 1962   101
8   Alternative Television Service and the Conservative
     Government   121
9   Alternative Television Service and the Liberal
     Government   147
10   Educational Television   175
11   Technology and Television Service   193
12   Channel 3 Barrie and the Toronto Market   203

III THE END RESULTS

13 The Board as a Regulatory Body: A Case Study 217
14 "Capture Theory" and the Board's Effectiveness 259
15 The Board of Broadcast Governors: An Assessment 273

Epilogue 293
Appendices 305
Notes 319
Bibliography 347
Index 351

PREFACE

IN THE SUMMERS OF 1962 AND 1964, I did contract research for the Board of Broadcast Governors (BBG) and came to know its Chairman, Dr. Andrew Stewart, many of its members and staff and, most particularly, a number of its problems. In the late 1970s, I learned of a manuscript written by Dr. Stewart about his experiences as the Board's Chairman for all but a few weeks of its life. The manuscript had been put aside when he and his wife, Jessie, proceeded to Africa with Canadian Executive Services Overseas. Eventually when I inquired about the future of the manuscript, Dr. Stewart graciously agreed to allow me to edit it for possible publication. Through an extended gestation period, the editing and revisions have unfolded in the midst of family death, the theft of an early draft, major alterations as the result of suggestions made by kind associates and finally, Dr. Stewart's own death in 1990.

Aside from the sterling histories of Frank Peers, the memoirs of Austin Weir and the provocative critique of Marc Raboy,[1] little in-depth academic work has been written about the life and times of the Board and its role in the development of public policy, especially that related to the expansion of television during the period 1958–1968.

Canadian Television Policy and the Board of Broadcast Governors, 1958–1968 follows the ebb and flow of the period—to witness the enhancement of the private sector of Canadian broadcasting, the diminution of the Canadian Broadcasting Corporation (CBC) and its difficulties in adapting to its reduced role in the broadcasting scene, the differing interpretations of ambiguous public policy, the notable gaps in that policy and the apparent inability or unwillingness of governments to clarify the situation.

Dr. Stewart's memoir provides an opportunity to be "present at the beginning" of a new Canadian television network. The creation of the new network marked a change in a major aspect of public policy and coupled with the technological developments of the period necessitated a reformulation of almost all aspects of broadcasting policy in Canada. Remarkably, governments initially seemed unwilling to accept the need or responsibility for consequential changes in public policy and finance.

Originally, my role was to provide an historical and theoretical context for Dr. Stewart's manuscript. I have in effect created, based on Dr. Setwart's memoir, a case study by which to test some of the hypotheses which have been developed about the workings of regulatory agencies in the Canadian context. The prime source of these hypotheses is the book *The Regulatory Process in Canada,* edited by G. Bruce Doern, and including contributions by Gilles Paquet, Andrew Roman, Michael Trebilcock, Richard Schultz, Caroline Andrew, Rejean Pelletier, Hudson Janisch and Peter Aucoin.[2] My analysis tests the performance of the BBG as a regulatory agency, while also measuring theory against practice in the development and application of television policy in Canadian broadcasting.

In the past two decades, a wealth of analysis and theorizing about public corporations and regulatory agencies has appeared in monographs, in royal commission research studies and in articles in learned journals. Many of these works are at odds with each other—even on such basic matters as definitions—yet arising out of this vast array are identifiable patterns related to regulatory agencies. In simplest form, these can be distilled down to four major areas: the purpose for their creation, the functions assigned to them, the tools at their disposal for the carrying out of their functions and, finally, their relationship to the government of the day and the public policy-making process.

Eschewing the thirteen definitions of a regulatory agency provided to the Royal Commission on the Economic Union and Development

Prospects for Canada,[3] reference is made to the relatively simple and straightforward definition provided by Lloyd Brown-John. A regulatory agency is:

> a statutory body charged with responsibility to administer, to fix, to establish, to control, or to regulate an economic activity or market by regularized and established means in the public interest and in accordance with government policy.[4]

Most regulatory agencies seem to have been set up to remove the object of the regulation from the direct impact of the partisan political process and/or to attract to the area concerned experts capable of dealing with the technologies concerned but beyond the interest or competence of the average politician.

The concept of regulation in itself is not necessarily a singular function and should be recognized as having at least three functions contained within it, those of policing, of promoting and of planning. As applied to broadcasting, the policing function could be seen as negative and reactive, precluding actors from doing certain things or heading in certain directions, for example limitations on foreign ownership or on the affiliation of Canadian stations with foreign networks. The promoting and planning aspects of regulation would presuppose a set of objectives for the system and entail more positive initiatives such as the second television network and the extension of service (promoting) or the regulation of Canadian content in the national interest (planning). The regulatory function often thought of as negative and proscriptive can now be seen as positive and prescriptive as well.[5]

Agencies function with specific tools at their disposal such as licensing, rates setting and standards setting. These tools or instruments permit the agency to control entry into the regulated area, to control pricing policies therein and to oversee the level of performance within the area.

If the establishment of the regulatory agency is designed in part to remove the area in question from partisan political pressures, how much authority or control can the executive branch of government retain over the operation of the agency and of the policy process surrounding it? As the parliamentary system requires responsibility of ministers to Parliament for their actions, how "independent" can the regulatory agency be in policy matters? And to whom is it accountable? Should the agency be regarded as merely the administrator of policy made elsewhere or should it be perceived as part of the policy-making process? What should be its relationship with the crown corporation operating in the regulated field?

All of these issues of purpose, functions, tools and independence in policy-making are considered in the work that follows, implicitly often in Dr. Stewart's portion thereof, more explicitly when the principles drawn from the Doern framework are considered in detail.

The bulk of the text was written by Andrew Stewart after his retirement from the Chairmanship of the BBG. The ten-year period which he spent in this office provided an ideal opportunity to observe the formulation of broadcasting policy in Canada, the implementation of the 1958 Broadcasting Act and the interrelationship amongst the various actors involved. The manuscript was, however, originally framed in a relatively impersonal tone. The passage of time since the late 1960s induced Dr. Stewart to add some more personal reflections to the manuscript. For the record, selected data about the BBG, its staff and the broadcasting industry during the period from 1958 to 1968 have been included as appendices.

The first chapter sets the framework for the study. Chapters 2 to 12, those which describe the formation and functioning of the BBG and its grappling with several specific policy issues, have been drawn largely from Dr. Stewart's original manuscript. Chapter 13, the analysis of the Board's activities measured against regulatory theory, was written by myself as was the first part of Chapter 14 in which the Bernstein "capture" theory is tested against the Board's activities. The second part of Chapter 14, the reaction to the comments of the Committee on Broadcasting, 1965 (the Fowler Committee) was written by Dr. Stewart while authorship of Chapter 15 was shared. Material cited from Cabinet documents and the Ouimet, Pearson and Spry papers was added on my own initiative after Dr. Stewart's death.

ACKNOWLEDGMENTS

CLEARLY THE GREATEST DEBT arising out of this manuscript is owed to Dr. Stewart himself for his foresight in writing the original, for his courage in allowing an erstwhile academic to edit and expand it and for his patience in wading through and adding to several revisions. For her warm encouragement and support through these many phases, Mrs. Stewart deserves deepest appreciation as well.

Many people assisted me immeasurably in the researching and development of the manuscript. The invaluable assistance of the staffs of the Brock University Library, the Manuscript Division of the National Archives and of the Library, the Legal Division and the Secretariat of the Canadian Radio-television and Telecommunication Commission is happily acknowledged. For service beyond the call of duty in reading and commenting generously upon the manuscript, thanks go to Rick Davidson, Professor J.E. Hodgetts, W.D. Mills, the late Alphonse Ouimet and the two University of Alberta Press reviewers. I am indeed grateful to Geoffrey Pearson for granting access to his father's papers and to Irene Spry for granting access to those of her husband, Graham.

The research and writing would have been for naught were it not for the tireless efforts of those who magically turned illegible manuscript into glorious typescript. To Amanda Hayne, Elaine Ross, Joan

Garnett and Jenny Gurski and the staff of Brock's Clerical Services, I am particularly grateful. The index could not have been completed without the invaluable assistance of Professor Barry Joe

Singled out for special praise must be my editor, Mary Mahoney-Robson of the University of Alberta Press, who provided expert assistance with the text, inspiration when the spirit flagged and forbearance when yet another delay loomed. Carl Wolff also has earned my gratitude for intellectual stimulation and for providing a quiet, comfortable place to work when my pack rat tendencies drove me out of my office and my study. Barb Magee was of incalculable assistance in too many ways to list. Finally, to my wife, Mary Ann and our children, Martha, Chris and Derek go heartfelt thanks for support and understanding. A challenging task was made less difficult because of them.

To this superb support system goes the praise for the virtues of the book. I must, of course, accept responsibility for its shortcomings.

I

THE BEGINNINGS

[1]

THE EVOLUTION OF
CANADIAN TELEVISION POLICY

THE YEARS 1958–1968 WERE watershed years in the development of Canadian broadcasting. The single system of broadcasting in which the publicly-owned Canadian Broadcasting Corporation (CBC) played the leading role was being seriously challenged by the growing economic and political power of the owners of the private broadcasting stations. Changing technology—colour and cable television for instance—was seeking a place in the system. Nationalists were demanding greater protection of Canadian culture against a perceived onslaught of American programming. Public demands were becoming more persistent for the extension of primary service to those regions of the country still without television and in the areas already served by the Liberal's single station policy for the provision of alternative channels. Some Canadians may have wanted to preserve the so-called "single system," but few favoured access to only a single channel. During the decade, these forces met head on and became the prime preoccupations of the Board of Broadcast Governors (BBG).

The Progressive Conservative party came to office in 1957 after 22 years in opposition. Even though fundamental policy decisions had been made by the previous Conservative regime under the Right Honourable R.B. Bennett (1930–35), the vast majority of broadcasting policy in place in 1957 had been the product of the King and St. Laurent Liberal Governments between 1935 and 1957.

The system which the Conservatives inherited had at its core the basic principle of public service broadcasting which could be traced back to the decision of the Bennett Government to accept the recommendations of the 1929 Royal Commission on Radio Broadcasting (the Aird Commission) for the introduction of public service broadcasting in Canada. This prompted the creation of the Canadian Radio Broadcasting Commission (CRBC) in 1932 and its successor the CBC, created by the King Government in 1936. Public service broadcasting implied a publicly-owned system of broadcasting mandated to provide high quality programs to satisfy a wide range of tastes in all regions of the country without slavish adherence to ratings figures.

Tempering the principle of public service broadcasting were the privately-owned, advertising-supported radio stations. Contrary to the Aird Commission's recommendations, but due to the financial exigencies of the Great Depression, these stations were allowed by the Conservatives to continue to function even if under the threat of expropriation. This threat was removed by the Liberals in 1938 when the private stations were guaranteed their place in the sun as the local segment of a single national system regulated and dominated by the CBC.[1]

Central to the system inherited by the Conservatives in 1957 was the dominant role of the CBC. Clearly the public corporation as established in 1936 was to be the prime force in Canadian broadcasting as the sole operator of the high-power transmitters and of national radio networks and as the regulator of all aspects of the system including the privately-owned stations. These stations were envisaged as playing a local role supplementary to the national role of the CBC stations—local outlets carrying the CBC program service to those parts of the country in which the CBC did not have "owned and operated" (O & O) stations. The private stations were tied to the CBC individually by affiliation agreements and collectively by the regulations which the CBC Board of Governors enunciated for the whole system. In those days, it was considered inappropriate to talk of the public and private stations as being in competition with each other. Their roles were seen not as competitive but as complementary in a single system in which the CBC was the driving force.

While not yet explicitly enunciated in legislation, another evident feature of the system was the element of motivation. The Aird Commission had claimed to discover that Canadians wanted Canadian radio broadcasting.[2] The creation of the CRBC in 1932 and then the CBC in 1936 was clearly designed to meet this desire in two respects—by joining Canadians from sea to sea through electronic bands as the Canadian Pacific Railway had joined them with bands of steel and by providing quality Canadian programming to all parts of the country, thereby filling a void or providing an alternative to the ever-present American offering.

This unique Canadian "single system" of broadcasting flourished from the thirties, through the wartime period and well into the post-war era. In the post-war years, however, the owners of the private stations started to flex their political muscle seeking a larger place in the scheme of things. The economic prosperity of the forties and fifties made them restive in the minor role into which they had been cast. The days of the "single system," of the "partnership" between public and private elements, were clearly numbered.

The defenders of Liberal policy through the forties and fifties consistently reinforced the "single system" concept and the necessity of maintaining the dominant position of the CBC. Several parliamentary committees and two Royal Commissions repeated and reinforced the orthodox incantations for radio and later television. The Royal Commission on National Development in the Arts, Letters and Sciences (the Massey Commission) in 1951 and the Royal Commission on Broadcasting (the Fowler Commission) in 1957 were particularly florid in their praise of the CBC and vituperative in their condemnation of the private broadcasters, primarily for their failure to make a meaningful contribution to the development of Canadian programming. In each report, the broadcasters were accused of neglecting their responsibility to develop Canadian talent and to assist in the process of Canadians saying something to one another. In spite of this, the private stations, under the umbrella of their industry association, the Canadian Association of Broadcasters (CAB)[3] began to make an impact on the federal Progressive Conservatives. As early as 1948, Conservative spokesmen—especially Mr. Donald Fleming, MP for

Toronto-Eglinton—were espousing the CAB claims of unfair treatment of its members by the Board of Governors of the CBC who, it was claimed, acted as both judge and jury in cases involving the private stations. The CAB claimed that the CBC Board regulated the system in the interests of the CBC and in effect denied the private stations natural justice. The only solution to the perceived iniquities, according to the CAB, was to strip the CBC of its regulatory powers and to create a new separate regulatory agency which would regulate both elements of the system in the public interest, not just in the interest of the public sector. Interestingly, the Fowler Commission, noting that the CAB had not been able to substantiate its claims with concrete examples of iniquitous treatment, rejected completely the concept of a separate regulatory agency yet recommended the creation of a new body to be called the Board of Broadcast Governors (BBG). This new body would not be involved in day-to-day CBC management, but would, acting on Parliament's behalf, receive regular reports from CBC management and would regulate both sectors of the system in the public interest. The Commission denied the CAB's major claim for policy change, restated the dominant position of the CBC and yet opened the doors to change by recommending the creation of the BBG which, while still presiding over a one-board system, would no longer be identified in name with the CBC and would perform a regulatory function while remaining at arm's length from the CBC's day-to-day affairs.

The election of June 1957 brought the Progressive Conservatives to power pledged to change the structure of broadcasting in Canada— and change they did—if not as radically as some might have hoped. Contrary to the wishes of some Conservative activists, the CBC was not privatized. The separate regulatory agency, however, was instituted, creating for the first time in Canadian broadcasting the two-board system and setting the stage for some of the difficulty Fowler had anticipated in recommending against such an arrangement. Regrettably, the new Board was named the Board of Broadcast Governors. The use of this name allowed some—even the Minister who piloted the legislation through the House—to argue that the recommendations of the Fowler Commission had been carried out. The name may have been Fowler's, but the spirit of the 1958 Act which created the separate regulatory agency was not. In Fowler's eyes, Canada had "a single system in which both public and private stations [were] all integral parts and which [was to be] regulated and controlled by a single public board, representing the public interest and responsible to Parliament."4

The creation of the separate regulatory agency by the new government should have come as a surprise to no one. The Conservative commitment had been a long standing one. What did come as a surprise to some were the problems that accompanied the creation of the separate agency. What was to be the appropriate relationship between the government and agency? Between the agency and the CBC? Between the agency and private stations? What role should the agency play in matters involving public policy formulation and federal-provincial relations involving subjects such as cable television and educational broadcasting? Many of these questions were to be answered only through the slow and sometimes difficult process of trial and error. Others remained unanswered throughout the period 1958–68.

The Board members (from left to right): Ivan Sabourin, part-time member, Quebec, Andrew Stewart, Chairman, Carlyle Allison, Vice-Chairman, and Joseph F. Brown, part-time member, British Columbia. *Photograph courtesy of Mrs. Andrew Stewart.*

[2]

THE BOARD OF
BROADCAST GOVERNORS:
CONSTITUTION AND FUNCTIONS

MEMBERSHIP: PERSONNEL AND PROCESSES

The Broadcasting Act, 1958, provided for establishment of the Board of Broadcast Governors, to have three full-time members—chairman, vice-chairman, and a third member—who would hold office for seven years, and twelve part-time members, all to be appointed by the Governor-in-Council to serve for a term of five years. Names of the members of the BBG were announced on Monday, 10 November 1958 by the Hon. George Nowlan, Minister of National Revenue and minister responsible for broadcasting.[1]

In mid-October 1958, Mr. Nowlan asked Dr. Andrew Stewart, then President of the University of Alberta, if he would be interested in the position of Chairman of the BBG. The suggestion was totally unexpected. Dr. Stewart knew that the newly-elected Conservative Government had brought down legislation on broadcasting, and that it favoured a policy of divorcing the supervision and regulation of broadcasting from the operation of the Canadian Broadcasting Corporation. Otherwise, he was relatively unfamiliar with the broadcasting scene. To the day of his death, he had no knowledge of the process by which his name was selected.

Dr. Stewart told Mr. Nowlan that he would be prepared to consider a change. On Friday, 24 October, Mr. Nowlan called again. The

Cabinet wished to offer Dr. Stewart the position. An answer was expected by 27 October. Before the 27th, Dr. Stewart discussed the matter with G.R.A. Rice of CFRN, Edmonton, who had been a member of the Senate of the University of Alberta, and the Hon. Sidney Smith, Secretary of State for External Affairs, who was in Edmonton to deliver the Henry Marshall Tory Lecture at the University. On the 27th, a telegram went to Mr. Nowlan accepting the Cabinet's offer.

The Chairman-designate had over the years been given appointments by different parties: Social Credit (Alberta Commission on Natural Gas), Liberal (Royal Commission on Canada's Economic Prospects) and Conservative (Royal Commission on Price Spreads for Food Products); political impartiality appeared to be one of the reasons for his appointment. That Dr. Stewart performed consistently with this expectation seemed evident from his colleague Carlyle Allison's description of him as a "political eunuch."[2]

Appointed as the Vice-chairman of the BBG, Roger Duhamel had been chief editor of *La Patrie*. He never became deeply involved in the activities of the Board and resigned on 12 July 1960 to become Queen's Printer.

The third full-time member, Carlyle Allison, was a native of Winnipeg and a graduate of the University of Manitoba. Upon graduation he began his newspaper career as a reporter with the Winnipeg *Tribune*. Apart from the period between 1928 and 1935 when he was attached to the Saskatoon *Star-Phoenix*, and a brief period with the Montreal *Gazette*, his life had been spent with the *Tribune*; in 1958 he had completed twelve years as editor-in-chief. The *Tribune* supported the Conservative party, and Allison's loyalty to Mr. Diefenbaker was well known. After Duhamel's resignation, Allison was appointed Vice-chairman of the BBG, effective 1 January 1961. His appointment expired 9 November 1965. The Liberal government did not reappoint him and he returned to Winnipeg to direct public affairs programs on the private television station CJAY-TV.

The failure of the Liberal government to reappoint Allison might have been expected. As editor of the *Tribune* he had attacked ministers who had to make the decision on his reappointment. When the Chairman discussed with Mr. Pickersgill the extension of Allison's appointment, the latter said it was a difficult request for him to accede to, as no one had done more than Allison to try to destroy Pickergill's career. Although understandable, Allison's claim to the position of Vice-chairman when Duhamel resigned was a mistake. It was not forgotten by the French-Canadian members of the Board. There was, however, no justification for the manner in which his services were terminated by the Pearson government.

As the end of his term approached, Allison and others sought the views of the Government on his reappointment. Most, but not all, of his colleagues supported a resolution recommending that he be reappointed, at least until the new legislation was brought down. On 18 October 1965 the Chairman had written the Prime Minister on the matter, referring to the announcement that the Chairman of the BBG and the President of the CBC had been reappointed for seven year terms, but noting the absence of any reference to Allison. The letter mentioned the expectation that, upon passage of the new legislation, the Broadcasting Act, 1958, would be rescinded, and expressed the hope that it would be possible to announce Allison's reappointment under the Broadcasting Act. The Chairman's letter to the Prime Minister of 15 November read:

I am sorry the Cabinet decided not to extend Mr. Allison's term on the Board; and I must express my profound regret at the manner in which his case was dealt with. As you know, Mr. Allison was advised that he would not be re-appointed on the day after his term expired. It seems inhuman to put anyone through this experience; and I cannot see how this kind of treatment can help in the problem of getting good people to enter the public service. I wish to record my appreciation of the valuable service which Mr. Allison gave to the Board of Broadcast Governors.

The Prime Minister's reply said that when the decision had been made the then Secretary of State Maurice Lamontagne had, through a misunderstanding, failed to advise Allison immediately.[3]

At the same time that Mr. Allison was made Vice-chairman, Bernard "Barney" Goulet, a former journalist and entertainment entrepreneur, was appointed as the third full-time member. He died, following an operation, on 1 December 1964. Barney Goulet's experience in the broadcasting industry was useful to the Board, and he was well liked by everyone.

From December 1964 to November 1965 there were only two full-time members, and from November 1965 to February 1966 Dr. Stewart was the only full-time member. On 7 February 1966, the appointments of Pierre Juneau, who held a senior position in the National Film Board, as Vice-chairman and David Sim, a retired civil servant, as the third full-time member were announced. The appointment of David Sim was clearly designed to bridge the gap until the new legislation would be passed and the new regulatory body named. Recognizing the imminence of the proclamation of the Broadcasting Act, 1968, Dave Sim tendered his resignation effective 29 February 1968. By agreement with the Prime Minister, Dr. Stewart's resignation became effective on 18 March 1968.[4] On the same day, Pierre Juneau became the Chairman of the BBG, and ultimately, Chairman of the new CRTC.

During its lifetime, the BBG had 31 part-time members. The original members were appointees of the Conservative government. By early 1968, all members had been appointed by the Liberal government, although two of the Conservative appointees, Claude Gagnon from Quebec and Joe Brown from British Columbia, had been reappointed—a fact attributable to their personal qualities.

No member worked harder than Joe Brown to become knowledgeable about broadcasting in his region, and to bring informed judgement to bear on decisions. He knew and was respected by all the broadcasters in British Columbia, and gave generously of his time in meeting with them. This helped to overcome the feeling of remoteness and isolation so frequently felt by people on the Pacific coast. A number of trying situations developed in British Columbia, placing Joe Brown under considerable pressure and tension and encroaching to an almost intolerable extent on his time. When he was satisfied the proper course of action was clear, or after the Board had come to a decision, he did not waiver in his position.

Claude Gagnon's contribution was of a different kind. He gave less time, outside of the regular business of the Board, to the problems of broadcasting in his area; but, in the consideration of cases before the Board, there was no one whose judgement was listened to with more respect. He shared with Jack Coyne the advantages of legal training and experience, and the ability to distinguish between the relevant and the irrelevant; and in his case justice was properly tempered with mercy. In December 1963, when the terms of the original appointees expired, seven members were appointed by the Liberal government. It was not until January 1966, however, that a firm majority of Liberal appointees was reached.

The Conservatives appointed 17 part-time members, the Liberals 14. Geographic distribution was maintained. Except for the Liberal failure to represent Saskatchewan, there was always at least one member from each province, with additional members from Ontario and Quebec. Vocational distribution was similar for Conservative and Liberal appointees with the largest group, in each case, drawn from business. The Conservatives seemed to prefer lawyers; the Liberals businessmen. Only the Conservative group included individuals who might be said to represent labour.[5]

The Royal Commission on Broadcasting, 1957 defended the concept of a "representative" board. The only way in which it was clear that the BBG reflected public opinion generally was that it was often divided. Having in mind the experiences and attitudes of the members, there was no reason to believe that the Board constituted a cross section of public opinion. Nor was there any reason to believe that they would, or did, act as Parliament would have done. Conformity to public opinion requires a disposition to seek to discover public opinion—not the opinion of some of the public—and to subordinate personal prejudices to it. This attitude was not necessarily found in an appointed group of 15 persons, or even in a larger group. Nor was there any guarantee that, without review by Parliament, an appointed group would consistently act as Parliament would act.

Although not applying to all, the dominant characteristics of the part-time members was their political affiliation. In two of the licensing cases, it was publicly charged that the Board's decision had been affected by political considerations. The first was the recommendation that the second television station licence in Toronto be granted to

Baton, Aldred, Rogers. The second was the granting of the CKVR-TV Channel 3 Barrie application. On the basis of the evidence available, it is doubtful if either of the charges could be substantiated. Members of tribunals such as the BBG are not likely to announce either publicly or privately that decisions have been influenced by political considerations.[6]

A number of the part-time members were, in their daily lives, actively involved in partisan political activities, and some clearly looked for some personal gain from this. In dealing with cases which involve a strong party element, it must have been extraordinarily difficult to resist partisan pressures or to be totally uninfluenced by them.

The process of appointment to the Board should have inspired confidence not only in the capacity of the members, but also in their disposition to seek objectivity and impartiality in carrying out the intentions of the legislation. The Chairman had no intimate knowledge of how appointments were made to the BBG. He was not consulted; nor was there any good reason why he should have been. Whatever the method was, it was not a good one. It failed to create the necessary public confidence, mainly because of the extent of the known political associations of most of the appointees. The original Board was heavily weighted with known supporters of the Conservative Government; the Board as constituted in 1968 was weighted with adherents of the Liberal Party. It would be unnecessary and inadvisable to restrict appointments to those without political associations, but the practice of loading Boards with the supporters of one political party can only bring administrative tribunals and administrative law into disrepute. There must be some better way of appointing persons to quasi-judicial national agencies.[7]

STRUCTURE AND FUNCTIONS

There were three periods in the life and activities of the BBG. The first, and by far the most productive, extended from the appointment of the members of the Board on 10 November 1958 to the federal election of 8 April 1963, when there was a change of government.

During this period, alternative television stations were established in the major cities and the private network was brought into operation. The regulations governing television were substantially revised, and conditions were formulated for the formation and operation of networks. This could be termed the period of expansion. The second period, the period of consolidation, ended with the publication of the White Paper on Broadcasting in mid-1966. Throughout this period, broadcasting policy was under continuous review. The discussions held amongst the Chairman and the Presidents of the CBC and the CAB (the group known as the "Troika") were followed by the inquiries of the Committee on Broadcasting 1965 (the Fowler Committee), and the preparation of the White Paper in the Department of the Secretary of State. This was a period of uncertainty and frustration, during which the activities of the Board declined. The White Paper and Bill C-163 were subjected to prolonged consideration in committees, and policy on some important matters remained obscure. It was apparent during this period, however, that the functions of the regulatory body would be significantly changed. In the third period, the denouement, from July 1966 to March 1968, the BBG was involved in preparation for the new dispensation.

The organization consisted of five branches—Secretary, Legal, Technical, Economics and Programs—each in charge of a senior officer. The Secretary to the Board occupied a central position in the organization. Such coordination of staff operations as occurred was undertaken by him. He was responsible for the calling of meetings, the maintenance of records and the processing of announcements. Counsel for the Board was responsible for the conduct of the public hearings and the examination of witnesses and thus, in an important way, for the relations between the Board and the broadcasters. As well, he drafted the regulations and watched over their observance. The Technical Advisor's role was principally one of interpreting technical matters to the Board. He advised the Board on the technical features of the applications, and of new technology such as colour television, cable distribution and space satellites. He maintained liaison with the Department of Transport. The Research Director-Programs was responsible for the categories of programs and the Canadian content regulations. The Research Director-Economics was concerned with market analysis and projections, and with the financial position of licensees.

In addition to these senior officers, the establishment in 1961 included: an assistant secretary and an administrative officer, two continuity clearance clerks, one central registry clerk, four log examiners, nine secretaries and stenographers, four clerks and one messenger. Entitlement to another six positions had been procured bringing the total staff establishment to 32. Five years later, the organization was essentially the same. Assistants had been provided to Counsel, Research Director-Economics and Research Director-Programs, and there were additional log examiners. The total number of staff establishment was 39.[8] By 31 March 1968, the staff complement had reached 120 persons.

Procedures required by the Civil Service Commission occasioned incredible delays, first in appointing senior officers and later in making replacements. However, by 1960 the organizational establishment and the budget of the BBG were set.

The Board's financial position was reflective as well of the three periods. In the fiscal year 1960–61, total expenditures of the Board (not including rental of space paid through Public Works) were roughly $280,000. The principal items were salaries, amounting to $181,000, and allowances and travel—$62,500, covering the $100 per diem allowance and the expenses of the part-time members. In the fiscal year 1965–66, the estimates of the Board were $493,000; of this amount $382,000 was actually spent.

After 1966, the period of preparation for the new dispensation, there were sharp increases in the budget and in expenditures. Funds authorized for the Board in 1966–67 totalled $814,000, with substantial increases for salaries, professional services and data processing. The amount provided in the 1967–68 estimates was $1,265,800, and a submission made in mid-1967 projected expenditures of $2,036,300 for 1968–69. The program review on which the submission for 1968–69 was based stressed that broadcasting was an expanding sector of the economy, with a normal expected increase of 40 to 50 stations a year. Licence fees paid by broadcasting stations had increased from $1 million in 1962 to $2.1 million in 1966-67, and further increases at the rate of $300,000 a year could be anticipated. The review outlined the additional functions to be expected under the new Act. These included the broadcasting of general licensing functions and the licensing and regulation of cable systems, both tasks previously performed by the Department of Transport. Additional planned functions included the development of educational television. A staff increase of about 60 was anticipated. Throughout the submission, emphasis was placed on an increased flow of information to the Commission and on more extended analyses of the information secured.[9]

The main activities of the BBG were related to licensing of radio and television stations and to the formulation of regulations related to the stations' operations. From time to time amendments to the regulations were introduced, and the work of administering the regulations was continuous. However, the procedures for dealing with licence applications and with changes in the conditions of licences established the normal rhythm of activities.

The Board announced the dates, approximately two months apart, at which it would hold public hearings. The Department of Transport then advised consultants of the dates by which applications should be filed. The interval of time between the filing of applications and the Board's hearings was sufficient to allow for the applications to be reviewed by the Department and considered by the Board. At a meeting of the review committee of the Department, which was attended by officers of the Board, the Board was officially informed of the applications which might be heard at the next public hearing. The review committee considered the reports on the technical aspects of applications, and forwarded to the Board those that were found technically acceptable. As the cleared applications were received, the process of distribution and study within the Board began. The Board's procedural regulations required that the announcement of applications be included in the agenda at least 20 days in advance of the opening of the hearings. Applications, once received by the Board, were distributed for study. The Secretariat began the preparation of a "blue book"—a summary of the information contained in each application; this "blue book" was sent to the part-time members in time for them to study it before they left to attend the meetings.

In the normal pattern of meetings, the Board began on Monday with an *in-camera* session at which each application was reviewed and Counsel received direction on examination of witnesses. The public hearings opened on Tuesday morning, and normally extended into Thursday. As soon as the hearings were completed, the Board began *in-camera* meetings to deal with the applications and with other matters on the agenda. It was usually late Friday afternoon before the part-time members left for home. During the period of expansion, meetings of the Board were frequent and longer than in subsequent periods; evening meetings became almost a habit. Under the reduced pressure of the consolidation period, it was possible to escape evening meetings, which had often proved to be trying.

After the part-time members left for home, the full-time members and the Secretary prepared the announcements, incorporating the decisions of the Board, and followed up on other matters which had been dealt with by the Board. The Secretary arranged for translation and printing of the announcements, which took some days. The announcement was usually released within a week to ten days after the completion of the hearings. It was delivered by hand to the offices of the Cabinet Ministers and, as soon as this was done, to the Press Gallery. An effort was made, sometimes unsuccessfully, to prevent any leak of information before the announcement had been delivered to the Minister. After a gap of two or three weeks the cycle started again.

Under Section 12 of the Broadcasting Act, the Board received for public hearing and recommendation to the Minister of Transport all technically acceptable applications for new broadcasting stations, including rebroadcasting stations, and for changes in facilities—mainly changes in power. These were not, however, the only applications on the agenda for public hearings. Under the general regulations pursuant to the Radio Act administered by the Department of Transport, applications for transfers of shares in licensed broadcasting companies were referred to the Board for a recommendation before being authorized by the Minister of Transport. Recommendations on transfers were made after consideration by the full Board. The Board, however, decided that all transfers which resulted in a change of ownership or control should be dealt with at a public hearing.

Other items appearing from time to time on the agenda of public hearings included, as required by the Broadcasting Act, applications to form networks or to disaffiliate from networks of the CBC. Public hearings of proposed amendments to the regulations of the Board were also mandatory. Applications for renewal of licences which expired on 31 March were judged to be applications for new licences, and at the public hearing preceding 31 March of each year the Board listed applications for renewal. Some licensees were called to the hearings. On its own volition, the Board placed on the agenda applications under Section 6(6) of the Radio (TV) Regulations. These were applications respecting educational programs. When colour television was introduced, the Board's approval was required, but the authority to approve was delegated to the full-time members. Reports were made to the full Board. When the Minister of Transport decided to seek advice from the Board on applications for CATV systems, the applications were discussed in the full Board. In addition to the regular meetings of the Board connected with public hearings, occasional special meetings were held to deal with urgent matters.

The Broadcasting Act made provision for an Executive Committee of the Board. This Committee met frequently during the first period; less frequently later. In 1959, the Board established two major committees—the Consultative Committee on Public Broadcasting, a joint committee with the CBC; and the Consultative Committee on Private Broadcasting, a joint committee with the CAB. There was also a joint committee with advertisers. The committees were particularly active in the first period.[10]

THE RECORD

The Board began its review of the existing regulations almost immediately, and public hearings on radio regulations were held in May

1959. On 18 July Mr. Nowlan, on behalf of the Government, declared himself on the introduction of a second television network[11] and the dates of hearing on applications were announced on 28 July 1959.[12] At the same time, the Board announced certain "basic principles" which it proposed to apply to television after second stations were licensed.[13] Public representations on the principles were heard in November 1959; in order to give applicants for licences an opportunity to prepare their submissions with a knowledge of the rules of the game, the Board announced its television regulations later the same month.[14] The hearings on applications followed. By June 1960 recommendations had been made for second television licences in the major cities. Interest in the formation of a network led to hearings on television network regulations in September 1960. The application by Spencer Caldwell to operate CTV Network was heard in April 1961.

However the decisions of the Board may be judged, the work completed in the first two years represented a considerable achievement. The increase in meetings of the Executive Committees after March 1961—and in those of the Consultative Committees—was related to the Board's concern with the problems of the private television stations and network, with the relations between private and public broadcasting and with the relations between the BBG and the CBC.

The decline in the number of applications for new (originating) television stations reflected the completion of the initial applications for second stations, and the slow progression of alternative service. There was, however, an increase in applications for television rebroadcasting stations and this resulted in an expansion of television coverage. There was some increase in activity in FM radio. The increase in applications for radio AM rebroadcasting stations reflected, in the main, the extension of CBC coverage to remote areas by low-power relay stations. The decline in applications for new AM radio stations was partly due to a more restrictive policy on the part of the Board.[15]

On 8 April 1963 the Government changed. The new Government was not committed to the BBG, nor to any of its decisions. On 1 May 1963 Mr. Pickersgill announced the setting up of the "Troika"[16] and, for the remainder of the second period, the entire policy for broadcasting was subject to review. The "Troika" was followed by the Committee on Broadcasting, 1965 (the Fowler Committee) and by the drafting and publication of the *White Paper on Broadcasting*. Only after mid-1966 did the shape of the new legislation begin to emerge. During this period, as the number of meetings indicates, the activities of the Board declined. The number of applications remained at about the same level as in the first period. There were few amendments to the regulations; a more cooperative relationship existed between the CBC and the Board, and there was a disposition on both sides to avoid sharp conflicts. Although the Board continued to deal expeditiously with matters coming to its attention, it refrained from initiating changes until public policy and its authority were more clearly defined. The Board had no reason to believe that the process of enacting legislation would take as long as it did. As the composition of the Board changed there was some disposition to undertake a complete review of policies and regulations established by the Board, for example, the Canadian content regulations. The process of a complete review by the Board, however, would not have been welcomed, and the Board intentionally avoided it.

The style of the BBG was set by the Chairman and he accepted responsibility for any defect in its performance. The style was probably best exemplified by the Consultative Committees. In the Consultative Committee on Public Broadcasting, the full-time members of the Board, along with two or three part-time members, met with officers of the CBC to discuss matters of mutual concern; and from time to time the Chairman had private lunches with Alphonse Ouimet, President of the Corporation. Ouimet was a proud man and a fierce defender of the independence and integrity of the CBC. It could be understood how Miss LaMarsh found him difficult. But the Chairman considered her charge of "rotten management" in the CBC unfair to Ouimet.[17] Personal relations with him were always cordial. In the Consultative Committee on Private Broadcasting, the members of the Board met with officers of the CAB. When Don Jamieson became President of the organization, a position he held for some years, he and the Chairman met frequently. Although they did not always agree, they came to respect each other's judgement. The Board also had a Consultative Committee with the advertisers. The style of the Committees was one of consultation and cooperation rather than bullying, a relationship between the regulatory body and the regulated that was really quite unusual.

Early in 1959 the Board suggested to the Directors of the CBC that it wished to maintain liaison with them. A dinner was held at the Chateau Laurier at which members of the Board of Directors and officers of the CBC were present. It turned out to be largely a social affair and in the brief discussion, the suggestion of a liaison committee received a cold shoulder. It was obvious that the CBC directors wished to maintain a position of detachment from the BBG. However, in a memorandum of 16 September 1959 to the members of the Board, the Chairman concluded: "Because of the final authority vested in the Board under the Act, it is recommended that the Board take the initiative in setting up machinery for regular consultation with the CBC and the Canadian Association of Broadcasters." The Board agreed, and on 13 October, letters were sent to the CBC and the President of the CAB.

The letter to Mr. Ouimet quoted Section 10 of the Act and expressed the view that the broad responsibilities conferred on the Board could be most effectively met by establishing Advisory Committees representing different facets of the national broadcasting system.

It is proposed that the Advisory Committee on Public Broadcasting should provide for a flow of information and views between the Corporation and the Board before decisions have to be made by the Board. A number of instances have already occurred, in which the Corporation has, at public hearings, sought approval of the Board for action already considered by the Board of Directors of the Corporation. The Board feels that in dealing with such situations the purpose of the Act can be more efficiently achieved if, prior to the public hearings, the Board has an opportunity to be fully informed on the position of the Corporation, and of the policies of the Corporation which are involved in particular cases.

The CBC did not contest the formation of the Committee, although the name was changed from Advisory Committee to Consultative Committee. The first meeting was held on 15 December 1959; between December 1959 and April 1963 there were sixteen meetings of the Committee.

It was hoped that a number of gains would follow from the discussions in the Consultative Committee. Not the least of these was that the Board would be better informed and therefore more capable of performing its functions. The Committee proved useful in informing the Board, and in assisting it in judging the consequences of proposed courses of action. The Board learned much from the experienced officers of the Corporation and developed a healthy respect for their knowledge of broadcasting.

Although the meetings disclosed, and dealt with, differences both real and apparent in the approaches of the Corporation and the BBG, the discussions always proceeded in a civilized manner; and the Chairman perceived a shared sense of integrity on both sides. Much of the early discussion was concerned with particular views reaching the Board from the private sector. The Board was receiving complaints from affiliates about the terms of affiliation agreements, and from the second television stations and CTV network, about what they claimed to be "unfair competition." These complaints occurred during the period when the private stations and network were incurring substantial losses.

The Board believed that clarification of some CBC policies was needed. Paramount amongst these were its policies respecting the number and location of stations to be licensed to the Corporation, the broad policies under which the CBC "O & O" stations operated in markets also served by private stations, and the broad character of the national package to be distributed by the CBC to private affiliates and contractual arrangements with private stations. The commercial policy of the CBC required clarification. The main concern was to have some policies clearly established and fully known to the Board. The Corporation thought that flexibility was necessary to its independence and that limitations on its flexibility would impair the service.

On 14 February 1962, the Chairman addressed the CBC Board of Directors and referred to four areas in which differences of opinion had become apparent. Conflicting applications for licences by the CBC and private applicants aggravated the conflict between the CBC and private broadcasters. A decision had to be made by the government on additional licences for the CBC. On affiliation agreements and the settlement of differences between CBC affiliates and the Corporation by reference to the Board, the Chairman confessed that he did not see the relationship between the CBC and its affiliates as that normally existing between a private commercial network and its affiliates. It was his view that when a private station accepted a licence subject to a condition that it "operate as part of the network of the Corporation" it accepted a condition that it distribute the national service. Actually, the Chairman favoured an arrangement in which the Corporation would contract, at a price, for the use of specified time on the station of the affiliate. The CBC was asked whether it was possible to spell out the required balance between imported, non-Canadian productions, Canadian commercial productions, and Canadian noncommercial productions and to determine the amount of time required of affiliates. The absence of a clear statement of policy and procedures by the Corporation led the private stations to suspect that public funds were being devoted to making the position of private licensees more difficult, and tensions were heightened. The Chairman was urging less commercial broadcasting on the CBC and in his "Troika" report recommended the eventual elimination of commercial activities by the CBC. Unfortunately, the meeting with the Board of Directors did not seem to help relations between the two boards.

After April 1963, when the position of the private stations and their ability to support the network improved, complaints from private broadcasters became less frequent and some of the sources of friction between the two boards was eased.

Over the eight years from 1959 to 1967, Board decisions had resulted in some significant changes in the structure of the broadcasting system, most notably the initiation of second television stations and the formation of an English-language television network serving private television stations. Television outlets had increased from 74 to

278. The CBC had added to its originating stations, and there were the new private stations unaffiliated with the CBC. The number of affiliated stations remained unchanged, but these stations and the CBC stations had considerably expanded their coverage by the installation of rebroadcasting stations. In 1960, there were 16 rebroadcasting stations carrying the national service. By 1967 the number had increased to 173.

After the publication of the White Paper, the Board became involved in reorganizing its structure and establishment in order to prepare for more substantial responsibilities under new legislation. Considerable activity centred around educational television and the opening up of the UHF band for television broadcasting. The attention of the Board was also directed to the possibilities of satellite distribution. The Board became involved in the deliberations of the Cabinet Committee on Broadcasting and of the committees of the House of Commons and the Senate.

II

POLICY ISSUES

[3]

CANADIAN CONTENT

ON 18 JULY 1959 THE MINISTER, Mr. Nowlan, announced that "As from 15 September 1959, [the Government] will be prepared to consider applications for additional television broadcasting stations in areas already provided with television service."[1] Prior to this announcement the Board had considered, and had discussed with the Minister, the conditions and regulations which would govern television after the introduction of alternative service. On 1 June 1959, subsequent to a preliminary meeting with the Minister in February of the same year, the Board supplied the Minister with a memorandum, "Regulations Governing Television." It proposed that:

> The Canadian content of the programs of any station shall not be less than 55% of the total program content during any week. (a) The Board of Broadcast Governors will provide standards for measuring Canadian content as referred to in this regulation. The standards will be similar to those applied by the Independent Television Authority in the United Kingdom. (b) The Board of Broadcast Governors will prescribe standards for measuring Commonwealth content. In the application of the regulation Commonwealth content will be counted as equivalent to 50% Canadian content.

At the same time the Board advised the Minister of discussions in meetings of the Board with the CBC and with the CAB and concluded that any regulations would be met with a show of opposition by the CAB.

Proposed ground rules were discussed by the Board at its meeting on 9–10 July 1959. On 13 July, the Board again wrote to the Minister stating that the Board had approved the ground rules and inviting the Minister to announce the rules should he wish to do so. He chose not to.

On 28 July 1959 the "basic principles" were announced by the Board in a press release. The announcement indicated that the public hearings for television applications would open in Winnipeg on 11 January 1960.[2] The Board invited submissions on the "basic principles" and public hearings on television regulations were called for 2–3 November 1959. Final television regulations were to be announced by 15 November 1959, in order to give prospective applicants for licences an opportunity to prepare their submissions. The "basic principles" as announced on 28 July 1959 included a provision that the total Canadian content on any station should not be less than 55% of the total program content during any week. The section of the regulation referring to Canadian content—as announced on 15 November 1959, following the public hearings held on 2–3 November—provided that during any four-week period, not less than 55% of the broadcast time of any station or network should be devoted to programs basically Canadian in content and character. Such requirements were to be phased in gradually with no minimum required before 1 April 1961, a 45% requirement up to 31 March 1962 and the full 55% requirement after 1 April 1962.

Programs considered basically Canadian in content and character would include:

(a) any program produced by a licensee
   (i) in his studio, or using his remote facilities; and
   (ii) to be broadcast initially by the licensee;
(b) news broadcasts;
(c) news commentaries;
(d) broadcasts of events occurring outside Canada in which Canadians are participating;

(e) broadcasts of programs featuring special events outside Canada and of general interest to Canadians;

(f) subject to Subsection (5), programs produced outside Canada:

(i) in Commonwealth countries, or

(ii) in French-language countries; and

(g) programs of films or other reproductions which have been made in Canada if:

(i) the producing company is incorporated under the laws of Canada or any province and has a majority of Canadian directors,

(ii) application has been submitted to the Board presenting evidence of Canadian and non-Canadian content in a form prescribed by the Board, and the Board, after consideration of the balance of the elements going into the production, has approved a Canadian content classification.

Programs produced outside Canada in either Commonwealth or French-language countries would be given 50% Canadian content credit not to exceed 1/3 or 1/4 respectively of the total broadcast time of a station or network.

On 18 November 1959, the Board released an announcement elaborating on the new regulations. The announcement noted that the "basic principles" as they referred to Canadian content, had, as a result of submissions made at the public hearings, been modified in two respects. First, Canadian content would be calculated on the basis of four weeks rather than one week. The announcement said: "The evidence presented during the public hearings satisfied the Board that the greater flexibility permitted by the longer period would assist stations in meeting the prescribed minimum Canadian content."[3] Second, stations were given a period of time to 1 April 1962 to "phase in" to full compliance with the 55% minimum.

The Board was informed by the CBC that the Canadian content was approximately 66% on the English network and 85% on the French. The regulation prescribing 55% Canadian content could therefore pose no significant problems to the existing networks. Other evidence before the Board indicated that many of the existing television stations, all of which were affiliates of the CBC, programmed between 45% and 50% Canadian content. The Board was satisfied that these stations would encounter no serious difficulty in raising the percentage to 55% by April 1962.

The announcement concluded that the condition of a minimum content of 55% was consistent with the intent of Section 10 of the Broadcasting Act which required the Board to ensure a broadcasting service "basically Canadian in content and character" and that, given certain other conditions, a minimum Canadian content of 55% could be attained on all networks and television stations without offending the further requirement of the Act that the service be of a "high standard."[4]

In the "basic principles" announced on 28 July 1959, the Board proposed that "A maximum of two hours of broadcasting time each day between the hours of 8 p.m. and 11 p.m. will be reserved for purposes to be prescribed by the Board of Broadcast Governors. Programming during the two hours in whatever way provided will have a minimum of 55% Canadian content."[5] This principle was incorporated in the regulations under Section 6(6). The announcement of 18 November stressed that especially in one station markets or in areas where VHF channels were limited in number, the licensee would be required to provide programming that was "comprehensive," "varied" and of a "high standard" as well as basically Canadian in content and character. The Board would not shy away from using this prescribed time to ensure that the above criteria were met and that the overall prime time (then 8 p.m. - 11 p.m.) met the conditions of the broadcast service required by section 10 of the Act.[6]

In the years which followed, every aspect of the regulations came under fire and was reviewed by the Board. Amendments were made from time to time, and alternatives were considered.

The original regulation provided that stations program a minimum of 45% Canadian content beginning 1 April 1961, and 55% beginning 1 April 1962. The stations had been meeting the 45% requirement without much difficulty, but as the time approached for full implementation of 55% Canadian content it was evident that this would put a strain on the stations—particularly the second stations, which were still facing financial problems. In 1962, following a review of the situation, a number of amendments were made to Regulation 6. In June, the regulation was amended to provide that during the summer months the required Canadian content would be reduced to 45% In reference to this amendment, in the Annual Report 1962–63, the Board said:

> In enacting this amendment for the summer of 1962, the Board considered that in view of the fact that during the summer months the television audience tends to drop off, advertising revenues decline and stations must pay for staff holidays, stations would experience particular difficulty in maintaining their Canadian content in this period. The Board considers that the summer of 1962 would be particularly difficult in this respect, and that some temporary relief should be provided to the stations.[7]

Similar amendments were passed in 1963 and 1964. In 1965 and subsequently, the 55% remained in effect throughout the full year.

The Board's announcement of 18 November 1959 noted the absence from the regulations of any specific Canadian content requirements in the peak viewing hours and said that the Board would keep this aspect of the station's performance under close scrutiny.[8] This scrutiny led to the conclusion that some minimum Canadian content should be prescribed for the evening hours. In May 1962, the regulation was amended to provide that the minimum Canadian content required during the period from 6:00 p.m. to midnight would be 40%. In its *Annual Report, 1962–63,* the Board noted that the purpose of the amendment was to maintain an acceptable Canadian content during the evening hours, to give a wider exposure to Canadian productions, to increase the revenues from Canadian productions, and consequently, to enable producers by greater expenditures on Canadian productions to improve their quality.[9]

An amendment was introduced in June 1964, extending the period of measuring Canadian content from four weeks to a calendar quarter. The quarters were: 1 January to 31 March; 1 April to 30 June; 1 July to 30 September; and 1 October to 31 December.

In its *Annual Report, 1959–60*, the Board elaborated on the reasons for giving credit to programs of Commonwealth origin, particularly programs from the United Kingdom. It pointed out that the regulations provided that English-language programs, up to 33 1/3% of the broadcast time, would count as 50% Canadian; and that French-language programs up to 25% of broadcast time would also count as 50% Canadian. These provisions would contribute to the variety of programming. The Board noted that the United Kingdom gave 100% British classification to Canadian productions.

Section 6(5) was amended in May 1962.[10] The effect of the amendment was to increase the allowable Canadian content, in the case of Commonwealth programs, to 100% for the first 28 hours of broadcast time in the four weeks devoted to them, and 50 percent for the remainder. French-language programs were still permitted to be calculated at 50%. The total broadcast time for Commonwealth or French-language programs which could be claimed as Canadian content could not exceed one-third of the total broadcast time of the station. The change made it easier for the stations to meet the requirements of the regulation, but a major reason for the change was the repeated representations from the Independent Television Authority in the United Kingdom that the acceptability of Canadian programs there might be endangered. The difference in treatment of Commonwealth and French-language programs led to the charge that the Board was discriminating against French-language broadcasting. The principal reason for the difference in treatment was that, while the United Kingdom offered British content status to Canadian productions, comparable recognition was never given in France.

The May 1962 amendment also provided that programs produced outside Canada in other than French-language or Commonwealth countries, and in which the audio portion was converted to English or French by lip synchronization done in Canada, were permitted to be calculated as 25% Canadian. Canadian artists, particularly French-speaking ones, derived considerable employment and income from "dubbing." However, the 25% credit was not changed.[11]

In August 1960, the Board issued a circular letter dealing with the classification of filmed and taped programs, and included notes for guidance in applying for Canadian content classification. The procedures called for a pre-production application, so that producers might have some reasonable expectation of the final classification, and for a final application after production was completed. The notes for guidance said:

> In seeking the balance of elements required for according a Canadian content classification, the following factors must be taken into account: (a) the nationality of the writer or writers; (b) the nationality of the executive producer, producers and directors; (c) the nationality of the artists and performers; (d) the nationality of the technicians required. No fixed ratio is set in respect of the above factors, but it is assumed that where the help of non-Canadians is required, at least two-thirds of the principals involved in the production will be Canadian. In certain cases the Board may decide that one or more of the programs in a series will be accorded a Canadian content classification while the remainder will be classified as foreign.
>
> The principal requirement is that the major production responsibility for programs accorded a Canadian content classification should rest with a Canadian individual or company, that is, a company incorporated under the laws of Canada or one of its provinces, the majority of whose directors are Canadian. Canadian producers are permitted to enter into co-production agreements with producers in other countries, particularly when such an arrangement is desirable to secure finances or to improve the prospects for international distribution. Particulars of such agreements must accompany the application for Canadian content classification.[12]

In the later circular letter of 15 June 1962, the Board recognized the need for further clarification of its attitudes to co-production agreements and to the productions undertaken outside Canada. With regard to co-production, its major concern was about the monies allocated, or spent, and about the proportion of the total budget devoted to the employment of Canadian talent and facilities. For extensive production work outside Canada, the Board was ready to weigh the elements involved, to arrive at a judgement regarding the appropriate Canadian classification, again considering both the personnel involved and the proportion of the total budget devoted to the employment and development of Canadian talent.[13]

A common format, particularly for children's programs, was a combination of live studio productions and film inserts, usually cartoons. In May 1961 the Board ruled that a station could claim Canadian content for programs of this kind up to a maximum of two hours for any single program without regard to the origin of the film inserts. The film inserts were not to exceed ten minutes in duration in each instance, and the total of the film inserts was not to exceed 50% of the program.[14] The identification of short inserts had proved difficult to administer. From time to time efforts were made to develop the production of animated cartoons in Canada, but the Board's ruling gave no incentive to use Canadian productions. In September 1962, the Board announced that the earlier rule would not apply after 14 October 1962.[15] Thereafter, Canadian content credit would be accorded only to the studio-produced part and to film inserts which had been assigned Canadian content by the Board. The change precipitated a dispute between broadcasters and producers and distributors of cartoons. The Board's regulation was not effective, and efforts to establish animation production in Canada did not succeed.

The Canadian content was determined on the basis of broadcast time. If a program to which Canadian content credit was granted ran for half an hour, the time credited was thirty minutes, without regard to commercial time. The commercials might have been produced in Canada or in the United States. As early as September 1960, the Board received representations that commercials should be dealt with separately; similar representations were received intermittently in later years. At 12 minutes in the hour, the amount of time represented by commercials was substantial, and the production of commercials was important to producing companies. The Board's method of handling commercial time did not offer any incentive to the production of commercials in Canada. Nevertheless, partly because of administrative problems of classifying every commercial, the Board did not accede to the requests for separate treatment for commercials.

The May 1962 announcement included a change in the commercial regulations allowing an increase in commercial time of 60 seconds in a half-hour Canadian production, with proportionate changes in programs of longer or shorter duration:

> The object of the amended regulations is to provide the sponsors of Canadian productions with more favourable terms, to induce an increased demand for Canadian productions, to increase the revenues accruing to Canadian productions, to increase the expenditure on Canadian productions, and thus to improve the quality of Canadian productions.[16]

Section 6(6), which provided for program contractors, was used in connection with educational television. The policy was dealt with in "The Statement of Policies of the Board of Broadcast Governors with Respect to Educational Television." Educational authorities could be recognized as program contractors and would be allowed the widest possible latitude in obtaining material and in devising programs. The stations could assume that the programs were one hundred percent Canadian.

There were repeated requests from churches—particularly those having production facilities in the United States—who wished to come under Section 6(6), on the same terms as educational authorities. These requests were not approved by the Board.

Public criticism of the "quota system" applied by the Board was directed to three main points. First, Canadian content classification was granted to many programs in which the actual Canadian content was considerably less than 100%; consequently the 55% was an unreal measure of Canadian content. This criticism was certainly not without validity. The credit given to Commonwealth, French-language, and education programs (other than those produced in Canada) distorted the true Canadian content. Assuming that the principle in each case was sound, it would have been preferable to provide credit outside the Canadian content regulations. With respect to other provisions, such as co-productions and "dubbed" programs, it could be argued that, in so far as these did not replace wholly Canadian productions, they contributed something to the use of Canadian talent. The second criticism was that the effect was to increase "quantity" rather than "quality." It may very well be true that the "quality" of Canadian productions was, on balance, lower than the supporters of Canadian broadcasting would have wished, but this does not seem to constitute a valid criticism of the Canadian content regulations. The regulations were designed to ensure the quantitative participation of Canadians in the broadcasting service. The "quality" of broadcasting was another matter, and was perhaps as much involved in non-Canadian broadcasting as in Canadian broadcasting. The third criticism came from organizations representing Canadian talent, who complained that expenditure by broadcasters on the use of Canadian talent was not enough. This criticism was related to the level of employment of Canadians, and therefore to the "quantity" of "real" Canadian content.

Various proposals for alternative approaches were made to the Board, and were given consideration by the members. The proposals included consideration of the cost of producing Canadian programs. It was suggested that either the credit given to Canadian productions should vary with the expenditure on them, or stations should be required to expend a specified percentage of their gross revenue on Canadian talent. It was proposed that the Canadian content credited to particular programs should vary with the "real" Canadian content. The suggestion of substituting a tax on non-Canadian productions was made from time to time. The Board considered a proposal that a special category of programs should be excluded from the calculation of Canadian content. This device was proposed in order to encourage the use of "quality" programs regardless of their origin. Finally, there was support for varying the percentages of Canadian content for particular stations or classes of stations according to local circumstances, for instance, the percentages for metropolitan stations might be greater than for small rural stations.

The concerns common to both sides were audience and revenue. The introduction of second stations into the markets served by CBC stations was bound to split the audience, and to reduce the audience of the CBC stations. The CBC had a mandate to serve national purposes. It had used its discretion in interpreting its mandate in terms of the program service it provided; and, except in those markets penetrated by signals from the United States, the audience had no choice but to tune in to its stations. The conditions were now changed. The audience the CBC could attract depended on the alternative service offered by the private stations. The CBC, therefore, had an interest in the obligations placed on the private stations. If the private stations were free to program solely with the object of attracting the largest possible share of the audience, and the audience of the CBC stations became small, both relatively and absolutely, the position of the CBC was endangered. Parliament would become increasingly concerned about the costs of the public service. The costs of television were relatively high; and the CBC was afraid that if it failed to maintain a substantial share of the audience served by its "O & O" stations, the public support available to it would be imperilled. The CBC believed that it should attract a minimum of 40 per cent of the audience. If the audience declined, advertising revenues would tend to decline and the problem would be compounded. The CBC was, therefore, concerned, first, that conditions should be imposed on the private stations which would restrict the program choices of the private stations; and, second, that the CBC should have flexibility in interpreting its mandate and in determining its balance of programming. Thus, the CBC favoured Canadian content regulations applied to the private sector which would require the private stations to produce and broadcast more of their own productions than they would otherwise do; but it did not wish to have a minimum Canadian content imposed on it. The private stations sought the largest possible audience because of the effect of audience on the revenues they could draw from the market. The private stations also wished flexibility, that is, the absence of regulations affecting their program choices. They were unhappy with the Canadian content regulations. They wanted, however, some assurance as to the programming on the CBC stations with which they had to compete and they wished more rigorous conditions imposed on the CBC.

After a number of years of experience with the Canadian content regulations, the Board was aware that the regulations required a thorough review. It was by no means clear what would emerge from such a review, however, and the Board was unwilling to proceed with it until the public discussions of broadcasting policy and the restatement of policy in the new legislation were completed.

The Canadian content regulations were part of the broad policy of directing broadcasting in Canada toward the achievement of national purposes. This policy had been stated and restated by successive Canadian governments and, as policy, it seemed to have the support of the majority of Canadians.

On 18 August 1958, in introducing a resolution for the establishment of the BBG, the Hon. George C. Nowlan quoted with approval the following words in a brief presented to the government by Professor Donald Creighton:

Canadian strength and Canadian unity ultimately depend on her autonomy and spiritual independence on the North American continent. Throughout our history we have persistently followed national policies devised to strengthen our unity from ocean to ocean and to maintain our separatism in North America... A steady flow of programs along the east-west lifeline will express Canadian ideas and ideals, employ Canadian talent, and help unite our people from sea to sea and from the river unto the ends of the earth.[17]

The Board subscribed to the broad policy, and the Chairman defended it in public:

As Chairman of the Board of Broadcast Governors it would be my duty to pursue the purposes of the Broadcasting Act, and the national policy indicated in it, even if I were not in sympathy with the policy or any part of it. It happens that I do subscribe to the historic Canadian policy for broadcasting as I understand it, and am prepared to argue for it on my own terms. This is what I propose to do.[18]

Toward the end of his term, the Chairman reiterated his support for the "national policy":

Neither would I wish to appear apologetic for the policy itself. I endorse it wholeheartedly; and, indeed, as you must be aware, nothing I have said today is inconsistent with, or reflects any significant change from the position we have taken over the past eight years. It seems to me particularly appropriate that the Report of the Standing Committee should be published and the legislation passed on it enacted during the Centennial Year.[19]

The Broadcasting Act said the broadcasting service was to be "basically Canadian in content and character." The concept of "Canadian content" did not appear too obscure; it was quantitative, and could be measured by the amount of Canadian participation. The concept of "Canadian character" presented greater difficulty, and the Chairman avoided the use of this phrase and also avoided reference to "Canadian identity." It seemed impossible to identify the peculiar characteristics of the Canadian culture and, in practice, it was unnecessary to attempt to do so. If Canadians had substantial opportunity to participate in broadcasting, their participation would tend to reflect the Canadian character and to maintain the Canadian identity. The emphasis was on participation and on the necessity of participation to the health of the nation.

The Canadian fact is indisputable; and I consider myself fortunate, among all the people of the world, that through circumstances I happen to be a Canadian. It is my firm conviction that no political unit, particularly a political democracy, can function effectively without communication among the people who comprise it. It is, therefore, obligatory that the necessary level of communication be assured, unless the country deliberately chooses to prejudice its existence by default. This is not my choice for Canada. Nor do I think it is the choice of private broadcasters.[20]

In his address on the place of government in political and social promotion of the arts, to the Canadian-American Relations Seminar at Assumption University, Windsor, Ontario, November 1961, the Chairman said:

What is important is that there must be communication at and between all levels of association or society cannot function satisfactorily. Communication ranges all the way from face to face communication by word of mouth and gesture to global communication using the available technical means. Face to face communication remains particularly important because it provides for "talk back" and we all have at least the opportunity to participate. The more distant the communications the more limited the opportunities for all to participate, and the greater the danger that the flow of communication is predominantly in one direction. It is, I think, essential to the health of society that in the closer associations of the smaller community people have an opportunity to communicate among themselves on matters that are important to them in these associations; that in relation to wider aspects of association within the nation, communities, through the people living in them, have a chance to communicate between each other, and that the flow of communication should not be only or mainly in one direction. The same necessity exists in the relations between people, living within national boundaries, in their inescapable associations with the nationals of other countries. This is what we must mean by free communication; and it is as important within nations as it is between them.

Inherent in this view of communications is the notion of a balance between local communications, communications within the nation, and international communications. Admittedly the appropriate balance between communications at these levels is not clearly determinable. Nevertheless, there is obviously a problem of maintaining a balance, and it seems to me quite certain that under some real conditions the balance which would be determined by the forces of the market is not the proper solution. Under these circumstances the only means to redress the balance is by intervention of government.[21]

The Chairman did express some doubts about the effectiveness of the control of broadcasting for political and cultural purposes. In the political democracies the capacity of broadcasting alone to contribute to the political and cultural purposes would seem to depend on, first, the availability, acceptance and use of broadcasting by the public; second, the extent to which the medium is diverted to the purposes; and, third, what might be called the disposition of the public to support the purposes.

The Canadian content regulations are a matter of controversy. In this debate we have a clear illustration of a conflict of objectives; a situation in which we cannot have our cake and eat it. From my contacts and experience with the public it seems quite evident that the vast majority of Canadians support the intention that broadcasting in this country should be basically Canadian in content and character. They believe that broadcasting is important to the life of the nation, and wish the broadcasting service to contribute to the national purposes of Canadian identity, Canadian unity, and the self-expression of Canadians through active participation in broadcasting. However, as listeners and viewers, when they turn to their radio and television sets, and a choice of program is open to them, they will frequently select the one which is not Canadian in preference to the Canadian program. While there are conflicts of interest, the differences which give rise to controversy are not so much between people as within the same people. At times, as members of the public, Canadians lend their support to Canadian content; at other times, as audience, they cast their votes against it.[22]

Notwithstanding the doubts, the effort had to be made!

Mr. Ernest L. Bushnell (left) and Dr. Andrew Stewart (right) at the official opening of CJOH-TV, Ottawa, Ontario, October 21, 1961. *CJOH Photography by Herb Taylor. Used with permission of CJOH-TV, Ottawa.*

[4]

THE INITIAL SECOND
STATION APPLICATIONS

FOLLOWING THE MINISTER'S POLICY statement in the House on 20 July 1959, the Board issued a press release referring to public hearings on applications for television licences.[1] The release noted that it would take two months for a would-be applicant to make all his preparations, including obtaining an option on a transmitter site, an engineering study, company organization and financing and necessary legal work. Once applications had been received, a further period of two months was required for the Department of Transport to process them and for a notice of a public hearing to be advertised in the *Canada Gazette*. So, under the new policy, at least four months would elapse between the time of the Minister's announcement and the first hearings by the Board.

The Board's announcement of dates for hearings was actually issued on 11 August 1959,[2] with the first hearing set for Winnipeg on 11 January 1960. Additional hearings were announced for Vancouver, Montreal (English and French), Toronto, Edmonton, Calgary, Halifax and Ottawa. The Board believed these centres would be found to be large enough to justify a second station, although there was some doubt about Halifax.

For some time prior to the Minister's announcement on licensing of second stations, the Board had been considering, and had discussed with the Minister, the conditions and regulations which could govern television after the introduction of the second stations. On 1 June 1959, Mr. Nowlan was supplied with a memorandum on "Regulations Governing Television." While the Minister's statement in the House made no reference to ground rules, the basic principles were announced by the Board in a press release on 28 July 1959.[3] In order to give prospective applicants for licences an opportunity to prepare their submissions on the basic principles, public hearings on TV regulations were called for 2–3 November 1959. An announcement by the Board on 8 October 1959 noted that inquiries had been received from prospective applicants for licences in Winnipeg and Vancouver and pointed out that, while applications for these centres had to be in the hands of the Department of Transport by 30 October 1959, the regulations would not be announced until 15 November. The press release stated that, should changes in the regulations as already announced occur, applicants would be permitted to make revisions in the non-technical aspects of their briefs.[4] In fact, the changes adopted by the Board following the public hearings were not such as to create any difficulties for prospective applicants.

After the hearings in Winnipeg and Vancouver, the Board published an outline of thirteen factors which it considered significant and to which it would give weight in determining its decisions on licence applications.[5] The factors were: coverage of the proposed station; nature of the facilities, including production facilities to be provided by the applicant; composition of the initial board of directors of the company; distribution of the voting stock in the company, and the location of effective control; general plan of financing; financial capacity of those involved in the application; experience and standing of those involved in the application; association of the applicants with other media of communication; estimates of expected revenue and of the capacity to meet the full costs of the service to which the licensee would be committed; establishment proposed by the applicant, and the capacity and experience of the personnel, particularly the management personnel, to be appointed; manner in which the programming policies of the station would be determined and implemented; the program commitments of the applicant in relation to the requirements of the Act and the regulations that the service be varied, of a high standard, and basically Canadian in content and character; characteristics of the community, the nature of the available broadcasting service; and, the capacity of the applicant to meet the varied needs of the proposed service area.

The Board engaged Special Counsel to hear applications for second television licences. As appeared to be the Ottawa custom, counsel names were selected from a list supplied by the Department of Justice. Frank O. Meighen of Brandon, Manitoba was the original choice of the Board. Mr. Meighen was available for the Winnipeg, Vancouver, Edmonton and Calgary hearings, and returned for the hearings in Halifax and Ottawa. Graeme Haig of Winnipeg acted in Montreal, for the English-language applications, and in Toronto. Claude Nolin conducted the French-language cases in Montreal. The Board followed the practice of meeting immediately before the hearings in order to instruct Counsel, and Counsel, along with senior staff, attended the meetings at which decisions were reached.

The order of appearance of applicants was arranged prior to the opening of hearings. Following the presentation of each case, the applicant was questioned by Counsel and by members of the Board. Rebuttals followed the reverse order and questions might again be asked. Submissions by other parties, if referring to a particular application, were heard immediately after the application. Submissions of a more general nature were taken after the several presentations had been received. The applicants were required to submit their supplementary briefs, in addition to their applications, in advance of the hearings, and these voluminous papers became public documents. Applicants were requested not to read, but to summarize, the material in their briefs. They were all, however, anxious to present their cases as effectively as possible, and most presentations were of considerable length. A substantial part of the time was spent on program proposals, with extensive use of visual aids.

WINNIPEG (13–16 JANUARY 1960)

The first hearings on second licences opened in Winnipeg. There were three applications for Channel 7.

R.S. Misener appeared on behalf of a company to be incorporated. Mr. Misener's associates included T.O. Peterson, President and General Manager, Investors Syndicate, Winnipeg, as principal investor. Three of the local radio stations were involved. Lloyd Moffat, Radio Station CKY, Winnipeg, would have substantial responsibility for the operation of the station; Roland G. Couture, Radio St. Boniface and Walter Kroeker, Radio Station CFAM, Altona, Manitoba were shareholders. The submission was made by Mr. Misener, assisted by Jack Davidson, who was to become general manager of the station. Mr. Davidson had 21 years' experience in broadcasting and, at the time, was Executive Vice-President of Radio Station CKY, Winnipeg.

The second applicant was J.O. Blick, the owner of Radio Station CJOB, Winnipeg. The initial directors of Perimeter Television Broadcasting were Mr. Blick, D.J. McDonald and Graeme T. Haig. Other directors were to be added after the licence was granted. It was proposed that shares would be offered to the public. Mr. Blick made his own presentation.

Red River Television Association had 16 members. Joseph Harris, Chairman of Great West Life, was President of the Association. The other members included: Clifford Sifton, Chairman of the Board of All-Canada Radio Television; Victor Sifton, publisher of the *Winnipeg Free Press*; J. Alvin Woods, Chairman of the Canadian Committee of the Hudson's Bay Company; five Winnipeg families engaged in the grain trade, including James A. Richardson and Kathleen Richardson; Herbert Moody and Robert Moore, architects; Herbert Bird, Bird Construction; J.A. MacAulay, QC; and Brigadier R.S. Malone, newsman. The case was led by W.A. Johnson, Counsel, and Harold Crittenden, Manager of CKCK, Regina—a radio station owned by the Sifton-controlled Trans-Canada Communications. Ernest Bushnell, former Vice-President, CBC, and engaged as a consultant, also appeared.

The Board, after reviewing the evidence, recommended that R.S. Misener and Associates be granted the licence, which was eventually issued.

VANCOUVER (18–22 JANUARY 1960)

The hearings in Vancouver attracted five applications, four of them for Channel 8. British Columbia Television Broadcasting Corporation applied for Channel 10.

The directors of Metropolitan Television were F.A. Griffiths, William Hughes and William Murphy, all of Radio Station CKNW, New Westminster. They had associated with them Fred Auger, Vancouver *Province* and Director, Southam Company; Lawrence Dampier, Assistant Publisher, Vancouver *Sun*, Sun Publishing Company; and T.E. Lachner, Counsel. Mr. Griffiths presented the case, assisted by William Hughes.

British Columbia Television Broadcasting Corporation was represented by M.J. Foley, Vice Chairman, Macmillan-Bloedel, and former Chairman of the Board of Powell River Company, as President; George Chandler, owner of Radio Station CJOR, Vancouver, as Managing Director; and Craig Munroe, Counsel. Other directors included Perry Willoughby, British Pacific Properties; C.N. Woodward, Woodward Stores; Ernest Buckerfield, Western City Company; Gordon Farrel, Chairman of the Board of British Columbia Telephone Company; Alan Hackett; C.A. Johnston, CA; and Ron Thom. William Jones, of Canastel, was the nominee of Associated Television, United Kingdom; and Norman Collins of London, England, appeared on behalf of ATV. Paul Nathanson, Sovereign Film Distributors, appeared as one of the directors. The presentation was made mainly by Mr. Chandler. Bernard Braden had been brought from England to speak about the use and development of Canadian talent and Allen Miller was under contract to assist in programming.

The youthful Art Jones had organized and was President of Vantel Broadcasting Company. Associated with him, as investors, were 11

Vancouver businessmen, including Peter Paul Saunders, President of Imperial Investment Corporation. The list was only slightly less imposing than those of British Columbia Television and Pacific Television companies. (Mr. Jones and Colonel Eakin would together own 34% of the stock; there were six shareholders with 8 to 8.5% each.) Others who appeared on behalf of the applicant were Norman Aldred, who was to be Operating Manager; Frederick Field, Economic Adviser, Faculty of Commerce, University of British Columbia; and Kenneth Bray, Production Consultant.

Pacific Television Company had as its President the redoubtable F. Ronald Graham. The principal shareholders were Colonel Victor Spencer (24.1%); Walter C. Koerner (19.2%); F.R. Graham (15.4%); Sir Denis Lowson (15.4%) and Frank McMahon (15.4%). Lloyd K. Turner was Vice-President; Allen H. Wainsworth was Secretary; and H.R. Jestley, Counsel. Ernest Bushnell had been engaged as a consultant.

Allan McGavin, Coast Television, had 47 business and professional people associated with him. The executive committee consisted of Mr. McGavin, President; Arthur J. Cowan, Secretary; and W. Stuart Johnston, Treasurer. Broadcast Operations, operators of Radio Station CFUN, Vancouver, had considered applying but had found this beyond their capacity. The syndicate had developed out of their interest. With the substantial number of investors, control was widely distributed.

In addition to the five applications, there were three other submissions. The Retail Merchants Association of Canada, British Columbia Branch, presented a brief specifically in opposition to the application of Metropolitan Television, on the grounds of control over advertising and communications. The B.C. Federation of Labour opposed all applications, claiming that if another outlet were required it should be licensed to the CBC. The brief expressed particular opposition to Metropolitan Television. Dr. Alan Thomas, then with the University of British Columbia, spoke in support of educational television, and advocated grants by broadcasting companies to the University for the engagement of staff and the creation of co-productions.

After considerable discussion, and some differences in the Board, the Board recommended for approval the application of Vantel.

MONTREAL (7–10 MARCH 1960)

The Montreal hearing considered two French-language applications for Channel 10 and two English-language ones for Channel 12.

With the consent of the City of Montreal, it was agreed that all television antennas would be placed on a common tower, to be constructed by the CBC, on Mount Royal. There were, therefore, no significant differences in the coverage patterns proposed by the several applicants.

Three French-language applications had been filed with the Board. At the opening of the hearings, however, Raymond Crepault, the licensee of a radio station in Montreal, withdrew his application with the simple statement:

> I have been authorized by my associates to advise the Board that after what I would call a great amount of soul searching we have decided to withdraw our application. The decision in fact was reached this morning. I had the choice of sending you a telegram, but I thought out of courtesy to the Board I would appear before you this morning and make the statement and this is what I have done. This is all I have to say this morning.

The Board understood the problem was financing.

The first French-language application was by Paul L'Anglais and Associates, with J.A. De Seve as President and principal investor. A.B.R. Lawrence of Ottawa, who had acted as counsel to the Board until the permanent Counsel was appointed, appeared as counsel to the applicant. The case was presented by Colonel Paul L'Anglais, as first Vice-President, with assistance on the program side from Andre Ouiment, second Vice-President, and Jean Paul Ladouceur, Production Supervisor. Both Mr. Ouimet and Mr. Ladouceur had had considerable experience with the CBC.

Although Mr. L'Anglais brought experience in the commercial side of broadcasting, the application was essentially an application by Mr. De Seve, who was initially to hold 60% of the voting stock. Mr. De Seve had been successful in the business of film distributing. It was proposed that the studio building would be leased from Cine World Corporation, one of Mr. De Seve's companies; the transmission facilities would be purchased by Compagnie France Film, and the studio equipment by Tele International Corporation.

The competing French-language application brought together the resources of Radio Station CKVL, owned by Jack Tietolman, and United Amusement Corporation which operated a chain of movie theatres. United Amusement Corporation was represented by William Lester, President. The Corporation had been selling theatres and was prepared to reinvest in the television station. The control would rest with CKVL, and thus with Mr. Tietolman. Mr. Tietolman's associates in the application were Marcel Provost, Program Manager and Robert Baulu, Manager.

On the Board's recommendation, the licence went to Paul L'Anglais and Associates.

The first English-language application was by Canadian Marconi Company, licensee of Radio Station CFCF, Montreal. The application was presented by S.M. Finlayson. With him were W.V. George, General Manager; A.G. McCaughney, Secretary-Treasurer; Richard Misener, Manager; and VinDittmer, Commercial Manager of CFCF. Canadian Marconi Company had a long history in telecommunications. It was organized in 1902 and established by an Act of Parliament in 1903. The company, in addition to supplying equipment, had started the first radio station in Canada, XWA, in 1919-20. This station later became CFCF and had been in operation for 40 years. Mr. Finlayson stated that their interest in television was first evidenced by an inquiry regarding a licence in 1938. Canadian Marconi was a public company with 22,000 shareholders. The principal shareholder was Canmar Investments, with 50.6% of the stock. The controlling interest in Canmar Investments, and therefore in Canadian Marconi, was held by English Electric which was incorporated in the United Kingdom. Mr. Finlayson was President of both Canmar and Canadian

Marconi. Canadian Marconi did not meet the "Canadian ownership" provisions of Section 14 of the Broadcasting Act, 1958. However, under the provisions of the Act, the Company had secured exemption by Order-in-Council PC 1959–1051. Mr. Finlayson claimed that the Government would not have granted the exemption by Order-in-Council if the Company had not been acceptable as a licensee, and that "We qualify under the recent Act." The capital costs of the project were to be met out of a public issue, which would also meet other requirements of the Company.

The opposing application was by Mount Royal Independent Television, 30% of whose voting stock was to be held by a group (Lewis, Keifer and Penfold) and another 30% by Geoffrey Stirling. Mr. Stirling was the principal shareholder (70%) in Maisonneuve Broadcasting, which had shortly before been licensed to operate Radio Station CKGM in Montreal. He was also the owner of almost 51% of the stock in the company owning Radio Station CJON in St. John's, Newfoundland. Other investors included Messrs. O'Brien and Veinberg, each with 13 1/2% of the shares. Dr. Wilder Penfield and Dr. David Thompson, Vice-President, McGill University, each held one percent. The Mount Royal case was presented by Crosby Lewis who was assisted by Mr. Stirling and by Don Jamieson, Mr. Stirling's associate in Newfoundland Broadcasting.

Canadian Marconi became the licensee of CFCF-TV.

TORONTO (14–21 MARCH 1960)

The hearings reached their climax in Toronto where there were nine applicants for Channel 9. Involved in the applications were: the three Toronto newspapers—*The Star*, *The Telegram* and *The Globe and Mail;* Maclean-Hunter Publishing Company; Consolidated Press-*Saturday Night* and *Liberty Magazine;* Southam Company; J. Arthur Rank, Canada; Sovereign Films, Granada Network and Associated Television, United Kingdom; Standard Radio, CFRB; and Radio Station CKEY. Eugene Fitzgibbons, Famous Players Canada, was engaged as a consultant to *The Star*.

The first presentation was made by Beland H. Honderick, Vice-President and Editor-in-Chief of *The Star*. The principals in the application were the six directors of *The Star*, J.S. Atkinson, W.J. Campbell, Ruth A. Hindmarsh, Harry A. Hindmarsh, Dr. Thorn and Mr. Honderick; and A.J. Mackintosh, lawyer. Eugene Fitzgibbons and Alan Savage, Cockfield-Brown Advertising Agency, had been engaged as consultants.

Maclean-Hunter was represented by Floyd S. Chalmers, Donald F. Hunter, R.A. McEachern, D.G. Campbell and Donald Hildebrand, who had been engaged as Program Director. Associated Television (U.K.) was to have 20% of the voting stock and was represented by William Jones of Canastel, the wholly-owned subsidiary of ATV.

Upper Canada Broadcasting included a distinguished array of patrons of the arts, creative artists and performers. Professor Anthony Adamson, architect, was Chairman and Blair Lang, Vice-Chairman. The list of directors included Sir Ernest MacMillan, dean of Canadian musicians; Mavor Moore, writer, actor, producer and executive; Tom Patterson of the Stratford Shakespearean Festival; Neil LeRoy, performer and immediate Past President of the Canadian Council of Authors and Artists; Frank Shuster and John Wayne. The President and principal spokesman for the company was Stuart Griffith, formerly for 16 years Program Director, CBC Television Network, and for the past two years Program Controller, Granada Television Network, United Kingdom. Granada was to have one director and 25 percent of the stock.

Jack Kent Cooke, of Radio Station CKEY and Consolidated Frybrook Industries had no partners. Mr. Cooke said, "I believe, and I am quite sincere about this, we have never given over our medium to the advertisers—it has been mine, good, bad, or indifferent, it has been mine, and this is precisely what I intend to do should we be fortunate enough to get this television station."[6]

Henry Borden, Brazilian Traction, appeared for the Toronto Telecasters Association—a group of 60 Torontonians and the Southam Company. Sir Robert Watson-Watt, the father of radar, was associated with the group as a special advisor.

Summit Television had as principal corporate investors *The Globe and Mail* and J. Arthur Rank, Canada. The presentation was made by

J.S.D. Tory. *The Globe and Mail* was represented at the hearing by R. Howard Webster, Chairman of the Board, and Oakley Dalgleish, Publisher and General Manager. L.W. Brockington represented the J. Arthur Rank organization.

Rogers Radio Broadcasting, Radio Station CFRB was represented by Joseph Sedgwick, Q.C., and W.C. Thorton Cran, President. CFRB was controlled by Standard Radio, which was controlled by Argus Corporation. The directors included Wallace McCutcheon, A. Bruce Matthews, W. Eric Phillips, J. Harry Ratcliffe, J. Ellsworth Rogers and Samuel Rogers.

Spencer W. Caldwell of S.W. Caldwell Limited, a company with considerable experience in television production and distribution, proposed a company composed of 95 Toronto residents divided into 38 shareholders' units. Mr. Caldwell would retain control of the company through ownership of the majority of the voting stock. He and his associate, Gordon Keeble, would be leaving S.W. Caldwell Limited to become President and Vice-President of the new company. The proposed directors included Kenneth B. Andras, Senior Partner in Andras, Atkinson and McCartney; H.E. Cochrane, Chairman of the Board of Cochrane, Murray and Company; W.F. McLean, President of Canada Packers; R.K. Martin, Partner in the firm of Martin, Lewis and Company; Donald Manson, the Secretary of the 1929 Arid Commission and Sidney Banks.

The presentation of Baton, Aldred, Rogers Broadcasting was a model of organization. Every aspect of the submission was meticulously dealt with. The visual presentation was provided through a closed-circuit system from Meridian Studios, with monitor sets in the hall. The presentation was led by E.A. Goodman, Q.C., with the principals, John Bassett, Joel Aldred, Foster Hewitt, Ted Rogers, Paul Nathanson and Rae Purdy appearing. Mr. Bassett, Publisher of *The Telegram* for seven years, appeared as Chairman of the Board and Chief Executive Officer. The majority of the voting stock (51%) was to be owned by *The Telegram*.

In addition to the applicants' briefs, four other submissions were heard. Arthur Chetwynd, Past President of the Motion Picture Producers and Laboratories of Canada, urged the Board to consider the extent to which applicants intended to use existing talent and facilities, thus making maximum use of available capital rather than tying it up in large buildings. Ralph Snelgrove, proprietor of CKVR-TV, Barrie, lodged objections, particularly against applicants whose facilities would effect the greatest penetration of his station's service area. For the Association of Canadian Television and Radio Artists, Alan King sought the greatest use of Canadian talent. Dr. Carleton Williams spoke for the Metropolitan Educational Television Association.

On the recommendation of the Board, the licence was issued to Baton, Aldred, Rogers Broadcasting.[7]

EDMONTON (10–13 MAY 1960)

The call for applications at the Edmonton hearings brought forth five applications including one from the CBC and one from CFRN-TV, the local CBC affiliate. The Corporation for financial reasons had to make a choice between applications in Calgary or Edmonton. Edmonton won out and when the Board recommended in favour of the CBC application, there were rumours of disquiet in the Cabinet and outright complaints from the private applicants that the Board, having prejudged the case, had wasted their time and money. The Board denied the claim. The Cabinet eventually approved the necessary order-in-council to award the licence to the CBC.[8]

CALGARY (16–17 MAY 1960)

The hearings in Calgary heard two competing applications for Channel 4.

Everett Chambers, Q.C., appeared as counsel for CFCN Television, but the submission was made by H. Gordon Love, who was Chairman of the Board of CFCN Television, assisted by his sons James A. Love and William Love and his son-in-law Gordon Carter. Robert Lamb, Technical Supervisor of Radio Station CFCN, also appeared. Gordon Love was a pioneer in radio broadcasting, having formed his own company and then acquiring CFCN in 1928. He was associated for a time with CHCT-TV, the CBC affiliate in Calgary. Mr. Love was the proprietor of the *Farm and Ranch Review* and had had a special interest in radio news broadcasting. There were no interests in the application other than those of the Love family.

Chinook Communications was represented by R.L. Fenety, Counsel-Secretary to the Company. A.G. Bailey, President, introduced the other shareholders. The main submission was made by Herbert S. Stewart who had been engaged as Vice-President and General Manager. Mr. Stewart was experienced in television broadcasting, and had left his position with CHCT-TV to assist in the application for Chinook. The shareholders of Chinook were all influential businessmen and citizens of Calgary. Mr. Bailey was Vice-President and General Manager of Bailey, Selburn Oil and Gas. Other shareholders included Frank McMahon and George McMahon of Pacific Petroleums; Eldon Tanner, President, Canadian Gas Association and a director of Trans-Canada Pipe Lines; Carl Nickle, President, Conick Petroleum and C.O. Nickle Publications; Mayor Harry Hays (who became associated before he decided to run as mayor); Ronald L. Jenkins, Jenkins Groceterias; Watson M. Hook, President, Hook Signs; Harry Cohen, Director and Manager, General Distributors; Harold Henker, President, McGee Drugs; Fred Mannix, President, Mannix Company; Gordon Elves, President, F. Gordon Elves Investments; Edward O'Connor, President, O'Connor-Bourougue Men's Wear; and Peter Rule, a partner in Rule, Wynn, Rule, Architects. None of the shareholders had any other interest in the mass media.

The Board recommended the application of CFCN Television for approval and the licence was issued to them.

HALIFAX (20–21 JUNE 1960)

The Board heard competing applications for Channel 5 in Halifax.

The first application, on behalf of CHAL Television, was an application by Mitchell Franklin and Peter Herschorn of Franklin-Herschorn Theatres. They referred to the impact of television on the motion picture theatre business, and their desire to diversify their investments. A.G. Cooper appeared as their counsel. Other directors of the television company who assisted in the presentation were Lloyd MacInnes, Vice-President and General Manager; William Piekarski, Technical Director; and John Cameron Graham, Program Director. These three had had experience in television in Halifax. J.B. Rogan, of Imperial Advertising, spoke to the question of the commercial potentialities of the market.

The second application was by CJCH-TV. The principals were Gerald Martin, Chairman of the Board; Finlay MacDonald, President; H.M. Standish, Secretary. Associated Television, United Kingdom, was a minor shareholder and was represented on the Board of Directors by William Jones of Canastel.

Representatives of the Halifax Board of Trade endorsed the establishment of a second station, and a brief from the Halifax-Dartmouth and District Labour Council opposed the application of CJCH-TV.

The licence went to CJCH-TV on the recommendation of the Board.

OTTAWA (23–28 JUNE 1960)

The concluding hearings opened were held in Ottawa with five applications for an English-language station operating on Channel 13.

Lawrence Frieman had associated with him Arthur Crawley of Crawley Films; the Southam Company, owners of *The Ottawa Citizen;* Ken Soble of Radio Station CHML, Hamilton and a group of Ottawa citizens. Mr. Soble was to be General Manager during the development period.

Frank Ryan, of Radio Station CFRA, based his case primarily on experience and performance. A unique aspect of the proposal was that the equity stock would be held by employees. The transmitter site would be in the Gatineau Park, on the site of the radio transmitter, resulting in substantial coverage. Reference was made to the early experience of CBOT-TV in bilingual broadcasting and to the establishment of CBOFT-TV. Mr. Ryan stressed that the staff of CFRA was mainly bilingual. He proposed a French-language program on Sunday evenings, and a children's program.

Roger Sequin appeared as the principal in an application by Inter-City Broadcasting, identified with both Ottawa and Hull. The 28 shareholders—both English- and French-speaking—were all residents of the Ottawa Valley. The Directors included Walter Herbert, Dr. Pierre Gendron, Dr. John Robbins, Mrs. A.F.W. Plumptre and Joe Feller. Bruce McLeod had been engaged as General Manager.

The corporate shareholders in Rideau Television Associates were FP Publications, owners of *The Ottawa Journal,* and Associated Television, United Kingdom. Gratton O'Leary appeared on behalf of the applicant.

The final application, by E.L. Bushnell and Associates, involved the participation of Granada Network, United Kingdom, represented by Stuart Griffiths, and NTA Television of Canada. NTA Television of Canada had been established by an agreement between Toronto International Film Studios, which operated a circuit of theatres, and NTA of the United States, for the distribution of film. NTA Television of Canada was owned 50% by the U.S. company. The participation of the two corporate shareholders was less than the 25% maximum provided for in the Broadcasting Act. In order to preserve control of the station in the hands of the individual shareholders, who were mainly Ottawa residents, a voting trust had been established. The three trustees were Mr. Bushnell, Raoul Landriault and G.E. Beament, Q.C. The trust represented 53.4% of the voting stock and could not be changed without the approval of the BBG. Mr. Bushnell was to be President and General Manager, and Stuart Griffiths, Assistant General Manager.

The Board recommended the application of E.L. Bushnell and Associates and the licence was duly issued.

AN OVERVIEW

The Broadcasting Act was explicit on the matter of non-Canadian participation in broadcasting stations, limiting this to 25% of the ownership of any station. The Board had not made any statement of policy on non-Canadian participation within the limits permitted by the Act. In the applications, however, participation by U.S. broadcasting interests was conspicuously absent, indicating that applicants did not believe such participation would advance their claims. Two private television companies in the United Kingdom—Associated Television and Granada—were parties to applications. Associated Television was involved substantially in an unsuccessful application in Vancouver but much less so in the successful application in Halifax. The Toronto application, in which Granada had a part, was unsuccessful—but they were involved in the successful application in Ottawa. There were two successful applications in which some interpretation of the non-Canadian conditions was required. These involved the Canadian Marconi Company in Montreal and NTA participation in Bushnell Broadcasting, Ottawa.

In the examination of applications, attention was directed to the participation in other media of communications by the organizations involved. On this matter, the legislation contained no direction to the Board and the Board had made no regulation or statement of policy. Several local radio stations applied, generally putting the case for combined operations of radio and television on the basis of broadcasting experience and of economies that could be affected by combined operations. In Calgary, and again in Halifax, the licence went to a radio station, and a local radio station was a major participant in the station licensed in Winnipeg. On the other hand, the applications by CKEY and CFRB in Toronto were unsuccessful. Film distributors were also frequent participants. The advantage claimed for film distribution was the availability of film material, without exclusivity. The successful French-language application in Montreal was by a film distributing company, and the successful Ottawa application included a film distributing company. J. Arthur Rank, Canada was associated with an unsuccessful application in Toronto. Sovereign Films was unsuccessful in Vancouver but Paul Nathanson had a piece of Baton, Aldred, Rogers, Toronto.

Newspapers or publishing companies were among the principals in a number of applications. The Board decided against the application in Winnipeg which involved the Sifton interests and against the application in Vancouver in which the Vancouver *Province* and Vancouver *Sun* were included. The application involving the Southam Company was unsuccessful in Ottawa. Newspapers—including the three daily papers—and publishers were widely represented in the Toronto applications.

The Toronto Star was in an unusual position. Mr. Honderick said:

> We would not normally be making an application for this licence. We have been prompted to do so by the principles which we think should govern the operation of a second Toronto television station and I would like to state now that if any other applicant unconnected with the existing media of communication is prepared to operate a Toronto station on a similar basis, we will withdraw in favour of that applicant.[9]

In reply to a question, Mr. Honderick said that in the ordinary course of events newspapers should not control any other form or media of communication.[10] *The Globe and Mail* offered no apologies for its application, and *The Toronto Telegram* suffered from no inhibitions. The *Telegram* spokesman said, "As the Board knows, there are presently in Canada many television stations—several of them even in monopoly areas—which are owned or controlled by newspapers, and this pattern has been well established."[11]

Mr. Honderick contended that broadcasting should be treated as a public utility with a limitation on profits. He proposed that, although the voting preferred stock and control should be held by *The Star,* the common equity stock would be held by a Foundation composed of people with general interests in the community. The initial trustees of the Foundation would be named by *The Star;* thereafter the trustees would themselves fill the vacancies. The investment would be amortized over fifteen years and subsequently interest would be limited to 7%. The surplus profits would be at the disposal of the Foundation for the production of programs which would contribute to public knowledge and enlightenment. If it were preferred that the Foundation should not control the station, *The Star* was prepared to meet the conditions of the Charitable Gifts Act by transferring the common stock to chosen charitable organizations, or to seek an amendment to the Act.

Licences were issued by the Minister of Transport, and the Department of Transport was responsible for the management of the spectrum. Applications for licences were made to the Department of Transport. They were vetted in order to ensure that they conformed to the technical regulations of the Department before being passed to the Board to go to public hearing. The Board did not have to concern itself with the technical aspects of the application. It was, however, naturally interested in the coverage of the proposed station; in some cities there were significant differences, depending on the siting of the transmitter and the engineering parameters. In Winnipeg two of the applicants applied for maximum power with omni-directional antennas, although differences in transmitter site made for differences in contour. The third applied for reduced power with a directional antenna. In Vancouver there were four applicants for Channel 8, a fifth for Channel 10. Among the four applying for Channel 8, two proposed to locate the transmitter on Burnaby Mountain, one on Mount Seymour and one on Mount Hollyburn. In Montreal, because of the advantages of the Mount Royal location and in order to avoid duplication of towers there, it was arranged that the two additional antennas would be placed on the tower already constructed by the CBC. In Toronto, S.W. Caldwell Limited planned joint use of the CBC tower. It was known that the CBC planned to move its facilities, but Mr. Caldwell implied that his company would either move with the CBC or continue to use the original tower. The antenna was directional, giving a strong signal for the main concentration of population but somewhat limited in geographical coverage. CFRA, in Ottawa, had been granted permission to construct its tower in Gatineau Park. The opportunity to use this site offered substantial coverage to the proposed television stations. The successful applicant in Ottawa was eventually able to negotiate the use of the site.

Considerable attention was given to studio facilities, equipment and location as factors affecting the capacity to produce live local programs. In Vancouver, two of the applicants proposed separate transmitter and studio sites, with downtown studios; the others proposed the same site, governed by the location of the transmitter. In Toronto, Mr. Cooke had built a new studio building with sufficient capacity for a television operation. On the other hand, Baton, Aldred, Rogers Broadcasting planned extensive new studio facilities, involving an expenditure of $1,358,536 on land and buildings and $2,021,185 on equipment. The successful applicants in Ottawa projected $800,000 for equipment and $700,000 for the station building to be financed on a lease purchase basis. Applicants were questioned on the provision they had made for conversion to colour and inquiries were also made about video tape equipment as a means of exchanging tapes between stations.

Understandably, the total investment proposed was generally greater in the larger centres; but even in the same centre the amounts differed substantially. The total estimated capital cost in the successful Calgary application was $881,000. In Toronto, Baton, Aldred, Rogers Broadcasting estimated initial capital costs—including land, buildings, equipment, preliminary costs and working capital—at more than $4.5 million.

The Board was interested in the methods of financing and in their effect on the location and stability of control. A great variety of financing methods were proposed and it was often difficult to determine the precise locus of control.

The Board concerned itself with the management team. Experience in Canadian television could be drawn either from the CBC or from private television stations. There were, of course, no applications from private television stations. In some applications there was an involvement by companies participating in television stations, for instance, Selkirk Holdings, Southam Company and FP Publications; they had little success. Some applicants had already engaged experienced management personnel. In other cases, contracts had been entered into but it was impossible to disclose publicly names and the Board received this information on a confidential basis. It seemed that any company receiving a licence would be able to attract experienced management personnel.

Perhaps the most striking feature of the hearings in cities with multiple applications was the wide range of estimates of revenues. The question of revenues was a fundamental one affecting both the capacity to survive and the ability to sustain the costs of Canadian production. What emerged generally was a projection of losses, not including preproduction costs, in the first year with profits in the third year. It was often difficult to compare the projections in the briefs. Sometimes the revenue figures were gross; in other cases they were net after agency fees. In the expenditure figures there was sometimes provision for amortization and depreciation, but the method of providing for depreciation varied. In other cases net revenues were presented "before depreciation." The profit and loss statement and the statement of each flow were relevant to the capitalization of the company, particularly to the provision of working capital. Applicants were questioned on their ability to acquire additional funds if their projections proved to be too optimistic.

It seemed apparent that applicants attempted first to estimate revenues and then, to some extent, expenditures—including expenditures on programming—were tailored to the revenues anticipated. The more generous the applicant's revenue estimates, the more he was prepared to offer in live Canadian production and Canadian content. Applicants knew that the revenue they could attract would depend primarily on the share of the audience they could deliver (especially in the peak viewing hours), the rates charged to sponsors and advertisers and the cost per thousand. In cities in which the only competing signals were those of the CBC station, applicants were generally optimistic on the share of the audience they could attract. Where the station would also have to compete the U.S. stations, for instance in Toronto, Vancouver and Winnipeg, estimates tended to vary more widely. The tendency was to set rates 10 to 20% below the rates of competing stations. Applicants indicated significant differences in the proportion of time they expected to sell, initially, and the rate at which sell-out would increase.

Both the Board and the applicants were aware of the relation revenue and costs bore to programming; the wide variations in estimates, however, gave the Board little assistance in making its own assessment. All applicants dealt with their proposed program schedule, some in great detail, summarizing them in terms of live Canadian programs and Canadian content in different time periods. The regulations required 45% Canadian content at the outset, advancing to 55%.

Some applicants offered the minimum required by the regulations, while others proposed to exceed the 55% Canadian content even at the outset. The Board had placed conditions on morning broadcasting but the proposed broadcasting times varied. Some applicants were anxious to get into morning broadcasting as soon as possible; others proposed restricted hours at the beginning. Frequent reference was made to the cost of producing Canadian programs and to the capacity of live Canadian programs—as against imported syndicated tape and film programs—to draw audiences. In assessing the competing applications, the Board had to weigh all these elements.[12]

As the hearings progressed and stations were licensed, the Board was informed of conversations which were proceeding on exchange of programs, and applicants showed interest in the possibilities. At the Toronto meetings, the prospective station was frequently referred to as the "anchor" or "flagship" of the second English-language network. Mr. Borden, of Toronto Telecasters Association, made a specific proposal for a video tape and film network. He proposed, 90 days after going on air, to make available seven and a half hours per week of good quality programs—14 half-hour live programs and two shorter programs. The distribution would be increased to ten hours in the second year.[13] In speaking to the Caldwell application Mr. Keeble said:

There has been a great deal of comment and speculation about the formation of a second network of some kind by second television stations. We have been very active in this speculation because of the very obvious advantages to all of us that some exchange of program service will bring. . . . However, there will be no reluctance on our part to share the load on some of our more elaborate and expensive productions.[14]

On questioning, Mr. Caldwell said:

I think we have discussed exchange programs with every applicant in Canada except Toronto, and with the Winnipeg licensee and the Vancouver licensee. In our brief we have listed the programs we think are suitable for exchange programs. We have costed these programs, we have sent a list of these out to the stations. We have had some letters back thinking they are quite good, and amazed at the rates for a market like Halifax or Ottawa. We have pages and pages of research on the video tape network and the microwave network. We could take the next two hours to explain to you our opinion, philosophy, and system we propose for private station network broadcasting in Canada. This is my field.[15]

In Ottawa, Mr. Bushnell said his company would be delighted to cooperate with any responsible group planning a network operation. However, he expressed opposition to further concentration in Toronto.[16] His company proposed to be makers, not takers, of programs and he believed that the station could make a substantial contribution in the network, particularly in news. Spencer Caldwell, who had failed to receive a station licence in Toronto, was a minor shareholder in the company,

The recommendation that the Toronto licence be awarded, in effect, to *The Telegram* had stirred up charges of political favouritism on the part of the Board. The charge was made openly in a letter to the press by Joseph Sedgwick, who had appeared for Standard Radio.[17] It is not possible to confirm or to deny the charge. The Board, as constituted by the Diefenbaker government, contained a predominance of committed Conservatives; the allegiance of *The Telegram* and of John Bassett was obvious. In meetings of the Board where applications were discussed, the political affiliation of the applicant was never mentioned. When members cast their votes there was no way in which the Chairman could determine whether or not their judgement was influenced by political considerations. The Chairman did not favour the application by *The Telegram,* principally on the grounds that it was unnecessary and that it would be a mistake to give the television licence to one of the daily newspapers; he himself did not vote in support of that particular application. Still, it has been noted that Baton, Aldred, Rogers did make a most effective presentation of their case.

[5]

THE TORONTO STATION AND
THE INVOLVEMENT OF ABC

THE IMPACT OF THE NEW stations on the market was substantial, but not unexpected. Prior to 1960 the revenues and net profits of private television stations had been increasing, and it was clear that in the major markets served only by a CBC station there was unfilled demand for advertising time. With the emergence of second stations in the eight major cities, the increase in revenues of established stations in the smaller centres was checked and profits were sharply reduced. The full effect was experienced in 1961. In that year about half of the established private stations experienced losses, and the aggregate losses exceeded profits.[1]

The general experience with the second stations was that, with respect to the initial years, the applicants had been overly optimistic. In 1961, the nine new stations obtained $15,000,000 in gross revenues; but in their first full year of operation, aggregate losses (before depreciation and taxes) amounted to $4,800,000. In 1962, the aggregate revenue of the nine stations increased 57%, and aggregate losses were reduced to slightly over $1,000,000. By 1963, aggregate profits (before depreciation and taxes) reached $1,400,000. In the case of particular stations, losses significantly in excess of those anticipated led to modifications in programming, and in some instances to substantial reorganization.

After 1963, the financial position of the new stations generally improved rapidly. Revenues rose to $27,896,000 in 1964; $34,388,000 in 1965; and $40,360,000 in 1966. All stations reported profits in 1967.

The case of reorganization which disturbed the Board most was that of CFTO-TV, Toronto. When it met on 21 August 1961, the Board discussed an application forwarded to it by the Minister of Transport, the Hon. Leon Balcer, for a change of shares in the company owning CFTO-TV, Toronto. The application provided for the purchase of stock by AB-Paramount Theatres (AB-PT), the owners of the ABC Network in the United States, and for the acquisition of the shares held by Aldred, Rogers Broadcasting. E.A. Goodman, counsel for the licensee, had asked for a meeting with the Board to explain the proposal. Everyone knew that CFTO-TV was experiencing financial difficulties and apparently there was public knowledge of the application. The Board had before it a letter from a Toronto lawyer claiming that, before dealing with transfers involving American interests, the unsuccessful applicants for the Toronto licence should be given an opportunity to present their cases again. The Board agreed to meet with representatives of Baton, Aldred, Rogers Broadcasting and of the American Broadcasting Company. The date was set for 24 August.

The meeting of 24 August was attended by Mr. Goodman, John Bassett, John Graham (representing the Aldred-Rogers interests) and Donald Coyle, Vice-President, International Division, ABC. The reasons for the proposal were presented by Mr. Goodman. First, differences on management matters had developed within the organization, specifically between Joel Aldred and Mr. Bassett. Mr. Aldred was the partner in the team with experience in television. Mr. Bassett seemed to attribute the financial difficulties of the station to the rather expensive advice from Mr. Aldred. The application from the Telegram Publishing Company to purchase the shares of Aldred, Rogers Broadcasting would resolve this problem. Ted Rogers, who later extended his radio operations in Toronto, would retain a minor interest in CFTO-TV. Mr. Graham assured the Board that his clients were supporting the application. Second, Mr. Bassett reported pre-operating costs of

$1,000,000 and an operating deficit over the first seven months of $1,200.00. The investment in facilities seemed excessive. The attempt had been made, unsuccessfully, to sell the building and arrange for a lease-back. In the application for the licence, the staff had been estimated at 305. It had actually risen to 400 but was now reduced to 311. The shareholders already had heavy investments in the station. Because of losses incurred, additional capital was required. The shareholders were either unwilling or unable to increase their investment. Alternative possibilities had been explored with the Southam and Thomson interests but, while additional capital was urgently needed, the control position of the Telegram Publishing Company was not negotiable. AB-PT was prepared to provide the capital without demanding control. Third, it was necessary to build up the resources of the station. It was hoped that through the association with ABC it would be possible to sell some of the station's productions in the United States; the experience that the new associates would bring to the operations would be of material help. Mr. Coyle stressed the experience of his company. He said they were not anxious to acquire control, had not sought a management agreement, and were not interested in CFTO-TV as an outlet.

The proposal was that AB-PT would buy some $300,000 worth of equity stock, and invest $2,000,000 in debentures. They would name three directors of the board of twelve. Their 25% of the equity common stock would represent 18.8% of the voting stock. Telegram Publishing Company would retain 36.3% of the voting stock with smaller proportions held by Ted Rogers, Foster Hewitt and Paul Nathanson (Sovereign Film Distributors).

Later in the discussion of the application within the Board, the first question raised was whether or not the application should be taken to a public hearing. It was agreed that the Telegram Publishing Company would still be in a position of control and that, as a change of control did not seem to be involved, the Board was not required under its normal procedures to hold a public hearing of the case. There was then a motion to approve the application. At this point the Chairman expressed his concern. While agreeing that the station did need management know-how, he believed that the participation of AB-PT did not advance the purposes of the Broadcasting Act and would make the pursuit of these purposes more difficult. There was little doubt that all three of the U.S. networks would be pleased to have direct participation in Canadian television if this was acceptable to Canada and that, if ABC were admitted, the other two networks would feel obliged to get in. Finally, it appeared that, the earlier experiences of the station notwithstanding, ABC apparently thought the station represented a good investment. The motion for approval was put and carried by one vote.

The Chairman then argued that the public was entitled to know the facts of the case and that a statement should be published. The mover of the motion that had just carried became concerned and wished to withdraw the motion. This was not allowed, but a motion to reopen the question was carried. Later, a draft of a recommendation was prepared by the Chairman in consultation with some of the members and was read to the Board. The statement proposed a deferment of thirty days to allow the licensee to obtain offers from experienced Canadian broadcasting interests on terms and conditions substantially as favourable as in the AB-PT offer. It was agreed by the Board to pass the recommendation to the Minister, and to advise Mr. Bassett that the Board would be prepared to deal immediately with a revised application providing only for the transfer of the Aldred, Rogers shares. The Board agreed to meet on 26 September to consider any alternative offer and also agreed that, if no alternative offers were before the Board in September, the Board would then recommend for approval the application before them.

A public announcement outlining the details of the agreement was issued on 28 August 1961.[2]

At the opening of the Board's meeting on 26 September 1961, the Chairman referred to letters in opposition to the proposal, and to a visit from the representative of the National Broadcasting Company—NBC Network. There had been a number of letters in opposition to the proposal. The NBC representative had come to say that, if ABC were permitted entry to Canadian television, his network would feel obliged to get in also. He talked about the possibility of buying into CHCH-TV, Hamilton.

The Board then proceeded to review the alternative proposals. Communications had been received from a group of Canadian investors in association with Granada of England; from Taylor Video with support from Associated Rediffusion, another English company; and from the Thomson interests. There was also a letter filed by Mr. Bassett on 25 September stating he had not had any offer as specified in the Board's announcement of 28 August. The Board agreed that no firm offer "on terms and conditions substantially as favourable to the station" had been made.

During the interval, opposition to the AB-PT proposal within the Board had been hardening. There were even threats of resignation should the AB-PT proposal be accepted.[3] Two questions were debated: first, could the Board refuse to recommend the sale of stock in a licensed broadcasting company which could legitimately be made under the provisions of the Act? Second, could the Board reverse itself from a position taken in a public announcement? There was some support for the view that the Board should not "go beyond" the Act. On the second point it was felt that the applicant had not, as a result of the announcement, entered into commitments which would result in loss if the Board reversed its decision, consequently, there would be no grounds for action; the Board could reverse its position.

A motion was then passed rescinding decisions taken at the August meeting. A further motion was carried recommending denial of the application and stating the Board was not prepared to commend any transaction involving participation by American networks in Canadian television stations. There was some dissent. Edward Dunlop registered his dissent and asked that it be made public.

On 27 September the Board wrote the Minister of Transport, referring to the application:

At its meeting on September 26, 1961 the Board considered this application and passed the following resolution: "The Board recommends denial of the application because on further consideration the Board was not prepared to recommend any transaction involving financial participation of American networks in Canadian television stations."

The recommendation of the Board is, therefore, for denial in this case.

Mr. Edward Dunlop wished his position to be recorded as follows:

> Mr. Edward Dunlop dissented, and wished to record his reasons. He referred to, and quoted from the Board's recommendation to the Minister, dated August 28th, "that approval of this application be deferred to provide the applicant an opportunity to receive offers from experienced Canadian broadcasting interests on terms and conditions substantially as favourable to the station as the offer which the applicant has received from the American Broadcasting-Paramount Theatres Incorporated" and "if, in the opinion of the Board, no acceptable offer as defined above has been received by noon on Monday, September 25th, the Board will at that time recommend the approval of the present application for the transfer of shares."
>
> In Mr. Dunlop's view, no such offer has been made or received, no new evidence had been introduced, and there was no new element in the case. He was also of the opinion that the denial of this application would impair the interests of the applicant and that the Board of Broadcast Governors, as an administrative body, should not reach a decision having such a result in a case where the applicant proposed to do only that which had been specifically provided for by Parliament. It was Mr. Dunlop's dissenting opinion that the Board should now forward its recommendation for the approval of the application in accordance with the decision announced on August 28th, 1961.[4]

Subsequently an agreement was entered into between Baton Broadcasting and AB-PT under which CFTO-TV received a loan in substantially the same amount as involved in the share transfer and which provided for participation by AP-PT in the profits of CFTO-TV. The loan agreement had the same effect as the transfer-of-share proposal.

In a letter to Mr. Bassett, the Chairman said: "I cannot agree that an arrangement 'the terms of which in no way infringe upon the Act' cannot evade the intent of the Act,"[5] but the Board had no authority with respect to loans. The Chairman saw the Minister of Transport on the matter of the agreement between CFTO-TV and AB-PT. The Minister suggested the Board draft a regulation which would place loan arrangements under the jurisdiction of the Board. The Board decided to enact a regulation requiring licensees to file with the Board the terms of any loan or management agreement. On 5 December they wrote the Minister, enclosing draft amendments to the Broadcasting Act. These amendments gave the Board authority to approve agreements under which the station was operated by someone other than the licensee or his *bona fide* employees, and applied to networks conditions respecting Canadian ownership similar to those already applying to stations. They were not pursued by the Government.

In January 1962 the Board learned, through a complaint from one of the CTV Network affiliates, that Mr. Coyle of ABC had attended meetings of the Directors of CTV Network. The following letter was sent to Mr. Coyle with copies to Mr. Goldenson, the President of ABC (New York), Mr. Bassett and Mr. Caldwell of CTV Network. "I understand that on two occasions you have tried to intrude into the meetings of CTV Network. I must make it clear to you that as long as you are an employee of ABC Network you have no recognized status in Canadian broadcasting. Your participation in the determination of the policies of any approved broadcasting organization in Canada could prejudice the status of the organization."[6]

Neither Mr. Coyle nor Mr. Goldenson acknowledged the letter. Mr. Caldwell and Mr. Bassett both wrote saying Mr. Coyle was invited to the CTV meetings. In reply to Mr. Caldwell, the Chairman wrote:

It goes without saying that you may invite experts to any meetings "if it is generally agreed by the network and affiliates that advice on certain matters would be helpful." Indeed if it is possible for the network to disassociate itself from the affiliates who are also shareholders in the network, I suppose it is possible for the network to extend invitations even if the affiliates do not agree.

I have not yet heard from Mr. Coyle. Mr. Bassett wrote. He also said that Mr. Coyle was invited. Neither Mr. Bassett nor you have said from whom the invitation came. As apparently you were not present the invitation must have come from someone else.[7]

[6]

THE CTV NETWORK

STATIONS UNAFFILIATED TO THE CBC network had been licensed in eight cities. Initially they were unconnected. The Board favoured the linking of the English-language stations by microwave as quickly as possible. Its view was that the private sector had a responsibility to lend support to the national broadcasting purposes, by providing and sharing Canadian productions, including news and live events. The Board did not support the idea of a regional network in the central provinces and wished to prevent the Toronto station from dominating the private network. The Board favoured the network organization which would give all of the affiliates a significant involvement, but preferred that final control should be exercised by nonbroadcasting shareholders. The stations preferred a "mutual" company and in the end this form of organization prevailed.

During the hearing of applications for second television station licences, applicants were questioned about exchange of programs as a means of increasing the exposure of Canadian productions and of spreading the costs. The applicants appeared interested and, as stations were licensed, conversations amongst licensees took place. These conversations led eventually to the creation of the Independent Television Organization (ITO) as a means of joint purchase of programs and of program exchange. S.W. Caldwell, having been unsuccessful in his application for the Toronto licence, kept his organization intact and transferred his interest to the formation of a network.

In May 1960, while the Board was meeting in Calgary for hearings on applications for second licences, the Chairman reported on conversations he had had with Mr. Caldwell. Mr. Caldwell's proposal was that the Company, financed by himself and his associates, should enlarge its Board of Directors to 16, eight from his own group and one from each of the eight second stations. The organization would provide a pool of program material on video tape, some of which would be produced, under supervision of the network, in the facilities of the stations. Although their basic concern would be the distribution of taped material, it was suggested that a news gathering service could be organized, and that microwave facilities for distribution might be found to be available by using existing microwave circuits when these were not otherwise required. Initially the organization would supply ten hours of programming a week, increasing to 25 hours a week as time was sold out. Mr. Caldwell wished his proposal to be dealt with formally in June.

The Board's interest in the proposal lay in the opportunity it appeared to present for wider distribution of Canadian programs. Each of the new stations was well equipped with production facilities and was committed to meeting the Canadian content regulations. It seemed to the Board that programs of network quality produced at the stations could obtain a wider audience, with greater opportunity to recover costs, through arrangements for exposure on a number of stations. At its May meeting, the Board agreed to issue a release indicating it was prepared to hear applications for the operation of a second network at its September meeting, and, in anticipation of this, to issue guiding principles in June.

The release of 17 May 1960 said that if, in the view of the second stations, network arrangements would assist them to implement their plans and to provide an improved quality of service, it would be the wish of the Board to facilitate such arrangements. It was noted that: "distribution of programs by video tape does not constitute a network as defined in the regulations, and arrangements for the distribution of programs by this means can proceed without reference to the Board."[1] The Board believed, however, that if the linking of second television stations by network on a basis which would be consistent with the provisions of the Broadcasting Act was feasible, the necessary arrangements should proceed as rapidly as possible so as to be of the maximum service to the stations which would go on the air shortly.

It was announced that the Board would, after 20 June, outline some general conditions which, in the opinion of the Board, a permanent private television network should meet, and that in September the Board would hear representations on the proposed conditions "and also applications which may be presented to the Board for the operation of a network, subject to such conditions as the Board may prescribe in keeping with the purpose of the Broadcasting Act."[2]

On 30 May the Board, at their request, met with the representatives of the second private stations. The first point discussed was the possibility that the CBC would apply for a second network to which they would be affiliated. The stations were opposed to this development. During the period of the single station policy, government policy was effective in determining the structure of the system. The determination of the pattern of program service, including commercial policy, and the relations between the public and private sector were left to the CBC. With respect to the service it was not clear that Parliament knew what it wanted the CBC to contribute; or, if it did, that it was prepared to meet the cost. When the single station policy was lifted and second stations were licensed, neither the BBG nor the CBC was given any directions on the way in which the structure was to develop.

On behalf of the Board, it was said that the Board had not considered the possibility of the CBC applying for the second network. If the Corporation came forward with an application at the September hearing, the Board would probably hear it, but the Board's thinking had not been predicated on the establishment of two CBC networks, and the expectation had been that if a second network were established it would not be owned or controlled by the Corporation. The second point raised by the stations had reference to access to private stations affiliated with the CBC for the distribution of programs of a private network. It was argued that the opportunity for wider distribution would enhance the prospects for a private network, and that private licensees should be free to take programs from both the CBC network and the proposed private network. The Chairman of the Board stated that, in general, the Board felt that if good programs were available from any network their distribution should not be artificially restricted, but noted that, as the CBC network was a truly national system, the widest possible distribution would probably mean distribution through the CBC network. Finally, the stations stressed that the development of another network should proceed from the bottom up rather than by a superimposed requirement of the Board, and the Board should not require any individual station to affiliate with any network without the agreement of the station concerned. The Chairman said the Board would not under normal conditions wish to exercise this authority. To ensure effective coverage, however, the Board would be interested in some minimum participation by stations in any new network; it would not be in favour of the setting up of a regional network, for example, between Toronto, Ottawa and Montreal, as an alternative to a more comprehensive network.

The spokesman for the stations, Mr. Bassett, then said the stations might appear at the September meeting to present an application and, if they did, there would be no other applications, it being generally accepted that the establishment of a network by the stations themselves would be preferable to any other proposal. If the stations were unable to appear in September, they would probably request a postponement of any decision until they were ready with their proposal. Mr. Bassett explained that, although the proposed organization of a station network had not been fully worked out, the present thinking of the licensees would be to set up a private organization in which shares would be held by the private stations presently licensed. An outside network management group would be brought in to operate the network on a fee basis. New affiliates would be added to the network without provision for ownership of new shares by them. These stations would perhaps be affiliated on a supplementary basis and programming would be sold to them. The Chairman emphasized that the Board must be in a position to deal with specific network proposals at the public hearing and that, if the private licensees intended to come forward, they should make every effort to agree on a network plan in time for the hearing in September. Mr. Bassett stressed that the private licensees were convinced that a new network was inevitable and felt that the existing private stations should form the nucleus of the network itself. He pointed out that groups such as that proposed by Mr. Caldwell might be in a position, if granted approval by the Board to form a network, to move in on the stations—with the Board's approval—and, in effect, to require them to become part of the network, while the company would bring to the formation of the network nothing more substantial than the necessary capital and the Board's approval.

The Chairman inquired as to what action the private licensees would take if, at the September hearing, they were not in a position to make application for a network and other groups would appear with applications which carried commitments from the private stations to affiliate with their proposed network. Mr. Bassett replied that, in his view, this would probably not happen, because the private stations would probably not give such commitments and every attempt was being made to have a network application ready for the September hearing. He suggested that any new network must inevitably depend on the facilities and plant of the private stations, as it was not economically possible to set up a program centre simply to distribute programs to affiliate stations.

In the discussion that followed, the Chairman indicated that, in his view, the Board would probably not look favourably on a proposed application by ABC in the United States, simply because of the ownership involved, and that the Board would oppose an outright formal affiliation agreement which would make a Canadian station a subsidiary part of a U.S. network. Arrangements that Canadian stations would take specific programs or packages of programs would not be opposed by the Board.

The introduction of second television service changed the relations between the public sector and the private sector. The new private stations had no attachment to the CBC. When consideration was being given to the formation of a network to serve the private stations, some supporters of public broadcasting proposed that the stations should be affiliated with the CBC in a second CBC network. The CBC itself recognized this as impractical. During the period when the second stations were getting established the Board considered the possibility that the CBC might supply some Canadian programs to them. The CBC showed some interest in the idea; but the private stations, although having difficulty in getting established and in meeting the Canadian content regulations, did not wish to be attached to the CBC in any way. For a time the Board explored co-operative arrangements which held out the possibility of reducing costs on both sides, e.g., common towers, co-operative purchasing of foreign syndicated programs, co-operative coverage of events of general interest. There was little disposition on either side to work together. Each wished to be independent of the other; that is, to maintain the position of competition. The CBC felt its position was paramount and the private sector (apart from its affiliates) was none of its concern. Further, the CBC felt it was quite capable of coping with the competition, provided the BBG imposed adequate obligations on the private stations. Although they claimed the competition of the publicly-supported CBC was often "unfair" competition, and wished more rigorous conditions imposed on the CBC, the private broadcasters were congenital competitors.

A release on 30 June gave some indication of the conditions which applicants could be expected to meet, subject to modifications following the September public meeting. The Board noted that while it had the authority to require television stations to operate as part of a network of the CBC, the Broadcasting Act enabled the Board only to permit television stations to operate as part of a network other than a network of the Corporation. "The Board does not have and will not seek the authority to require stations to affiliate with or to prevent stations from disaffiliating from a private network."[3] The conditions proposed covered assurances of a minimum amount of time of actual microwave connection, participation by a minimum number of stations, and affiliation agreements between the stations and the network. No minimum amount of time of microwave connection was specified. "It now appears to the Board that a private television network should include a provision that (a) at least six "second" television stations should hold voting stock in the company; but the stock held by all stations may not exceed 49% of the voting stock authorized or issued; (b) it is provided that one-half of the Directors of the

Company are to be elected by the six or more stations holding stock in the Company."[4] The minimum of six stations was set in order to ensure that the operation was more than a regional network in the central provinces. The Board favoured substantial participation by stations in the network company, short of actual control. Affiliation agreements, to be approved by the Board, were to be required. "No television station may be affiliated with more than one network, but the affiliation agreement between a network and a station may not prevent the station from securing particular programs or series of programs from another network in Canada."[5] No network might have any exclusive contract to take programs from one program supplier or non-Canadian network; and a network must observe the regulations of the Board that apply to stations, final responsibility for the programs and program policy of the network resting upon the network company.

The question of a second network was the principal item discussed at a meeting of the Consultative Committee on Private Broadcasting on 28 July 1960. The Chairman of the Board referred to the fact that the second stations had met on 18 July and had established the ITO, and that representatives of ITO had reported orally to the Chairman and Mr. Allison on their meeting. The Board expected to receive later, in writing, the views of the stations on some matters affecting a second television network. It was understood there was some doubt in the minds of some or all of the stations as to the appropriateness of proceeding with a network organization at the time.

In the discussion, the Board's representatives reiterated the views they had expressed at the meeting on 30 May. The principal questions raised by the representatives of the CAB had to do with affiliations. With reference to the possible disaffiliation of stations from the CBC, so that they might affiliate with a private network, the Board's representatives said that an application for disaffiliation from the network of the CBC would be affected by the policy principles established by the Board, and particularly by its view that the Corporation's programs should be available to all communities receiving service. The Board would not approve disaffiliation in areas where no CBC network service was available from other sources. Reference was made by the representatives of the CAB to a move by the CBC to revise its affiliation agreement to include a clause requiring that the CBC affiliates may not take programs from another network. In response, the representatives of the Board indicated that they would not look favourably on such exclusivity. One of the owners of a station affiliated with the CBC then pointed out that, since affiliation agreements between a network and a station would permit the station to secure particular programs or series of programs from another network in Canada, second stations would be able to meet their Canadian content requirement by obtaining programs from the CBC for broadcasting during Class "B" time, thus leaving Class "A" time available for purely commercial use. CBC affiliates, on the other hand, would be required to carry the Corporation's sustaining program during Class "A" time, and would thus be placed at a competitive disadvantage. He said he felt very strongly about this.

After the meeting of the Consultative Committee on Private Broadcasting, a memorandum was prepared for the Board members, dealing with the several conditions proposed in the release of 30 June. The memorandum made reference to the problem of defining a network, and referred to controversy over the proposals with respect to station participation and affiliation agreements. It seemed possible that distribution of programs by video tape would be important. If ITO functioned for the purpose of distributing programs by video tape, should it be seen as a "network"?

Because of the difficulty of arriving at a definition of a network appropriate to future conditions, it seemed best to proceed under the existing definition as an organization or arrangement employing or involving electronic connections between two or more stations.

It was noted that the section on station participation indicated a preference for a company in which final control rested with non-broadcasting shareholders, rather than a mutual company controlled by the stations. This condition was bound to be controversial. The Board had not favoured a mutual company mainly on the grounds that the control of such a company could be expected to be exercised by the Toronto station. Such was the expectation of the Toronto station, but the other stations were not anxious to place the Toronto station in a dominant position. In addition, there appeared to be reason to doubt the effective operation of a mutual. Station operators were highly individualistic, and the interests of the stations were not identical. Experience raised doubts that under a mutual arrangement the stations could work together smoothly and effectively. On the other hand, it was clear from the views expressed by the stations that they would wish to have a substantial say in the operation of a network. The proposal of the Board would place them in a position to protect their interests and to influence the operations of the network to a substantial degree. Their final protection was that they could not be compelled to remain in affiliation with the network.

There was bound to be controversy on the condition that, while no television station might be affiliated with more than one network, the affiliation agreement between a network and a station may not prevent the station from securing particular programs or series of programs from another network in Canada. What was proposed was that, through affiliation, a station would identify itself with one network—either private or the CBC—but that this condition would not prevent a private network from selling programs to stations affiliated with the CBC or the Corporation selling programs to stations affiliated with a private network. It was not anticipated that any "cross-programming" would occur during the time reserved to another network under an affiliation agreement. The memorandum referred to discussions which had taken place on this point.

In earlier discussions with the Corporation, Mr. Ouimet had been reluctant to agree to a proposal that stations affiliated with the CBC should take programs from another network or to the idea that the CBC might offer program to nonaffiliated stations. The Board was later advised that the CBC was prepared to agree to the proposed condition. Apparently some of the Directors of the CBC felt that the CBC should make a substantial effort to provide programs to nonaffiliated stations. The CAB, in a brief to the Parliamentary Committee, had suggested deletion from the Act of the condition which required the approval of a network before a station could take a program from another network. However, in a meeting of the Consultative Committee on Private Broadcasting, representatives of the CBC affiliates had expressed concern about the possibility that the CBC would provide programs to affiliates of a private network. They seemed to fear that the private affiliates would fill the peak hours with U.S. programming, and would then rely on the CBC to give them Canadian content material for release at other times.

In a memorandum to the Board the Chairman said that there was obvious friction between the Toronto station and the other stations. The Toronto station was proceeding rapidly and aggressively to get itself established. It was understood to be asking the other stations to reserve time for programs being supplied to or produced by itself. "However, there is no evidence of willingness on the part of the Toronto station to reserve time for programs that can be made available by other stations; and it should be a matter of concern to the Board that the Toronto station seems to be endeavouring to develop its activities as, in effect, a 'network'."[6]

Members of the Board had been advised that it seemed best to proceed with hearings on the proposed television regulations on 1–2 September. The CBC indicated their intention to present a brief. The ITO might decide at its meeting on 21 August to submit a brief. The CAB had decided not to appear. Some of the new stations had joined the CAB; others had not. It was clear that within the CAB there were differences between the CBC affiliates and stations not affiliated with the Corporation. The CAB was advising member stations that they might make individual submissions if they wished to do so.

At the time there was no assurance that the Board would receive applications for a network under conditions the Board would announce following the September hearings. It was thought that the Board might receive applications for permission to organize a network. There was a feeling in some quarters that if the Board gave the nod to some organization and indicated the Board might approve a later application for a network which met the necessary conditions, a sufficient number of stations would be prepared to join up.

At the hearings on 1–2 September, substantial submissions were made by the CBC, the ITO, Mr. S.W. Caldwell and the CBL. In an opening statement the Board said its concerns were that good quality programs of Canadian origin should have the widest possible exposure in Canada and elsewhere, and that new stations should have the fullest opportunity to get established and to compete effectively. The Board recognized that the initial period would be difficult for the new stations, and wished to facilitate their establishment; the capacity of the CBC and of its affiliates should not be prejudiced; in some markets the most rigorous competition would be from U.S. stations. The 12 conditions previously announced were reviewed and it was stated that, following the hearing, general regulations governing the operation of networks and procedures for applications would be announced.

Mr. Ouimet said the CBC's view was that its national network could not be duplicated by anyone on a purely commercial basis. The CBC was not opposed to second networks, but would oppose any development which was detrimental to the national service or to the partnership between the CBC and its affiliates. New ground was being opened up and it would be wise to make haste slowly. He agreed that the definition of a network was fundamental. Electronic connection was vitally important but was not of itself what constituted a network; therefore, the existing definition was inadequate. A network must provide programs either by production or acquisition, must distribute programs by one of a variety of techniques possible, and must actually broadcast programs. These characteristics were essential but did not constitute a network. Three other conditions were required: First, the network operator must be accountable, but to whom? Second, there must be a contractual arrangement providing for costs of a specified time, and third, the pattern of programming must be designed to meet the objectives of the network. Mr. Ouimet said the CBC was not directly involved in the question of ownership of the network. He felt that there should be close connections with stations, and that the network should own stations. He could not see that control in the hands of a third party was necessary. The condition dealing with affiliation was perhaps the most important. The use of time must not be left to the discretion of an affiliate. Although there might be an exchange of programs, one Canadian network should not in any way operate as part of another network. If the affiliate of one network was sold as part of a package of stations affiliated with another network there would be two affiliations. Network identity and integrity, which were important in promotion, must be maintained. Cross-network programming could hurt this. The CBC accepted as desirable competition between two networks with their own component parts; they opposed competition between two network operators for the time of a single affiliate in the market.[7]

Richard Misener appeared as President of the ITO and was accompanied by Joel Aldred, CFTO-TV, Toronto; Jack Davidson, CJAY-TV, Winnipeg; and E.L. Bushnell, CJOH-TV, Ottawa. The Organization was made up of nine licensed second stations including CFRN-TV, Edmonton and the French-language station CFTM-TV, Montreal. Each station had a Director and was an equal owner. Action was being taken to incorporate. ITO was not seen as a second network. It had the following objectives: to further the development of TV broadcasting; to extend the use of Canadian productions; to facilitate production exchange and purchase in Canada of programs on video tape or film; to expedite exchange of information; and to study the development of an additional Canadian network through the use of film, video tape or electronic means. The ultimate objective was the formation of a network. This would involve electronic connections. In the meantime, no one could prove to the Board that it could get microwave connections on any practical basis, except on a most limited regional basis. The primary function of a network was to move program material. With prevailing recording techniques and jet travel, program material could be moved quickly and more cheaply by these means than by electronic means, and the bulk of material would not suffer from a time lapse. It was hoped that in one year ITO would have a predetermined network schedule, with reserved time commitments by stations. Program choice within reserved time would be made by the network management. The members of ITO felt strongly that program distribution should be controlled by the member stations. A network with electronic connections was not a profitable investment. Microwave costs were too high. The stations did not like the idea of someone wanting a share of their profits. It was desirable, however, to have a strong mutual organization for the acquisition, distribution and sale of programs. The costs would be shared on the basis of the size of the market.[8] The matter of affiliations and of cross-programming came up during questioning. Mr. Aldred made a case for access to network option time of affiliates of the CBC.[9] Mr. Dunlop replied that this would be a dangerous assumption to make.[10] Mr. Bushnell asked if CBC contracts with its affiliates were going to be so tight that CBC affiliates could not take any ITO programs.[11] The Chairman of the Board replied that this would not be the case but that reserved time would be inviolate and programs would not be shown under the label of ITO.[12]

Mr. Caldwell and his associate, Gordon Keeble, claimed that microwave connection was essential and should be considered from the beginning, and produced expert evidence on comparative costs of microwave and video tape distribution. It was said that when facilities were available, and on the basis of four hours per day, Trans-Canada was prepared to offer a rate of $1,025 per hour, Halifax to Vancouver and $125 per hour Toronto, Ottawa, Montreal. Taking into account costs of recording on video tape, preparation of copies, checking tapes at stations, tape depreciation, express and insurance, distribution of tapes, Toronto, Ottawa, Montreal would be more costly than distribution by microwave. Tape distribution, Halifax to Vancouver, might cost $1,325 per hour; although if copying and playback costs could be minimized, tape distribution costs could compare favourably with microwave costs.[13] Mr. Rhind, appearing for Trans-Canada, said the estimates of microwave costs might be on the high side.[14] Mr.Caldwell argued that the network company should be a public company which would act as the management group for the network. The stations should have participation without having control. He did not think that an applicant should have to bargain with the stations before an application was approved. The network should not have access to CBC reserved time, but should be able to do business with CBC affiliates.[15]

John Robbins and Graham Spry appeared for the CBL. The official position of the League was that informed public discussion of the issues was needed and that no action should be taken immediately. Mr. Spry, speaking personally, said that the operation of a private network should be a national trust, and should not be allowed to hurt the CBC. He flatly disagreed with Mr. Ouimet that the network should be owned by the stations.[16]

On 9 September 1960 the Board released an announcement containing its proposed amendments to the regulations. The definitions of a "network" and of an "affiliation agreement" were to be changed and new definitions of "network reserved time" and "temporary network" were to be added. A "network" would now be defined as "a person having affiliation agreements with two or more stations to broadcast on the facilities of such stations and within specified periods of broadcast time a specified program or package of programs in a manner determined by such person but does not include the operation of a licensed satellite station or a temporary network."[17] The definition no longer was based on electronic connections; rather, a network was defined in terms of a contract, the essential conditions of which were control of specified periods of broadcast time by a person other than the licensee of the station. The contract was the "affiliation agreement" which, under the new definition, included the condition "that within specified periods of broadcasting time the facilities of the station will be made available for the broadcast of a program or package of programs in a manner determined by a network company."[18] The specified periods of time represented "network reserved time."

The regulations applicable to licensees of stations were to be amended wherever necessary to apply to "networks," and the section governing networks was to be replaced. The significant features of the new section on "networks" were that the network, rather than the station, would be held responsible for all program material carried by affiliated stations during network reserved time; no station might enter into an affiliation agreement with more than one network; no station should represent itself as operating as part of a network except when it was broadcasting programs supplied to it by the network to which it was affiliated; affiliation agreements were to be approved by the Board; and the Board might revoke the approval of an affiliation of any station if, in its opinion, the station was not maintaining a service which was basically Canadian in content and character; no network might have an exclusive contract to take programs from one program supplier or non-Canadian network.[19]

The Board's announcement outlined for the guidance of applicants some of the factors which the Board would weigh in considering applications.

(1) Non-Canadian Interests

The maximum participation by non-Canadian interests is specified in Section 14 of the Broadcasting Act. The Board will give preference to a company which is wholly Canadian-owned.

(2) Means of Distribution of Programs

A network company may distribute programs by any appropriate means. The Board will give preference to a company which is prepared to assure some microwave or co-axial cable connection between affiliated stations.

(3) Number of Stations Initially Affiliated

The Board will give preference to the company with the largest number of affiliates and which plans to include additional stations as they may seek affiliation.

(4) Number of Hours of Network Reserved Time

In the opinion of the Board, the number of hours of reserved time should not be fewer than ten hours per week, and affiliation agreements should provide for an increase of hours as circumstances permit.

(5) Incorporation and Organization of a Network Company

In dealing with applications to form a network the Board will give preference to a private company which provides the opportunity for participation, without control, by affiliated stations.

In expressing the above preferences, the Board wishes it to be understood that no one factor should be considered of overriding importance, and that in dealing with applications the Board will be concerned with the balance of factors, including program proposals, included in each application.[20]

It was announced that representations on the proposed amendments would be received at a public hearing, opening on 26 September, and approved amendments would then be announced as soon as possible; no network applications would be received until approved regulations had been announced; the first hearing on applications would be toward the end of November or early in December 1960; and in the meantime no one, other than the CBC, or a station affiliated with the Corporation, had permission to operate a network or as part of a network.

Following the September hearing, the Board, on 14 October, announced the approved regulations, which appeared in the *Canada Gazette* of 26 October.[21] This announcement referred to the unique position of the CBC which was established to provide a national broadcasting service—interpreted to mean nation-wide in extent.

Because of the authority vested in the Corporation under the Act, the CBC did not require permission from the Board to form and operate networks. The Board noted, however, that "because the Board is responsible for imposing on licensees the condition that their stations operate as part of the networks of the Corporation, the Board cannot escape responsibility for the terms of affiliation between licensees and the Corporation."[22] The Board urged the Corporation and stations to work out amicably agreements consistent with the Act and the regulations without Board intervention. It warned all concerned, however, that failure to reach voluntary arrangements could lead to agreements, the conditions of which would, under Section 72(1) of the *Radio(TV) Broadcasting Regulations,* be determined by the Board.

It was noted that there was no provision in the Act giving the Board authority to require licensees to operate as part of a network other than a network of the Corporation; the Board had no authority to intrude into the negotiations between a private network and licensees:

A private network can thus be formed only through the voluntary affiliation of licensees on terms acceptable to them, subject only to the condition that the agreement must be consistent with the Act and the regulations. However, in order to contribute to the orderly operation of networks, both private and those of the Corporation, and thus to ensure the efficient operation of the national broadcasting system, the Board is enacting Section 14(6) to provide that the

Board may adjudicate disputes between network operators and affiliates during the time of affiliation agreements.[23]

The announcement referred to an addition to the amendments as proposed earlier which provided for two steps in the process of applying for permission to operate a network: first, permission to form a network, and second, permission to operate a network as defined, that is, by the completion of affiliation agreements. Applications might be presented to the Board separately or concurrently, but permission to form a network would be granted only after a public hearing on the application. The purpose of this provision was to enable an applicant and potential affiliates to know whether the network proposal, in respect of conditions other than affiliation agreements was acceptable before the applicant endeavoured to secure affiliation agreements.

With reference to the section restricting stations to affiliation with one Canadian network, and specifying the conditions under which a station might represent itself as operating as a part of a network, the announcement pointed out that—these conditions notwithstanding— the way was left clear for cross-programming between networks outside of reserved time. The Board also excluded from its definition of the affiliation agreement any arrangement which involved fewer than eight hours per week of reserved time on any station. As a safety measure, however, the Board provided in Section 14(10) of the *Radio (TV) Broadcasting Regulations* that "where, in the opinion of the Board, a licensee is operating his station as part of a network without having filed an affiliation agreement with the Board, the Board may require him to show cause at a public hearing why he should not either file an affiliation agreement or modify his operations."[24] Sponsors of programs offered to stations frequently specified the time at which these programs would be aired, and the time so established became reserved time under the definition. The Board did not wish to bring these arrangements under the definition of a network, unless the amount of time so pre-empted became significant. The announcement of 14 October repeated the Board's preferences on non-Canadian

Interests, Means of Distribution of Programs, Number of Stations Initially Affiliated, Number of Hours of Network Reserved Time, and Incorporation and Organization of a Network Company.

The definition of a "network" continued to present difficulties. The definition of an "affiliation agreement" as contained in the amendments gazetted on 26 October was: "Affiliation agreement means an agreement between any person and a station that includes a provision for reserved time, but does not include an agreement that provides for less than eight hours of reserved time per week."[25]

A further statement on "Administrative Policy Regarding Television Networks" was issued on 19 December, that is, after the hearing of 29 November.[26] The Statement said that the Board's definition of a "network" was designed to take into account the effect on the public interest and the change in the normal exercise of responsibility which a licensee has for the programs which he presents over his station. The greater the amount of time placed under the control of the distributor of the program material, the greater the effect on the public interest and the greater the impairment of the responsibility of the licensee. However, there was a minimum amount of time below which the effects might be considered insignificant. For the purpose of administration the crucial time was now set at four hours. Regardless of the means of distribution, any arrangement providing for reserved time of more than four hours per week would be seen as involving network operations; permission would be necessary and the distributor, as a network operator, would have to comply with the regulations. In the case of arrangements involving electronic means of distribution, even if the agreement provided for less than four hours, permission would have to be obtained; but because of the relatively small effect each application would be dealt with on its merits and exemptions from some regulations might be approved. Where the agreement called for fewer than four hours per week, and distribution was by nonelectronic means—giving the licensee the opportunity to review the program before it was broadcast—the effects appeared to be so negligible as to make it unnecessary to deal with it as a network operation.

Three years later, in its *Annual Report 1963–64*, the Board referred to its attempts to define a network in terms of the responsibility for the material broadcast and noted that the Federal Communications Commission in the United States had developed a similar definition: "'Network' means a person or organization which, as part of its regular business, by contract or agreement, expressed or implied with two or more affiliated broadcast stations gives or supplies program service to such stations under prescribed conditions for the purpose of identical programs by such stations."[27] The statement in the *Report* admitted that the Board's definition might be contested and might not cover all situations which could be interpreted as involving the operation of a network. It stressed the need for a definition of a network in the Broadcasting Act.

The problem of definition was important in two connections. First, in the early stages, was the ITO operation (which was an alternative to the second "network") to be construed as a "network" and to be brought under regulations? Later, there emerged an organization of the Hamilton television station, the affiliates of the CBC and the CBC "O & O" stations for the acquisition and distribution of syndicated programs. Was this to be treated as a "network"? The answer seemed to depend on whether there was reserved time. There was also the question of responsibility for programs broadcast during reserved time. The CBC stations were frequently unhappy with the programs supplied to them by the CBC, and which they were required to carry under the affiliation agreement. During the controversy over the "Sunday" program of the CBC, the English-language licensee in Quebec City advised the CBC and the Board that it refused to broadcast further programs in the series. The Board advised the station that, under its affiliation agreement, which was approved by the Board, it was required to carry the program, and that it would be in breach of the regulations if it refused to do so; but that the CBC as the network operator was responsible, under the regulations, for the material broadcast. This was the legal position, and the station complied. The licensee, however, was not satisfied with the legal position. He believed that the audience held his station responsible, and the program could alienate his audience.

Controversy continued to centre around the concept of cross-programming. An announcement by the Board on 7 December 1961 outlined the conditions under which, consistent with the regulations, cross-programming might occur.[28] On 3 January 1962 the CBC responded with a statement which expressed concern at the possibility of CBC affiliates taking programs distributed by CTV Network. The BBG's statement noted that, under the regulations, an affiliate of the CBC could broadcast programs supplied by the CTV Network, provided they were not broadcast within time reserved to the CBC under the affiliation agreement with the CBC, that the arrangements between CTV Network and the station were not such as to constitute an affiliation agreement, and that the station did not at any time refer to itself as being part of a CTV network. The regulations recognized the CTV Network as a potential supplier of programs to affiliates of the CBC, as long as it did not interfere with the operations of the CBC Network, and the CBC as a potential supplier of programs to CTV affiliates—provided it did not interfere with the operations of the CTV Network. The BBG's announcement said that cross-programming, when Canadian programs were involved, "can assist in the production and widest possible exposure of Canadian programs of a high standard"; the Board's primary object was to keep open to the new network means of assisting it in the production and distribution of Canadian programs. The CBC, although noting that the regulations specifically prohibited "double affiliation," was afraid of "network splitting" and expressed its apprehension. In a letter to the Chairman, Mr. Ouimet said:

> While we doubt the long-range desirability of cross-programming in the public interest, in view of the present situation and its difficulties we would not presently oppose an experiment in cross-programming through the use of recordings, be they tape or film, under certain conditions. This might be regarded as an experiment to be assessed at the end of a one or two year period. We believe the use of network-controlled cross-programming, other than programs of true national, regional, or local importance, should be postponed indefinitely.

The regulations continued to permit cross-programming under the defined conditions. The CTV stations were not interested in using the

CBC as a supplier of programs; and, although some CTV programs were accepted by CBC affiliates, the number was minimal.

The CBC affiliates were not particularly interested in the Canadian programs of the CTV network, and the network offered no advantages over other sources of supply of tape or film material. Cross-programming to CBC affiliates by electronic means was limited by the reserved time conditions of the affiliation agreement, and "network splitting" or "double affiliation" was prohibited by the regulations.

At its public hearing on 13 April 1961, the Board considered an application by S.W. Caldwell on behalf of a company to be incorporated as CTV Television Network Limited for authority to operate a television network in Canada. The application provided for the affiliation of eight television stations to the network. The *Annual Report 1961-62* noted:

> In a Public Announcement dated 21 April 1961 the Board announced its approval of this application under the provisions of Section 13(4)(a) of the Broadcasting Act.
>
> By agreement with the Board, the CTV Television Network began its operations on 1 October 1961. As the result of the establishment of this network, an alternative network service is provided by video tape and microwave in the eight cities in which the affiliated stations are located and the surrounding areas representing some 60% of the population of the country.[29]

On 10 January 1962, the full-time members of the Board met with representatives of CTV Network, and of each of the affiliated stations. Although facing great difficulties, the network had held together. The main areas of discussion were the financial position of the network, the need for access to a larger audience, the policies and regulations of the Board, and the competition of the CBC. Mr. Caldwell reported that losses being encountered would result in a total loss over the first full year of operation of $630,000, and this would be increased to $1,000,000 as a result of additional distribution costs when the microwave circuit came into use. As a commercial network, CTV must be able to produce and distribute programs in such a way as to realize a revenue greater than the production and distribution costs. To attract advertisers the cost per thousand homes should be about $3.50. CTV was producing programs at one-third of the cost of many CBC programs, and there was no possibility of significantly reducing costs. The cost per thousand was, however, too high to attract advertisers. Panel and games shows were low-cost. One of these shows cost $2,200 and delivered 363,000 homes. The cost per thousand was $4.42. It was possible to sell this show because advertisers got some bonuses through extra mentions. On the other hand, a variety show which was produced for $3,400 and cost advertisers a total of $7,800, reached 200,000 homes at a cost of $9.75 per home. The program was cancelled after the network had lost $50,000. This moneyloser was the most expensive show produced by CTV to that time, yet it cost the network less to produce than any other show created by sister Canadian producers. The most effective way to reduce the cost per thousand was to increase the coverage of the network.

Mr. Caldwell asked whether the Board would analyze the coverage of the stations making up the CBC network to see if there were areas of duplication where a station was making no real contribution to CBC coverage and could, therefore, be permitted to joint CTV and provide an alternative programming service. Possible areas might be Charlottetown-Moncton-Saint John, Toronto-Kitchener-London, and Moose Jaw-Regina. In the end, the Board was prepared to consider an application as long as the disaffiliation from the CBC would not lead to the withdrawal of the national service from any listener in the area. The Board, however, was adamant on the principle that the national service would not be withdrawn from Canadian listeners now receiving it. There was some discussion of extending coverage by cross-programming. The Board emphasized that it was thinking only of Canadian shows. The CBC did not appear to be adamant in its opposition to the use of film or tape in cross-programming, but were reluctant to commit themselves to it until they were able to assess all the implications. Mr. Caldwell said that the practical possibilities were limited to tape or film distribution.

Mr. Caldwell listed nine ways in which modifications of the Board's policies and regulations would assist the network. These were: deferring the effective date of the 55% Canadian content to the fall; averaging the Canadian content over a full year; granting Commonwealth programs 100% Canadian content classification while reducing the total time for such programs from one-third to one-sixth; giving 50% Canadian content to programs which could not qualify as Canadian content, but which were of unusual or exceptional interest to Canadians and therefore had value in the schedule of the network and the stations; relaxing the commercial restrictions in a number of ways, including increased commercial content in Canadian productions; support by the Board for appeals to the Department of National Revenue for alleviation of the application of the sales tax to various broadcasting functions; encouraging and helping foreign producers to work in Canada; discontinuing the affiliation of the CBC with U.S. networks; and disaffiliation of some CBC affiliates so that they might join CTV network.

In turn, the Board listed amendments to the regulations or modifications of administrative procedures which it might be prepared to consider. The Board had given some consideration to amendments to the regulations respecting Commonwealth programs, the commercial content in Canadian productions, special consideration to programs of wide public interest, weighting the Canadian content of certain Canadian productions. They had also considered changes in administrative arrangements affecting combined film and live programs, dubbed programs, Canadian-produced commercials, educational programs, religious programs, programs produced by organizations of which Canada was a member, e.g., specialized agencies of the United Nations; news commentaries and public affairs programs; film series produced by Canadian companies where some of the episodes are produced in Canada and some are not; and cross-programming.

Mr. Caldwell expressed concern about some of the competitive activities of the CBC and their effect on CTV Network. Specifically he referred to an increase in local discounts, increase in CBC advertising and promotional budgets, special rates for local advertising business, introduction of spot advertising on Sundays, opening up of time before and after sustaining programs for the insertion of spot advertising, acceptance of back-to-back commercials, increased prices paid for U.S. films and, particularly, discontinuance by the CBC of the "one-for-one" policy, i.e., the requirement that advertisers buying a U.S. program must also buy a Canadian program. Reference was also made to the use of the microwave circuit for the subsidiary network of the CBC "O & O" stations.

The points raised by Mr. Caldwell respecting CBC commercial competition were later discussed with the CBC in the Consultative Committee on Public Broadcasting. A number of the points involved rate setting and the legitimate efforts of the CBC to protect its revenue position against the competition of the private sector. It was doubtful if the Board had authority to become involved in rates, and the Board did not wish to become involved in setting them. There was no evidence that the policies of the Corporation were having the effect of reducing its net revenues. The principal problem of the CTV Network and its affiliates was that, because the CBC had more extensive coverage, national advertisers were inclined to buy the CBC network rather than the CTV Network; because the CBC could command more revenue, it could afford to pay more for the programs it acquired. In other words, the problems which the network and the stations were encountering were inherent in their position in the market rather than being engineered by the CBC. Mr. Caldwell's problems were more those of his relations with the stations than with the CBC, and he later expressed regret that he had brought his complaints about the CBC to the Board. As the market expanded and the revenues of the stations improved, less was heard about "unfair competition," but private operators wholly dependent on the market can never be entirely happy in competition with an operation substantially supported by public funds. The network continued to seek additional coverage either by access to new second television stations or by the licensing of rebroadcasting stations to its affiliates.

The life and times of Mr. Caldwell and the CTV Network were not easy ones. On Wednesday, 23 February 1966 a public hearing on an application for a transfer of shares in CTV Network was held. In the application, the stations affiliated with the network proposed to purchase the shares owned by the nonbroadcaster shareholders in such a manner as to provide each station with an equal number of voting shares and to contribute to the financing of the operation of the network in the ratio of the commercial rates of the stations. Moncton Broadcasting, the licensee of CKCW-TV, Moncton, New Brunswick, an affiliate of the CBC, appeared in opposition on the grounds of exclusive contracts entered into by CTV Network.[30] The CBL opposed the application on the grounds that the network should be operated either by the CBC or under a public trustee.[31] The Association of Canadian Television and Radio Artists (ACTRA) urged the greater use of Canadian talent.[32] Mr. Kenneth Soble and his associates in Power Corporation requested that no action be taken on the application respecting CTV Network unless they had had an opportunity to present an application to form a network.[33] The Board announced approval of the application on Friday, 4 March 1966.[34]

The stations continued to own and operate the CTV Network. To the eight original stations were added stations in St. John's and Moose Jaw. One of the problems in expanding second service into Saskatoon was the difficulty being encountered in reaching an agreement between CTV Network and the Saskatoon station on the nature and extent of the station's participation in the network.

Another form of BBG/CBC competition. Andrew Stewart (left) and Alphonse Ouimet (right) at a game of chess. *Photograph used with permission from the Archives of Ontario, #66–2080–9, C 109–2, Herb Nott Collection.*

[7]

THE GREY CUP GAME, 1962

IT WAS INEVITABLE THAT THE second television stations would want a piece of the popular and commercially desirable sports events. The distribution of football broadcasts by the CBC had served the public well, and the CBC was probably correct in its conviction that television had assisted materially in developing public support for the Canadian game. Given the responsibility of the CBC to provide a varied service there was, even in the Corporation, some feeling that complete coverage distorted the proper balance of programming in the public service. For their part, the football clubs were restive in a situation in which there was only one buyer. They claimed that the price paid by the CBC was too low and that they were anxious to exploit the possibility of competitive bidding for television rights.

Prior to 1958, the CBC, although confined within the single station policy, had enjoyed a very substantial degree of autonomy and capacity to make decisions affecting the entire broadcasting system and service. The principle of independence of the CBC from direct control by the government was endorsed by the public and defended by Parliament. But tensions were beginning to develop between Parliament and the Corporation. Television was proving more costly than radio. When the revenues from receiving set licences proved to be an inadequate source of monies for the public service, the CBC had to take its requests for financial support annually to Parliament. Parliament was becoming increasingly concerned about decisions of the CBC which affected the public purse. Further, there was a feeling among parliamentarians that television was a more powerful force than radio in its influence on public attitudes; and there was a growing concern about the nature of the influence which might be exerted through the independent decisions of the CBC. There was, for these two reasons, a disposition on the part of government to reduce the autonomy of the CBC.

Prior to 1958, when the CBC combined the operating function with the function of regulating all broadcasting, the Corporation had the authority to make decisions both directly and indirectly affecting private broadcasting stations. It had no contractual agreements with its affiliated stations. It did not need them. The stations were the creations of the Corporation. Affiliation was a condition imposed by the CBC; and there was not much the affiliates could do but accept the decisions of the Corporation. The unaffiliated (at that time radio) stations were also "in the hands" of the CBC. They resented being regulated by a Corporation which was, in a real sense, competing with them for audience and revenues. They were successful in securing the passage of legislation which introduced a separate regulatory body. There was no doubt that under the Broadcasting Act, 1958, the CBC no longer had authority to make decisions directly affecting the private sector. The CBC never disputed this; and the President and others expressed the view that they were relieved no longer to have the responsibility for the private sector. What, however, was not clear was how far the capacity of the CBC to make decisions affecting its own operations but bearing upon and indirectly affecting the operation of the private sector was diminished; also unclear was how far the BBG could or should become involved in decisions of this kind.[1]

Differing interpretations of Section 10 of the Broadcasting Act, 1958 were at the heart of the matter. The Board interpreted Section 10 as giving it wide powers which could be used, if the Board so chose, to affect the operations of the CBC. The CBC resisted this interpretation of Section 10. The Bill had been hurriedly drafted. Officials of the CBC along with the Department of Justice had been involved in the drafting. Mr. Ouimet contended it was not the intention of those drafting the Bill that Section 10 should give full and final authority to the Board in all matters affecting the relations between stations and between networks and stations. In his opinion Section 10 was intended to indicate the objects and purposes for which the Board should strive; and not to state the powers and authority of the Board. The specific powers, he pointed out, were contained in the subsequent sections. We were told that Section 10 was introduced by the government after the rest of the Bill had been drafted; and that the words "have the final determination of all matters and questions in relation thereto," were added by the Prime Minister. If this is indeed what happened, Section 10 could be seen as reflecting the intention of the government; but the specific sections were not rewritten so as to conform clearly to the intention of Section 10.

The government never publicly took a stand in support of the apparent intention of Section 10. It was evident in the Chairman's conversation with Mr. Nowlan before his appointment to the BBG that there was no unanimity in the government. After the "Preview Commentary" affair, in which the Minister acted without reference to the BBG, the Conservative Government showed no stomach to tangle directly with the CBC. The determined stand of the producers of "Preview Commentary," with the threat of mass resignations, was a principal factor inducing the government to back away from the issue; but they were conscious of the capacity of the CBC to mobilize articulate support when its autonomy appeared to be threatened. There was at the time an organized, articulate section of the public that was suspicious of the designs of the government and of its creature the BBG, and was ready to react to any move which seemed to them prejudicial to the CBC. This section of the public was represented by the CBL, and its associated organizations, principally the Canadian Labour Congress and the Canadian Federation of Agriculture. The CBC also found strong support from within the universities.

The private broadcasters had sought the basic changes which were introduced into the Broadcasting Act, 1958; and although in principle opposed to controls, they were disposed to give the BBG a chance. They were, generally, pleased to have a body other than the CBC to which they could express their concerns and make their representations. But they were not a homogeneous group. The unaffiliated radio stations had no reason to support the CBC. The second private television stations and CTV network were in direct competition with the CBC stations and the CBC network, and, in the early years, found the competition rigorous. They turned to the BBG. The position of the CBC affiliates was more equivocal. Among the radio affiliates there were many who would have preferred disaffiliation and the opportunity to compete with unaffiliated stations on equal terms. The television affiliates found the paternalism of the CBC irksome, and were not unwilling to turn to the BBG when it appeared to be in their interest to do so; but they had prospered under their relations with the CBC, and the CBC was clearly anxious to maintain good relations with them. There was a general feeling in the private sector that a showdown between the CBC and the BBG was inevitable.

The authority and capacity to make decisions resided finally in the Directors of the Corporation, who were appointees of the Government. They were, however, inexperienced in broadcasting. The officers of the Corporation, however, had had long involvement with the CBC, were experienced and knowledgeable, and had strong institutional loyalty. In the early days, differences within the Corporation were apparent. R.L. Dunsmore was appointed by the Conservative Government and, in June 1959, elected Chairman by the Directors of the Corporation, although the Act made no provision for a Chairman. Mr. Dunsmore displayed concern about the level of expenditures of the CBC, and was unhappy about some of the *avant garde* programming of the Corporation. The appointment of Mr. Dunsmore as Chairman was undoubtedly intended to strengthen the position of the Directors who shared Mr. Dunsmore's concerns, and the concerns of the Government. However this did not mean that the Directors were sympathetic to any intrusion by the BBG. They, no less than the officers of the Corporation, were jealous of such authority as they had; were unwilling to have their decisions reviewed or reversed by the BBG; and feared any tendency on the part of the BBG to extend its authority to affect the decisions of the Directors.

The opportunity for the football clubs to exploit competitive bidding for rights appeared with the licensing of the second stations and the formation of the private network. The two networks—CBC and CTV—were not, of course, in an equal competitive position. Its own stations, supplemented by its private affiliates, enabled the CBC to deliver a larger audience. By 1963 the networks finally came to agreement on division of football broadcasts with duplicate coverage of the Grey Cup game. The football clubs were unhappy with this arrangement, and the 1963 rights were sold to a Montreal advertising agency whose efforts to break the agreement between the networks proved abortive and expensive. Order was eventually established in football broadcasting, but only after matters were moved along by the traumatic events of the Grey Cup game, 1962.

The first move by the private stations to engage in football telecasting had occurred in 1961. John Bassett, the proprietor of CFTO-TV, Toronto, himself a sports enthusiast with interests in football in Toronto, bid for and was successful in acquiring the 1961 Big Four football television rights on behalf of his station. Mr. Bassett was not in a position to broadcast games except over the facilities of his own station, and blackout conditions limited his opportunity to broadcast the games played in Toronto. In order to broadcast games outside of Toronto, it was necessary to apply to the BBG for permission to form a temporary network. However, as the available microwave facilities were committed to the CBC and Spencer Caldwell of CTV Network, Mr. Bassett could not himself make such an application. At the time of Mr. Caldwell's application to operate CTV network, affiliation agreements had been entered into with eight television stations; it was proposed that the new network would be in operation in September 1961. As part of his application, Mr. Caldwell applied for permission to distribute telecasts of the Big Four football games commencing August 11. The stations to be included for the purpose of these telecasts were CFTO-TV Toronto, CJOH-TV Ottawa and CFCF-TV Montreal. Later CFTM-TV Montreal was added. These four stations were the only second stations it was possible to link by microwave. CTV Network was in a position to provide the coverage to the four stations, having entered into an agreement with the Bell Telephone Company for microwave facilities between the three cities. Mr. Caldwell had also made an agreement with Mr. Bassett.

Even if the games were to be carried in the three cities, the coverage would be considerably restricted in comparison to that of the previous year and to the coverage the CBC could offer. The only way in which comparable coverage could be obtained was by incorporating into the CTV network stations affiliated with the CBC. Mr. Bassett announced his readiness to make the football telecasts available to CBC affiliates outside the cities of Toronto, Ottawa and Montreal. Under the Act, however, stations affiliated with the CBC could not operate as part of another network without the approval of the BBG, and the BBG could not grant approval without the permission of the CBC. The CBC quickly made it known that they would not give permission to their affiliated stations to join a private football network; it offered to purchase the football rights from Mr. Bassett.

When the application for the football network came before the Board, Mr. Bassett said the CBC offer was not acceptable to him. However, as there appeared to be no possibility of including the CBC affiliates, Mr. Bassett later disposed of the 1961 Big Four football rights to the CBC. He then requested that the Board direct the CBC to permit CFTO-TV Toronto, CJOH-TV Ottawa and CFCF-TV Montreal to pick up the CBC feed for coverage of the Grey Cup game on December 2. This request was considered at the Board's meeting of 27 November 1961. As early as 9 March 1961, the Board had issued the following statement:

> In the opinion of the Board, the Grey Cup Game and the play-off games of the Big Four and Western Interprovincial Football Conference are of general national interest and should be broadcast to the widest possible national audience. It is also the opinion of the Board that the other games of the Big Four and W.I.F.U. Conferences are of general interest in their respective regions and should be broadcast to the widest possible regional audiences at least.
>
> The Canadian Broadcasting Corporation has the facilities and the affiliation agreements to provide complete national coverage of

the Grey Cup Game. In the view of the Board, it would be in the public interest that the Grey Cup Game should be carried by the Corporation, but that the game might be made available to all stations wishing to broadcast it.[2]

The CBC opposed the request by Mr. Bassett.

The Board's statement, issued 20 November 1961, said:

Under arrangements now completed the Grey Cup Game will be carried on the complete network of the CBC. Additional broadcasting of the Game by stations unaffiliated with the Corporation might extend coverage to some people who would not otherwise be able to see it, but would deprive viewers who did not want to watch the Game of any alternative service on Canadian television stations. The Board sees no reason to change the position taken in the release of March 9; but does not feel that the public interest requires that it direct the CBC to make the game available to unaffiliated stations.[3]

The statement went on to stress the national importance of such sporting events, the Board's unhappiness at the uncertainty and confusion surrounding the 1961 Grey Cup game and the Board's willingness to use its authority under the Broadcasting Act if negotiations for future football rights did not proceed in a manner more amenable to the public interest.

The broadcasting of the 1961 Grey Cup game, distributed exclusively on the network of the CBC, proceeded without further incident; but the permanent problem was no nearer solution.

In the spring of 1962 football rights were again on the market, and both the CBC and CTV Networks, the latter in association with CFTO-TV, were bidders. The CBC bid $125,000 for the nonexclusive rights to the Grey Cup game, and $175,000 for exclusive rights. Exclusive rights to the game were sold by the League to CFTO-TV and CTV Networks for the same price as offered by the CBC. At this point the CBC declared it was prepared to buy the rights at the prices it had bid.

When Mr. Bassett bid away from the CBC the rights to broadcast the Grey Cup game, the resulting confrontation seemed, so the Chairman thought, to provide a clear case for intervention by the Board. After all, Section 10 of the Act cast the Board in the referee's role. The full responsibility for the decision to intervene lay on the Chairman. The decision was supported by the full-time members and the part-time members were asked to give their unanimous approval.

Proposals and counterproposals were then made by the owners of the rights and the CBC with respect to terms and conditions of broadcasting the game. The Board was kept informed of these negotiations but took no part in them until 30 May, when the problem was reviewed at a meeting at which the Board heard from both Mr. Ouimet and Mr. Caldwell. Immediately after this meeting, the following letter was sent to CTV Network, with a copy to the CBC:

> The Board is not prepared, even if it were in a position to do so, to require the Corporation to release its affiliated stations for the purpose of carrying a broadcast of the Game by CTV Network. The Board believes it is possible to resolve the situation which has developed this year by arrangements which would permit both networks to broadcast and distribute the Grey Cup game. The Board suggests that CTV and the Corporation cooperate in an effort to resolve the problems of the 1962 Grey Cup game within this framework.[4]

Mr. Bassett then became involved in a bizarre incident. On 7 June, he sent a letter addressed to the Board, copy to the CBC, in which he referred to certain proposals for the telecasting of the Grey Cup game. The Chairman, without consulting with the CBC, replied on 11 June:

> I presume that negotiations between the parties involved will proceed.
> I must say that the possibility that the Corporation would make its network available on a sustaining basis to carry a CTV feed was not considered by the Board when it discussed the problem at its recent meeting. This arrangement would make the extensive net-

work of the CBC which is maintained at public expense, available to serve the interests of a private organization.

The Board hoped that the problems of the 1962 Game could be resolved without its intervention. However, the Board is giving serious consideration to a regulation, similar to the provision in the U.K. legislation prohibiting any broadcaster from entering into an exclusive contract to carry certain sports events of outstanding national interest.[5]

The CBC did not receive a copy of this letter; but, also on 11 June, the CBC, without consulting with the Board, wrote Mr. Bassett accepting his "offer."[6] Later, during a public hearing, the Chairman expressed surprise that the CBC had replied to a letter addressed to the Board, without being in touch with the Board, and his regret that he had written his letter without consulting the CBC.[7] Better communications at this point might have made a difference to the outcome. In any case, on 12 July, CTV network, co-owner of the rights, referring to references in the press to the CBC carrying the broadcast on a sustaining basis, formally advised the CBC that the CTV network had not granted such rights to the CBC.[8]

On 4 July, Mr. Caldwell advised the Board that no agreement had been reached between the owners of the television rights and the CBC. From the outset Mr. Ouimet, in conversations with the Chairman, maintained that public opinion would eventually force CTV Network to deliver the program to the CBC on terms acceptable to the Corporation, and that there was no need for the intervention of the Board. The Board, however, continued to be assured by Mr. Caldwell that CTV Network and its affiliated stations were fully prepared to carry the game alone. This was confirmed by CTV affiliates including Mr. Bushnell of CJOH-TV Ottawa. Although the Board had urged a negotiated settlement, Mr. Caldwell's letter seemed to imply that negotiations had failed, and that there was a real danger that many Canadians would be deprived of the broadcast of the game.

The Board considered carefully an adamant refusal of the CBC to accept the commercials for British American Oil, Nabob and Labatts, under any conditions. The Corporation was engaged in commercial operations and had been increasingly aggressive in its commercial policy. The Corporation had recently, because of reduced government funding and advertising revenue, found it necessary to cut its costs and to curtail its services. The Corporation had carried the broadcast of the Grey Cup Game in other years on a commercial basis. The three companies had all been acceptable sponsors of the CBC over the years. The CBC was willing to take the commercials of the three companies in the pre-game and post-game programs, but not within the body of the broadcast of the game.

Somewhat later, in annoyance over a reporting error on the 11 o'clock national news, referring to the controversy, the Chairman wrote Mr. Ouimet. "The people you are dealing with now are respected Canadian business firms. Why not complete a deal with them; cut out this nonsense in our national news, and get on with the business of producing shows like *The Gondoliers*. We are sure you would be happy; and we would try to keep out of your hair." Mr. Ouimet took the Chairman to task for releasing a "personal" letter to him. His defence was that the Board lacked the substantial public relations potential of the CBC.

On 6 July a memorandum was drafted, setting out the conditions the Board felt necessary to effect a solution. Copies of the draft were provided to Mr. Caldwell and the CBC, with the advice that copies of the official memorandum would be in their hands by 11 July. The Chairman personally delivered the draft copy to the CBC. Unfortunately Mr. Ouimet was away at the time and the draft was presented to Mr. Briggs, Vice-President of the CBC. The Chairman also met with Mr. Dunsmore. Both Mr. Briggs and Mr. Dunsmore were bitterly resentful of the BBG's intrusion.

Copies of the Board's memorandum were mailed to Mr. Ouimet and Mr. Caldwell on 10 July. The memorandum referred to the failure of negotiations to produce a solution acceptable to both parties and said, "The Board is therefore convinced that, under the authority vested in it under Part I of the Broadcasting Act, it must now move to protect the public interest."[9] The proposal contained two essential conditions; first, that the owners of the rights would not impede, and must exercise their rights so as to facilitate the solution, and secondly, that the Board would have such assurances as necessary that the telecast would be sold to sponsors under the normal conditions. Given these two conditions the Board would then name a producing authority. In the first instance, the Board would ask the CBC to originate the telecast using some of the personnel of the CTV network, credits would be given to both networks and the CBC could insert such public announcements as it might choose. If the CBC were unwilling to proceed, the CTV network would have the second chance. Failing this, the Board would seek another producer. The Board would require both networks to distribute the broadcast without addition or deletion. Should any question of the Board's authority arise, the Board would move, at a public hearing, to pass necessary regulations under the authority of the Act.

As mentioned, the Board found its authority under Section 10 of the Broadcasting Act. In a memorandum prepared for the Minister, Mr. W.C. Pearson, Counsel to the Board wrote:

[The Board] relies on the authority of Section 10 dealing with its power to regulate the operation of networks, the relation between public and private stations and the provision of a final determination of all matters and questions in relation thereto. The Board takes the view that Section 10 not only sets out the purpose for which regulations are to be made, but vests the Board with broad regulatory powers. These powers are not diminished by the enactment of Section 11 and the Board here relies on the opinion of Mr. Justice Duff in the case of 'Re: Grey' 57 Supreme Court Reports which held that the enumeration of certain powers does not limit the general terms but rather emphasizes the comprehensive character of the general terms and suggests the intention that the powers are to be comprehensively interpreted and applied.[10]

The CBC was unwilling to proceed with the broadcast of the game under the conditions prescribed in the Board's memorandum of 10 July. On 12 July a telegram was sent to Mr. Caldwell advising him of the recommendation which would be made to the full Board at its meeting on 18 July.

After the Board meeting, the following telegram was sent to both the CBC and CTV Network:

At meeting today Board decided to announce the following amendments to the Radio TV Broadcasting Regulations for public hearing on Saturday August 18: Sixteen (1) All licensees shall broadcast the following network program of public interest namely the CTV network program of the 1962 Grey Cup Football Game. (2) the terms and conditions for the broadcasting of the CTV network program of the 1962 Grey Cup Football Game shall be as follows (A) All broadcasting stations shall broadcast the program in its entirety and shall not omit or increase any portion of the entertainment or advertising content of the program (B) The sharing of the revenue of the program shall be in accordance with such agreement as may be made between the Corporation and CTV Television Network Ltd and in the absence of such agreement then such revenue shall be shared as the Board upon the application of any broadcasting station made on or before the first day of November 1962 shall by regulation prescribe. (3) the CBC and CTV networks shall be operated so as to make the program referred to in this regulation available to all stations that form part of the respective networks.[11]

In a public release of the same date, the Board announced a special hearing on the amendments for Saturday, 18 August.[12]

The CBC position on the regulation was most forcefully put in a release of 15 November.

This regulation, as enacted, would compel the CBC to accept the advertising messages of another network. This is the crux of the whole matter and on this point the CBC is in firm disagreement with the BBG and CTV. . . .

The CBC does not intend to allow CTV or any unauthorized person or organization, either directly or indirectly, to use the national broadcasting service as a sales tool. . . . The BBG in its regulation has categorized advertising messages as being in the same category of national importance and interest as the program itself.

The CBC not only disagrees with this as a matter of principle but is also advised that the BBG regulation in question is invalid.

In August of this year the CBC stated publicly it had received a legal opinion which stated that the BBG did not have the authority to pass such a regulation. That legal opinion was written by Mr. E.A. Driedger, Q.C., Deputy Attorney General of Canada.

Before adopting the position it is taking today, the CBC sought further legal advice on this matter. It has consulted Mr. C.F.H. Carson, Q.C., of the Toronto law firm of Tilley, Carson, Findlay and Wedd. It is Mr. Carson's opinion that the regulation is invalid.[13]

Mr. Carson's letter to Mr. Ouimet read as follows:

You have asked for my opinion as to the validity of Section 16 of the Radio (TV) Broadcasting Regulations enacted by the Board of Broadcast Governors on the 7th instant.

The effect of the regulation is to require all television broadcasting stations forming part of the CBC Television Network to carry the CTV Television Network broadcast of the 1962 Grey Cup Game including all advertising sold by CTV Television Limited in connection with such broadcast.

While the matter is not entirely free from doubt, I am of the opinion that the regulation is invalid for two reasons.

First, the power conferred upon the Board under Section 11 1(f) to require licensees to broadcast network programs is in terms limited to "programs of public interest or significance." The word "programs" in this paragraph does not, in my opinion, mean units which include both entertainment and advertising. In this very same section there is a distinction drawn in paragraphs (b) and (c) between "programs" and "advertising." A similar distinction is drawn in paragraph (d) between "programs" and "advertisements." These, I think, indicate that the word "programs" in paragraph (f) is not to be construed as including advertising. That being so, advertising is not a part of a network program of public interest or significance and the Board cannot, in my opinion, require licensees to broadcast advertising material under paragraph (f). The advertising material cannot, in my opinion, be regarded as of public interest or significance. Accordingly, the regulation in my opinion goes beyond the power of the Board of Broadcast Governors insofar as it purports to require licensees to broadcast advertising matter.

Secondly, Section 13 4(b) of the Broadcasting Act prohibits the Board from granting permission to a licensee, operating as part of one network, to operate as part of another network for a particular program, without the consent of the operator of the network of which the licensee is ordinarily a part. This restriction on the power of the Board would be entirely ineffective if the Board had power to direct that a licensee carry a program originating with another network. Sections 10 and 11 must be read along with Section 13, and the result of reading those Sections together, is, in my opinion, that the Board has no power to make regulations directing that a station forming part of one network must carry a program originating in another network, without the permission of the operator of the network of which the station is ordinarily a part.

The considerations to which I have referred in relation to Section 11 and Section 13 4(b) are, I think, helpful in determining the true interpretation of the general language to be found in Section 10.[14]

The regulation was not immediately enacted after the public hearing of 18 August. The Board continued to hope that the several parties could find a voluntary solution. During the hearings, the Chairman said to Mr. Ouimet that he appreciated the efforts made by the CBC and CTV to reach a solution in the short run (1962) and that all must keep an eye on solutions for the long run (1963 and after). The Board in its wisdom had tried to facilitate a short-run solution by devising the draft regulation. "This has developed out of a series of events, the settlement of which nobody can give us any assurance at this time. . . . If we can clear up the current situation, the really pressing matter is for us to get a permanent solution for these problems, and . . . we would welcome any proposal which might help to move us in this direction, and we but seek the cooperation of everybody involved."[15]

Mr. Ouimet replied: "Well, you can be sure, Dr. Stewart, that we will continue in the months that are left—I indicated there were quite a few—to try to somehow show the Grey Cup on TV stations all across the country. This is our duty."[16]

On 24 August, the Chairman wrote Mr. Ouimet proposing a meeting of representatives of the CBC, CTV Network, Canadian Football League, Canadian Association of Advertising Agencies and the CAB. "It may be you have already given consideration to the problem [of a permanent solution] and would be prepared to indicate the general lines of your thinking. In this event you might, in replying to this letter, outline the possible solutions which have occurred to you. This would assist the Board in deciding whether or not a meeting would be fruitful."[17] The proposal was not acted on.

On 22 October the Board issued a press release. It read in part: "The Board remains of the opinion that the public interest can be served only if it is possible for television viewers in all parts of the country to see this event; and that, if no arrangements have been made which would ensure this result, the public interest can be served only if the Board enacts a regulation."[18]

The press release of 22 October was issued following information received by the Board on discussions between Mr. Ouimet and Mr. Caldwell. The Chairman's notes in reference to this said:

The President of the CBC approached the President of CTV Network to discuss an agreement over a term of years which would incorporate the principle of dividing the distribution of football broadcasts. This responsible approach to the problem nearly succeeded. It failed in part because of unreconciled but negotiable differences on the conditions for the future; it failed mainly because the agreement would have provided for a solution of the 1962 problem, the CBC carrying the commercials of British-American

Oil, Nabob and Labatts. The CBC Board of Directors refused to accept this condition for a long run settlement. It is obvious that further efforts must be made to establish a basis on which the two parties will be prepared to distribute football broadcasts—a basis which includes division of the broadcasts.

Mr. Ouimet brought the interested parties close to a solution of both the immediate and permanent problems. The CBC Board of Directors failed to give him their support.

The amendment to the Regulations was published in the *Canada Gazette* effective 7 November.[19] On 14 November, the Chairman wrote Mr. Ouimet:

> May I remind you of the urgency we feel, in view of the fact that tenders for 1963 football broadcasting rights are called for November 27, that further efforts be made to complete an agreement between the networks which would avoid a repetition of the difficulties already encountered.
>
> We are, I believe, agreed that the most promising approach is based on the principle of sharing the broadcasts.
>
> I am sure you appreciate the responsibility the Board feels to ensure that effective arrangements are made before November 27. However, we agreed on Monday that the Board would not move at this time, so that you might renew your efforts to arrive at an agreement with CTV Network.
>
> The Board is prepared to lend any and all support it can to your efforts in conjunction with Mr. Caldwell. I expressed concern to you that an agreement between the networks might be rendered ineffective if other parties involved in the disposal and acquisition of the rights felt that the agreement was prejudicial to their interests. We hope that in some way their cooperation could be assured.
>
> I hope it will be possible for you to resume your discussion with Mr. Caldwell at the earliest possible moment.
>
> May I ask that the Board's view as expressed in this letter be brought to the attention of your Board when it meets tomorrow?[20]

The Directors of the CBC met the following day and issued the statement of 15 November, to which reference has already been made. The statement, after reviewing the various conditions, short of accepting the sponsors arranged by CTV Network, concluded:

Finally, the CBC has again repeated its offer directly to CTV sponsors or their agencies, that while it would not carry their sales messages it would provide them with five courtesy announcements at no charge during the course of the Grey Cup game. These messages would make it clear to all viewers that they were seeing the game on the CBC Network through the cooperation of the commercial firms to be named in the announcements. In addition, the Corporation was and is prepared to sell them time for sales messages in the programs immediately preceding and immediately following the Grey Cup broadcast.

This offer still stands. If it is accepted, by agencies and sponsors, advantage could be taken immediately of the BBG's offer to rescind their regulation should a satisfactory agreement be reached.

If the CBC offer is not accepted the CBC still intends to broadcast the Grey Cup game. The CBC intends however to omit the commercials of CTV sponsors, and this is technically possible and feasible.

Any attempt to block the CBC from carrying the game will be construed by the Corporation and, in its view by the public also, as additional proof that commercial interests surrounding the Grey Cup telecast have been placed above the public interest.[21]

On 19 November, Mr. Ouimet supplied the Board with copies of the statement of the CBC Directors. The Board's reply said:

The Directors having made an irrevocable decision not to comply with the regulation, we appreciate the helpful intentions of your letter of November 19, in which you refer to two ways in which the Board can make the CBC broadcasts of the 1962 Grey Cup Game possible.

(1) By recognizing any special arrangements which might be made between CBC and the holder or holders of the rights through rescinding regulation 16, as you have already stated.

The Board has maintained a position from which it would be possible to render the regulation inoperative if a workable agreement providing for complete coverage was reached. Time is running out, but the Board hopes that efforts to reach an agreement will continue and will prove successful. Under the terms of the Regulation Act the last date at which the Board would be able to allow the regulation to lapse would be November 27.

(2) By advising the CTV Television Network Ltd. to provide CBC with a feed of their 1962 Grey Cup Game program.

This implies that CTV Network will be bought by the owners of the rights. If the owners of the rights buy the CBC network alone the regulation does not apply.

As your letter correctly points out, if CTV network is bought by the owners of the rights the Network would be in breach of the regulation if it did not make a feed, complete with commercials, available to the CBC. The Board has, on inquiry, so advised the owners of the rights. The Board has no indication that CTV Television Network Ltd., if it sold its network to the owners of the rights, would intend to violate the regulation. However, the Directors of the Corporation have said that, having received a feed from CTV Network, they propose to proceed contrary to the regulation. The Corporation appears to be asking the Board to condone a breach of the regulation. Obviously, the Board cannot do this.[22]

About this time, after receiving a letter from Mr. Ouimet forwarding "useful background information," the Secretary of State, Mr. Halpenny, moved in. The events surrounding the problems of the broadcasting of the 1962 Grey Cup game had received a vast amount of coverage, and the editorials in the newspapers were almost uniformly adverse to the Board's regulation.[23] The Minister was subjected to questioning in the House and had avoided taking any position.[24]

Mr. Halpenny had decided that the appropriate solution was the proposal referred to in the CBC release of 15 November, namely, that the CBC would provide the sponsors with five courtesy announcements, at no charge, during the course of the Grey Cup game broadcast, and would sell the sponsors time in the program of the CBC immediately preceding and immediately following the Grey Cup game broadcast. The sponsors and owners of the rights then accepted this proposal. The game as produced by CTV Network was broadcast on all stations, including stations of the CBC network, under these conditions. The Board later rescinded its regulation.[25]

The Board did not expect the Minister to support its position although, in view of the direct involvement of the Government in the insertion of Section 10 in the Act, the supporters of the Government on the Board thought that the Minister might, without necessarily supporting the particular actions of the Board in this case, have conceded that the Board had a statutory responsibility to resolve disputes in the public interest. His failure to do this finally convinced the Board of the necessity for a review of the legislation.[26]

As was noted in a Board memorandum after the fact:

The particular point at issue in the dispute over the television broadcast of the 1962 Grey Cup Game appears to be whether or not the CBC will carry the game on its network including the commercial messages of the sponsors under contract with CTV network. It must be obvious now that this is not the real issue. The real issue is whether when unsolved disputes develop between broadcasters in which the public interest is clearly involved, there exist effective means to bring about a solution consistent with the public interest.

The situation had happened once. It could happen again. It was, therefore, imperative that effective means be provided to solve problems arising out of relations amongst the private broadcasters or between the CBC and private broadcasters.

Viewing new equipment of CFTO-TV, Toronto, are (from left to right) John Bassett, Andrew Stewart, Joel Aldred and Foster Hewitt. *Photograph courtesy of Mrs. Andrew Stewart.*

[8]

ALTERNATIVE TELEVISION SERVICE AND THE CONSERVATIVE GOVERNMENT

THE SETTING

The initial selection of eight centres in which second television licences were approved was based on population. Only Quebec City had a population greater than Halifax, the smallest of the eight cities. Six of the cities had CBC "O & O" stations. Edmonton and Calgary had private stations affiliated with the CBC. The decision of the CBC to apply for a station in Edmonton, but not Calgary, indicated that at this time neither the Board nor the CBC were committed to any long run pattern, or policy for extension of alternative service. By 1961 the Board was concerning itself about the extension of service into additional, and smaller, markets. The CBC and its private affiliates registered their opposition to extension of service by rebroadcasting facilities of CTV stations. The Board believed there was a need to establish a policy for expansion. The experience with the Quebec City applications was not helpful. In December 1962, the Board announced it would support a policy of one CBC station in each province, preferably the capital city. The CBC applied for a station in St. John's. This application had not been disposed of by the time of the election of the new Liberal government; and there was still no government policy on extension.

When television was first introduced into Canada in 1952, the Liberal Government made licensing of stations subject to the policy that, until television service had been extended to a substantial proportion of the population, not more than one station would be licensed to serve any one area. Under the single station policy, it was provided that the CBC would own and operate stations in six cities, one in each of the major regions of the country: on the Pacific Coast, Vancouver; in the Prairie Provinces, Winnipeg; in Ontario, Toronto; in Quebec, Montreal (French- and English-language); in the Atlantic Provinces, Halifax; and in the national capital, Ottawa. All other communities were to be served by stations provided by private investment, but these private stations were to be affiliated with the CBC in order to distribute the national network service. The main production centres for the CBC were established in Toronto (English-language) and Montreal (French-language); other CBC stations were to have production facilities, primarily to feed material of regional origination into the network, to meet the objectives of inter-communication between all parts of the country. Under the single station policy, the total system changed and grew only as private entrepreneurs found it possible to establish stations in locations not already within the signal range of existing stations. The introduction of new private stations was governed mainly by market conditions, although the CBC was in a position to influence the rate of expansion and the establishment of stations, in particular situations, through the terms and conditions of the arrangements it made for providing service to private stations.

The original plan was clear, and the Government adhered strictly to its policy. The policy was remarkably successful in achieving its objective. By 1959, 55 stations had been licensed and television service was available to some 85 percent of the population.

In July 1959, after consultation with the BBG, the Conservative Government announced the lifting of the single station policy, opening the way to second stations and alternative television service. The announcement of the change in policy was made by the Hon. George Nowlan, in the House of Commons, during the debate on the estimates of the BBG.[1] The Minister noted that the Conservative Party had opposed the single station policy on the grounds that it created "local monopolies." The Party favoured competition. Since assuming office the government had, he said, re-examined the situation, with consideration to both the current circumstances of the CBC and the private broadcasters and to the review and recommendations of the Fowler Commission. The Commission, while warning of potential difficulties, had recommended the licensing of competing stations under suitable conditions. The Minister recognized the effect of competition on the revenue of existing stations, particularly CBC stations, but emphasized the benefits to the consumers of television service. It was announced that, from 15 September 1959, the Government would be prepared to consider applications for second stations and to give approval, provided all the requisite conditions were met. "It is unlikely," the Minister said, "that the size of the market to be served will justify additional stations in many of the areas already served. This is a matter which the BBG no doubt will wish to take carefully into account in considering the proposals put before it. Nevertheless, as time goes on, we would assume that more and more areas in Canada would justify a second station." The Minister had consulted the Board before announcing the policy of the Government to receive applications for second television licences, and the Board had more than one conversation with the Minister on the conditions to be applied to television stations after second stations were licensed. Neither the announcement by the Minister, nor the general rules as outlined by the Board made any reference to the position of the CBC as a potential applicant. There is no record of the matter having been discussed with the Minister.

By May 1960, when the public hearings were held in Edmonton and Calgary, the Government had not disclosed any policy, and neither the CBC nor the Board had established a policy with respect to the CBC. Conversations had occurred between the CBC and the Board on the licensing of additional stations to the Corporation. Some awkwardness, under the provisions of the Broadcasting Act, had been disclosed. Section 12 of the Act provided that a licence might not be issued by the Minister of Transport without a recommendation by the BBG, after a public hearing, and an order-in-council. Section 29(1)(b) provided that the CBC could establish stations as it considered desirable. The CBC claimed that, as an agent of the Crown, the Corporation could not, or need not, be licensed, and therefore that Section 12 did not apply to the Corporation. As far as the CBC was concerned, the operative section was 29(1)(b). The CBC, however, indicated it was prepared to follow the procedures set out in Section 12 and have its applications go before the Board at public hearings. The Board for its part was aware that, under the Act, the CBC was required to submit a five-year budget to the Government, and that the Corporation's annual budget had to be approved by Treasury Board and Parliament. It might have been plausible to assume that an application would not be forwarded to the Board by the Minister of Transport if the licensing of additional stations to the CBC was contrary to government policy. If the CBC ever submitted a five-year budget to the Government, the BBG was never advised of it, and the Board did not have access to the Corporation's annual budget.

During the public hearings of the 1959 Parliamentary Committee on Broadcasting, that is, before the hearings on second station applications began, the Chairman of the Board was asked what the Board would do if it were confronted with competing applications by the CBC and a private applicant. As there had not been—as far as the Board knew—any determination of policy by the Government, and the Board had not established a policy, the discreet and proper answer would have been that the Chairman did not know. He made the mistake of replying that he thought the Board would probably recommend the CBC.[2] This answer was picked up by the press and received some unfavourable editorial comment. It did not draw any reaction from the Government.

EDMONTON

The Board announced and proceeded with applications for second licences. It had become clear from conversations with the CBC that the preference in the Corporation was to apply for stations in both Edmonton and Calgary. The Board counselled against this but did not advise against an application in one of the cities. The CBC chose Edmonton. The public hearing of applications in Edmonton proceeded without any commitment on the part of the Board to favour the application of the CBC. The CBC was aware of this, and the private applications proceeded in the expectation they would receive a fair hearing.

The Board opened its public hearings on applications for a television licence in Edmonton on 10 May 1960. In addition to the CBC application, there were four private applications.

The principal in the application of North Gate Broadcasting Company was Dr. Charles Allard. Dr. Allard was Head of Surgery at the General Hospital and also a highly successful businessman. Associated with him were Dr. Rene Boileau, also a practising surgeon, Vice-President. The list of shareholders included five doctors. Don Mackay, Secretary of the Edmonton Chamber of Commerce, who had previously been General Manager of Radio Station CHED, was to be General Manager of the station.

Selkirk Holdings was the principal shareholder in Edmonton Video. Selkirk Holdings had extensive participation in other broadcasting stations, radio and television, in the west. The submission was made by Gerry Gaetz of Radio Station CJCA, as President and Chief Executive Officer of Edmonton Video.

Radio Station CHED was also an applicant, with a list of shareholders which read like a roster of the Edmonton Burns Club.

Mayfair Broadcasting brought together Michael and Alex Starko, the operators of Page Cleaners and Furriers; Sydney Wood of Wood, Haddad, Moir, Hyde and Ross, lawyers; and a group of Edmonton businessmen.

Other presentations included one by G.R.A. Rice of CFRN-TV who wished to be assured that if the CBC were successful there would be orderly transition from his status as an affiliate, and if a private application were successful his status as a basic affiliate would be maintained.[3] A.F. Shortell, of CHSA-TV Lloydminster,[4] and G.A. Barclay, CHCA-TV Red Deer,[5] appeared to protest the encroachment of the signals into their service areas and to request that the power of any new Edmonton station be limited. A.M. Dechene spoke for the French-Canadian Association of Alberta, asking for a minimum of French-language broadcasts and expressing a preference for the CBC.[6]

The CBC application was supported by briefs on behalf of the Alberta branch, Canadian Association of Consumers, the Alberta Federation of Labour, and a group of University staff members who had circulated a petition in the University of Alberta and the schools. The Television Committee of the Grande Prairie Chamber of Commerce and Associated Chambers of Commerce of the Peace River District contended that public funds could be better expended by establishing a CBC station in the Peace River area.[7]

Alphonse Ouimet presented the case for the Corporation. He stated that, for financial reasons, the Corporation had been faced with the difficult choice between Edmonton and Calgary, and had chosen Edmonton because it was the Gateway to the North, the larger of the two cities, the provincial capital and the university centre. The station in Edmonton was seen as essential to assist in distribution of the full national network service, to help Canadians know their country better and to develop program production for regional and national network distribution. On the local front, it was contended that the combination of a station of the CBC and a private station would offer a better choice to the audience than would two private stations, one an affiliate of the CBC. It was claimed that if service was to be extended into the Peace River area—and this was in the CBC's plans—this would be facilitated by a CBC station in Edmonton. In response to the representations from Lloydminster and Red Deer, Mr. Ouimet said they would encounter less difficulty from a CBC station in Edmonton and, with reference to CFRN-TV, that it would find the CBC competition less rigorous. The CBC expected that, in terms of its local operations, the station would generate sufficient revenue to meet its expenditures.[8]

At various points in the hearings, reference was made to the possibility of the CBC maintaining two affiliates and to supplying the second station with network programs not carried by CFRN-TV. Mr. Ouimet saw the first as impractical; on the second point he expressed an open mind, but saw considerable difficulties. The Corporation was questioned on the need for transmission facilities. Mr. Ouimet argued that it was impractical to suggest that the CBC operate only as a program producer: this would cost more to the public treasury, and it was not possible to represent a community without being a part of it. There was considerable discussion of the policy of using local stations as program producers. The Corporation's view was that they were prepared to use programs produced by local private stations, but that private stations underestimated the difficulty of producing programs of network quality. Even more attention was given, during the hearings, to the extent to which the Corporation could, or would, originate local programs for the national network. Mr. Ouimet stated that, at the time, of the English-language national network service 70 percent originated in Toronto and 30 percent elsewhere. He agreed that the CBC should strive to originate more from outside Toronto, but claimed that even the small amount which could be taken from the several other centres was not inconsequential to the national purposes.

Immediately after the hearings concluded, the Board voted to recommend the issue of the licence to the CBC. The next day the Chairman was advised by a member of the Board that the Government had learned of the Board's decision and wished to see the decision reversed. The proposal that the question be reopened was rejected. The issue of the licence required an order-in-council. The Government eventually passed the order. The licence was issued to the Corporation.[9]

Following the recommendation of the Board that the licence be issued to the CBC, some of the private applicants protested that the case had been prejudged by the Board and that they had wasted their time and money in proceeding with their applications. Perhaps this was an understandable reaction. Notwithstanding the Chairman's earlier statement it was, however, unfounded.

After the Edmonton hearing the Board drew to the Government's attention the fact that, under existing legislation, it was awkward for the Board to deal with applications by the CBC. Nothing was done about it, and the problem continued to plague the Board.

In a release dated 11 December 1961, the Board expressed the view that, in the light of the experience of second stations in major markets, extension of second stations into other and smaller markets could only proceed slowly.[10] CTV Network had been approved and it was in the interest of the network to offer its advertisers a more extended coverage. The private network's coverage was considerably less than the CBC network coverage. This represented a serious disadvantage to the private network, both in purchasing programs and in selling network time. The second private stations, affiliates of the CTV Network, were getting established and it was in their interest also to extend coverage, preferably by the least costly method: rebroadcasting stations. The CBC feared and consistently opposed the extension of alternative service by rebroadcasting stations of the CTV affiliates. The Corporation realized that the effect of this development would be to give the private stations greater coverage than their own stations and to make it difficult for the CBC to compete for local and national selective revenue. The Corporation shared the concern of their local affiliates at the prospect of competing with a rebroadcasting station. The CBC was afraid of the increased payments which might have to be made to affiliates for carrying the national network service. The local CBC affiliates were afraid that they might not be able to compete with an alternative service which did not share the obligation to provide local programming.

QUEBEC CITY

Before the end of 1961, the Board received an application for a private television station in Quebec City from Jacques LaRoche, who had been awarded a licence for a radio station. The number of households within the "B" contour of the proposed station was 125,000. The French-language CBC affiliate, in which Famous Players held a controlling interest, was a profitable undertaking, but it carried on its shoulders the unprofitable English-language service. When the CBC became aware of the LaRoche application, the Corporation submitted a competing application. The issue of the place of the CBC in the extension of alternative television was reopened. The Board had no more knowledge of government policy than it had at the time of the Edmonton application. The Board had to choose between a private applicant and the CBC. The dilemma eventually led to the resignation of two Board members.

The two applications were heard at the public hearing in March 1962, in an atmosphere of marked hostility between the supporters of the private application and those supporting the application of the CBC.

The CBC had not, at March 1962, enunciated any long-run policy. The Chairman of the Board's position at the time was that an issue of broad national policy was involved: the Board could not continue to deal with applications for second stations, including CBC stations, on an *ad hoc* basis, and submission of conflicting applications by the CBC and private applicants was undesirable. It was his view that the decision on the role of the CBC in the extension of second service, because of its profound effect on the structure of the system and its financial implications for the government, should be made by Parliament. If it was not possible to get a declaration of policy from the government, and there seemed to be no disposition on their part to take a position publicly, the Chairman felt the Board should have a long-run policy of its own, and should declare it. He was reluctant to deal further with applications until a policy was established.

At the meeting of the Board following the March hearing, a number of the members felt that, the two applications having been received and heard, the Board was required to make a recommendation; but the first motion was to deny both applications. In terms of the capacity of the market to support another outlet—at least an outlet of the CBC—there was no justification for denial, thus leaving the predominantly French-speaking audience without alternative service. A Quebec member of the Board, Dean Hudon, said that if the motion passed he would be forced to resign, and he was supported by Dr. Forsey. The motion was put off to the next day. A poll of the members indicated no support for the denial of both applications; the motion was withdrawn. The majority appeared to favour reservation of the decision on both applications, but the members left for home without any action being taken. Following the meeting, the Chairman sent a letter to all members of the Board stressing the importance of clarifying relations with the CBC in areas such as the principles on which the "O & O" stations were to be operated, the material package and affiliation agreements and the commercial policy of the CBC. He declared his belief in the primacy of matters of this sort over and above the immediate disposal of the particular problem in Quebec City.

At the same time the Chairman, in correspondence with Dean Hudon, was attempting to dissuade him from resigning if the Board did not approve the CBC application. He noted that the Board was badly divided and admitted that he did not know what the outcome would be. As Dean Hudon felt that sometimes the English-speaking members of the Board lacked an understanding of or sympathy for the views of French-speaking members on cases in Quebec, the Chairman referred to this point:

> In this country with its two languages and two cultures there may very well occur cases in which the collective judgement of the Quebec French-speaking members of the Board would differ from that of the English-speaking members of the Board from other parts of the country. I cannot think of a case in which the issue of biculturalism was involved in which the French-Canadian members of the Board were in a solid minority. If there have been such cases, I cannot recall them. I would certainly feel that the English-speaking members of the Board would be most reluctant to force a decision contrary to a solid opinion of their French-Canadian colleagues on matters of vital concern to the French-Canadian interest in this country.

The Chairman also referred to the principal of "Board solidarity" which had been approved by the Board; when a decision was reached members all supported it regardless of their personal positions, and "minority decisions" were not normally announced. The policy had been breached on two occasions. While supporting the policy, the Chairman said, "it seems to me that breaches of the kind we have experienced are to be preferred to the resignation of any member of the Board because of Board action in a particular case. However, I concede that, even in relation to a particular case, a member of the Board may feel so strongly on the matter that he may, in the face of an adverse decision, feel obliged to tender his resignation. The Board returned to the Quebec City applications at its meeting on 7 April 1962. Dean Hudon referred to the correspondence with the

Chairman, and took the position there was no reason to postpone further action on a decision favourable to the CBC. He was supported by Dr. Forsey. Two French-speaking members then moved approval of the LaRoche application. The motion was defeated. A motion to take no further action was eventually carried. Hudon and Forsey both recorded their dissent which they wished to make public.

The Board met again in late May. At an evening session on 29 May, notice to make a decision was carried by a substantial majority. A motion to approve the private application was defeated. A motion to approve the CBC application was also defeated but by a slightly smaller majority. The Chairman said the only conclusion he could draw from the votes was that there was a preference for approval of the CBC application but a reluctance to make an immediate decision and to announce it. The Chairman adjourned the meeting at 11:00 p.m. The outcome was not surprising. The Chairman had learned of the intervention of Hon. Jacques Flynn, the Member of the Cabinet from Quebec City. With a federal election coming up and because of the strong feelings on both sides in the city, Mr. Flynn hoped a decision could be avoided until after the election. This word had got to some of the members.

The subject was reopened on 31 May. Dean Hudon and Dr. Forsey did not attend this meeting. They had written their resignations but had not submitted them. The meeting adjourned without any action, a member having given notice of motion to be put the following morning to rescind all motions on the Quebec City applications. When the Board met on 1 June, a motion to reserve decision on the CBC application was approved by a substantial majority. A motion to deny the LaRoche application was carried. On the same day, Dean Hudon and Dr. Forsey submitted their resignations and their statement was released on 7 June. It was unfortunate. They were both good men.

The federal election was held on 18 June 1962. The Conservative government lost its majority in the House. Mr. LaRoche resubmitted his application. At the meeting of the Board on 19 January 1963, the CBC application was approved unanimously; the LaRoche application was denied.

THE POLICY CONTRADICTIONS

In the meantime, discussions with the CBC were proceeding in the Consultative Committee on Public Broadcasting. One of the topics was the extension of alternative television service. Before the Board had disposed of the Quebec City applications, a statement had been received from the Corporation outlining its policy. The CBC committed itself to a national policy providing for a combination of CBC-owned and privately-owned stations, implying that in the remaining markets served by the private affiliates of the CBC, the second licence would be issued to the CBC. Three principal reasons were offered in support of this policy. First, bearing in mind the nature of the public service, the combination of a CBC and a private station would offer a better choice of service than would a combination of private stations. Second, it was necessary for the national service to draw upon material from all parts of the country. Third, the CBC contended that all Canadians were entitled to a full public service, whereas it was not reasonable to expect affiliates to carry more than one-half of the total program service broadcast by CBC-owned stations. Within the long-run policy, the immediate goal was to establish at least one major station in each of the provinces, preferably the capital city. To make the long-run policy effective it was proposed that channels should be reserved for CBC use at all points presently served only by private stations.

The CBC realized that the basic problem was the availability of funds to the Corporation. They also recognized the problem of the capacity of the single station markets to sustain a second station. The CBC claimed that in terms of 1962 dollars it would be possible to install transmitters to serve all the areas covered by CBC affiliates at a total cost of $25 million, and to add small studios at a few points at an additional cost of $5 million. The capacity of the markets would limit the rate of expansion, and capital expenditures would be spread over 15 to 20 years. The decision as to when an area was ready was seen to be a responsibility of the BBG. The existing stations had the right to a public hearing should they wish to contest an application.

Concerns for capital financing aside, the balance of programming affected costs as well as operating revenues and the overall relations between a public and a private sector station. As a generalization, it cost more to produce programs than to purchase foreign programs having the same audience appeal. Program production costs were the principal item in the expenditures of the CBC. The main part of these costs was associated with the national network service carried on both CBC and private affiliated stations. Other costs were incurred in producing programs for the "local" service of the CBC stations. Competition at the local level became a contentious issue. Initially, and until the network was formed, the second private stations met the Canadian content regulations by producing programs for local broadcasting only. The CBC urged that the principal function of the private stations was local service; but the CBC was concerned to maintain the local service of its stations. The private stations believed that the CBC's principal function was to provide the national service, and that the CBC should leave the local service, or leave it more largely, to them. One of their complaints was that while they were being held responsible for service to the local community, the CBC was able to pick and choose the local service it provided. The CBC could neglect some aspects of local service, but when some event of more than ordinary interest occurred in their locality the CBC would move in to cover it for regional and even national distribution.

Part of the "local" service of the CBC "O & O" stations consisted of syndicated foreign programs, and the private stations also bought and broadcast syndicated material. The costs of these programs were relatively low, and if judiciously selected they appealed to the audience and generated net revenue. The CBC was able to buy collectively for their stations, and the private stations acting independently were in a less favourable position as buyers. The CBC was able to outbid the private stations. The private stations claimed this was possible because the CBC was supported by public funds, and was therefore not subject to the same limitations on the prices it could pay. The principal reason, however, was the capacity of the CBC to buy for the system of "O & O" stations; and eventually the CTV made arrangements with its affiliates for co-operative purchasing through ITO. This improved their competitive position.

There was contention over the rates charged to advertisers. The CBC was not disinterested in the rates charged by the private stations; but the main complaints came from the private stations with respect to the rates charged by the CBC. There were broadly two sets of rates—rates charged to national advertisers for national network coverage, i.e., "national" rates, and "local" rates charged for exposure on a single station. The latter rate might be paid either by a strictly local business with no interest in exposure beyond the local community, or by a firm with wider interest wishing to buy exposure on particular stations selectively. The CBC sold on both the "national" and the "local" basis. The private stations were more involved in selling on a local basis. They were therefore particularly concerned with the CBC local rate. During the hearing of applications for second stations most of the applicants proposed rates lower than the CBC rates. The new licensees were particularly incensed when the CBC stations reduced their local rates; and the private stations again claimed this was possible because of the public funds available to support the CBC. The complaint was particularly strong in the early stages of the operation of the second stations when they were operating in the red. It passed as the revenue position of the stations improved, and they began to raise their rates.

The national operations of the CBC were not beyond the concern of the private stations; but it was the "local" operations of the CBC "O & O" stations they were most exercised about. They claimed that the CBC was in a position to change its local operations, programming and commercial policy, so as to strengthen its competitive position without regard to the net revenues of the local station. The evidence was not available to the Board; only the CBC had any idea of the net revenues from local operations of its several "O & O" stations.

The Board expected that the CBC "O & O" stations would perform three distinct functions; carry the national service that is also carried by the affiliates, contribute to the national network service, and provide a "local" service.

It seemed desirable that the CBC "O & O" stations should be incorporated in a separate division of the Corporation. The station division should, on behalf of the individual "O & O" stations, enter into affiliation agreements with the network division, the terms of affiliation being determined on the same basis as used in arriving at agreements with private affiliates. Under the affiliation agreements the stations would receive revenue from the network division for distributing the national network service. They would also receive revenue from the network division for material supplied by them and used in the national network package. In the latter connection, the payments made by the network division for material provided by the stations might be based on the computed costs determined by approved accounting procedures.

The local service would consist of the broadcast service outside the time required to carry the national network package. The local service need not necessarily be produced in the facilities of the station and might be acquired from a variety of sources. The cost of the service should be charged to the stations rather than to the national network service. The revenue from the subsidiary network operation should be credited to the stations carrying the programs. The policy with respect to the relation between costs and revenues in the operation of the subsidiary network of the "O & O" stations should be clearly enunciated. It was suggested that the subsidiary network should "break even." The remaining function of the "O&O" stations would be to produce or acquire programs for broadcasting on the individual station.

Against the total costs of carrying on the operations of a station in a particular market, the station would receive revenue from four sources:

1) As an affiliate, revenue from carrying the national network package;

2) Revenue in payment for services rendered to the national network service;

3) Net revenue, if any, for subsidiary network service to "O&O" stations; and,

4) Revenue from sale of local programming.

The Board believed that the policy of the Corporation should be to operate each station so that the revenue from these several sources would cover the total costs of the operation of the station.

The Board's approach required a definition of the national network package to be distributed to "O & O" stations and affiliates alike on comparable terms. The distribution of the national network package was seen as the principal function of the public service. The definition of the package would impose obligations on the Corporation in the production and distribution of Canadian programming; and it was expected that there would be a substantial net cost to the public treasury from performing this essential function. Given the separation of the network division from the station division, and the accounting procedures required, it would be possible to identify the net costs of operating the national network service. The accounting procedures proposed for the station division and the individual "O & O" stations would make it possible to compare the revenues and costs associated with the "local" operations. It was suggested that the policy should be to break even on the local operations.

The proposals involved certain accounting procedures, and allocation of revenues and expenditures between the network division, the station division, and the individual stations. Maxwell Henderson, the Auditor General, who had previously been the Comptroller with the CBC, informed the Board that he had evolved accounting procedures within the Corporation in line with those involved in the Board's proposals. The CBC agreed that the procedures could be followed, and informed the Board that, in fact, they were being applied for purposes of internal management. They questioned the validity, for policy purposes, of the allocation of revenues and costs and consistently considered the information from their internal accounting procedures as confidential.

On the presentation of their views to the CBC at a meeting of the Consultation Committee, Mr. Ouimet expressed surprise that the Board felt that the policies of the Corporation were not well enough defined. Mr. Dunsmore, however, said that the CBC would wish to study the views carefully and that more discussions should be held.

In the continuing discussions with the CBC, the Board's proposals designed to define the CBC's mandate in more precise operating terms were met by the CBC with arguments in support of flexibility, i.e., the opportunity to modify its policies, priorities, and decisions as seemed best to it. The CBC saw the issue as affecting its "autonomy" or "independence" and genuinely believed that reduced flexibility would impair the public service. The view the Board expressed was that the public service was not an island unto itself in the total broadcasting service, and that it was impossible for the Corporation to have complete authority and flexibility in determining the national service, unless the Corporation were sensitive, and willing to adapt itself to considerations outside its own operations. The operations of the CBC must be influenced by its dependence on private stations to achieve nation-wide distribution of the national broadcasting service; its commercial policy must be influenced by the fact that, although receiving public funds, it was in competition for commercial revenues with private unaffiliated stations operating wholly on commercial revenues; and, it must accept an overall view of the total broadcasting service of which its own operations were only a part. Finally, the Board noted that the operations of the CBC must be influenced by the need to secure the support of Parliament.

It was the Board's view that the insistence by the CBC on complete flexibility was one of the factors affecting the relations between the CBC and Parliament. The emphasis on flexibility made it difficult for the CBC to describe to Parliament what the CBC was doing, and for Parliament to get a clear sense of what it was voting money for. The Board believed that, if the mandate of the CBC were more clearly defined, it would be possible to persuade Parliament to provide assured support over a period of years; and the Board could urge on Parliament the advantage of so doing.[11]

The Broadcasting Act required the BBG to ensure that the total broadcasting service conformed to criteria expressed in the Act in quite wide terms; and it was necessary for the Board to have some concept of what was required of the broadcasting service as a whole. The service provided by the CBC was, both qualitatively and quantitatively, a highly significant part of the total broadcasting service. Complete flexibility would leave the regulatory body without any assurance of the nature of the contribution to be made, within the total broadcasting service, by the CBC. The amount which already existed was making it difficult for the Board to devise its regulations governing the private sector or expanding the overall system. In seeking a better functioning of the two board system, the Board noted that if it was not to become involved in the functions of the CBC it would be necessary that the nature of the national network service be defined more clearly than had so far been done, and that the essential features be approved by Parliament. If a definition of the CBC program package could be determined and the Board were satisfied that the package was of a kind that would enable the Board to regulate the operations of the private stations so as to secure a satisfactory broadcasting service overall, the Board would lend the full weight of its support to securing the approval of the package and maintaining it.

During 1962, however, the situation became increasingly confused. Public pressure for alternative service in single-station markets was building up, promoted by second stations seeking to expand their coverage through rebroadcasting stations. The CBC, having established its policy of applying for second station licences whenever they might be granted, announced it was preparing applications for St. John's, Newfoundland and Saint John, New Brunswick. The "austerity" measures of the Conservative Government made it uncertain just when the CBC might be able to proceed with further applications. With this in mind, the Corporation approached the Board to determine whether the Board would recommend favourably on applications based on "phasing in," that is, an initial application for a transmitter to be followed later, as finances permitted, by one for approval to construct studios. The CBC affiliates in second-station markets, alarmed at the prospect of competition from rebroadcasting stations, proposed what became known as "twin stick" operations—the circumstances in which the licensee of the local private station would be licensed to operate in conjunction with its service, as a local CBC affiliate, a repeater station, on another channel, carrying the programs of CTV Network.

It appeared that some statement of policy would reduce the uncertainty and create a greater measure of stability. On the relation of the CBC to expansion of alternative service, a statement of policy by the Government would have been most helpful; but the precarious position of the Government made the possibility of this more remote than ever. It seemed that the Board had to come to grips with the problem. The Chairman advised his colleagues that the Board should announce support for the policy that the CBC should have at least one station in each province—preferably the capital city—without implying any commitment beyond this. The situations in which this short-run policy would apply included St. John's, Quebec City, and Saskatoon. It appeared that apart from Saint John, these were the only locations in which an application for a second station might be expected in the next year or two. It was proposed that the Board establish this short-run policy by announcing that it was prepared to hear applications from the CBC for reservation of channels in these areas.

The discussions of the Board led eventually to the release of a public announcement entitled, "The Extension of Alternative Television Services." A section on "The Structure of the Two Station System" set out the long-run objective as the Board saw it:

> Under the single station policy, the unit in the system was the local station. The Board reaffirms an earlier statement of policy which indicated that in extending alternative service through second stations, the Board believes that, as in the development of primary coverage, the basis of the second coverage must be the local station providing local service as well as, no doubt, being affiliated with a network. Except where there are substantial changes in the distribution of population or other good causes, the ultimate pattern of the second service should closely duplicate the facilities established to provide the primary service. The Board wishes to state emphatically that it does not intend to approve any developments, whatever their short-run advantages, which would appear to hinder or prevent the achievement of this long-run objective.[12]

The statement went on to say: first, that the conditions in the small markets did not, with one or two exceptions, offer the prospect of further second local stations at the time; second, that extension of alternative service by means of rebroadcasting stations would create unfair competition between the local station and the station operating the rebroadcasting facilities, which would prejudice the primary service and which could easily impede the establishment of a second local station at the appropriate time; third, that the operation of relay stations by the network offered earlier prospects of extending alternative service; and, finally, that adoption of the "twin stick" proposal would represent an extension of monopoly in the medium, a move which in the opinion of the Board would require more stringent regulations of the kind governing public utilities.

> The Board is not prepared to state a long-run policy with respect to the licensing of additional stations to the CBC. The Board has noted that, within the framework of the "single station" policy, the Corporation was licensed to operate one station *in each region.* The Board believes it is within its competence to determine that, within the "two stations" policy, additional licences should be issued to the Corporation to enable it to operate at least one station *in each province,* preferably in the capital city.

In conclusion, the announcement of 20 December 1962 emphasized the limitations on the rate of expansion of alternative service.

> The Board is aware of the desire for alternative service and choice of channels in those parts of Canada now served by one television station; but the limitations to the rate of expansion must be realized. Television service is costly. The additional costs of extending service must be paid for. Payment must come either from the public treasury or from advertising revenues. Neither source is unlimited."[13]

ST. JOHN'S

By the time the announcement was released, the public was aware that the CBC was applying for a station in St. John's, Newfoundland. Following the announcement, channels were reserved for the Corporation in the Fredericton-Saint John area, Saskatoon, and Sudbury, in addition to St. John's.

Strong local support was generated for the CBC application in St. John's. The Board's announcement of 20 December 1962 was misinterpreted, however, and the Board came under attack for having prejudged the application. The paragraph which lead to the misunderstanding read: "The Board cannot at this time concede that the potential national advertising revenue and the local conditions justify alternative service by any means, in any of the remaining 'single station' markets (other than Quebec City). In the opinion of the Board this can be established only after the submission of briefs and public hearings." The actual wording of the statement made it clear that, while the Board had decided that the CBC application for Quebec City would be approved, it was refraining from committing itself on other locations until after public hearings. Unfortunately the initial news report conveyed a different impression. A citizens' committee was formed to promote the CBC application in St. John's. In early January 1963, the committee published an "open letter" accusing the Board of prejudging the application and of capitulating to the pressure of the licensee of the private station.

After the introduction of television and the establishment of the single-station policy, the CBC had responded to an application for a private station in St. John's by seeking to establish its own station in Newfoundland. Consistent with the policy at the time, the government of the day rejected the CBC's claim. The applicant for the private station was Geoff Stirling and, as his support for the Liberal Party was already known, there was some feeling that the Government had been influenced by political considerations.[14] The CBC certainly believed that the decision had been a political one. CJON-TV was established as an affiliate of the CBC. The conditions in the island province were such that coverage of the population appeared possible only by the development of a single system having its centre in St. John's and extending service by rebroadcasting stations. The conditions predisposed to a provincial monopoly, and the logical development on the introduction of second service was two parallel systems. At the time of the CBC's second application, one of the co-owners of CJON-TV was Don Jamieson, then President of the CAB. The St. John's market was substantially smaller than the Quebec market and, in comparison with other potential markets, raised the question of why the CBC selected St. John's for its next application. Jamieson was not unnaturally concerned about the effect of the division of the audience. On the other hand, the CBC seemed determined to introduce its "presence" into the Atlantic province and had little difficulty in generating local support.

After Quebec City, the Chairman had developed a distaste for public hearings on conflicting applications by the CBC and private applicants. The atmosphere created was nasty. Each side attempted to develop support where it could. The supporters of the private station attacked the CBC and the supporters of the CBC attacked the local private station. Neither in Quebec City nor in St. John's had the Board been aware of any strong objection to the service being provided by the local station and, in the opinion of the Board, both stations were giving a comparatively good local service; however, in each case the application of the CBC brought out latent hostility. The local support for the CBC seemed curiously like the local support that would have been given to a new fish canning plant—it was an important public works project. The investment in the facilities would stimulate local business and the operations would expand payrolls in the city, with similar effects. It would provide additional earnings for local people, particularly university professors. All this would be provided from federal public funds. Anyone who stood in the way was a public enemy.

The Board replied on 11 January 1963 to the "open letter" of the Citizens' Committee in a letter to the Committee's secretary. The letter referred to the charge that the BBG had prejudged the St. John's case:

The Board was certainly not helped by the way the release was handled in the news. As I told you in reply to your wire, I do not know what was carried on the broadcasting stations. I do know that CJON broadcasts the CBC national news; and this is what the CBC carried to every part of Canada: "The Board of Broadcast Governors says potential revenues from national advertising do not justify alternative television service in any of the remaining 'single station' areas, with the exception of Quebec City. In a statement of policy, issued today, the Board says that, with one or two exceptions, conditions in smaller markets do not offer the prospects of further second TV stations." You will notice that the first sentence is not what the Board said; and the second sentence, which is a correct report, contradicts the first. . . .

The Board surely had to make it clear that although it was prepared to make a commitment that the CBC would have a second station in certain places, this must not be construed as meaning that the Board was committed to approving an application from the Corporation for a licence to operate. This would indeed have been prejudging cases which the Board is bound to recommend on only after public hearings.[15]

The Board met the following week and, at the meeting prior to the public hearing, on 18 January 1963, the Chairman reviewed the developments. The CBC had, immediately prior to the hearing, submitted a revised brief changing its estimate of revenues and operating expenditures in a manner which projected a more substantial operating deficit. The Board agreed that the economic considerations should be the principal concern of the hearing. It seemed desirable to get the evidence of the economics of the market and of the proposed operation on the public record. The Board favoured probing into the estimates of capital costs and revenues included in the CBC application. It was further agreed that the Board should neither attempt to establish whether the funds had been assured to the CBC nor comment on the procedural irregularities in the late submission of the CBC brief.

Following the public hearing, after discussion of certain features of the presentation—including the last-minute revision of the financial estimates, and the proposal that the CBC modify its commercial policy so as to reduce the impact on the private station—the Board agreed to announce that a decision was deferred. A letter was sent to the Secretary of State on 31 January 1963 inquiring as to the responsibility of the Board to comment on financial aspects of CBC applications.[16]

The election was imminent and the Board received no guidelines from the Minister on the questions put to him.

The Board was not opposed to the establishment of a CBC outlet in St. John's, although it was evident that the loss of network service could create substantial difficulties for the local private station. One possibility was the establishment by the CBC of a network repeater transmitter without facilities for local origination. This would leave local revenue exclusively to the other station. The CBC consistently opposed the discontinuous service which would be provided by a network repeater outlet, on the grounds that it was bad broadcasting practice. The local demand for CBC service in St. John's was largely directed to local service. The alternative was some form of "phasing in" to full operation of a local station with production facilities, in order to give the other station time to make adjustments. The Board realized that if the principle of "phasing in" were adopted in the St. John's case it would become a precedent in later cases involving small markets. The Board was therefore concerned about procedures. After the announcement that the decision was reserved, the Board wrote both the CBC and Mr. Jamieson indicating that if the Corporation and CJON-TV could agree upon procedures, the Board would without a further hearing make a favourable recommendation to the Minister incorporating the procedures agreed upon.

The case was reviewed by the Board at its meeting 29 March 1963. The CBC had made proposals for the "phasing in" to full operation of their station. The proposals were: first, that transmission facilities would be in operation by the fall of 1964, broadcasting network programs from which the CBC could obtain network revenue; second, that studio facilities would be completed by 1965 with local origination beginning at that time, but the CBC would seek only "national advertising;" and third, that in the fall of 1966 the CBC would be free to obtain revenue from all sources including local advertisers. Mr. Jamieson did not oppose these conditions. He was concerned about alternative network service. No microwave was available except by agreement with the CBC. The possibility of an arrangement with the CBC was being explored. The Board decided to recommend approval of the application, subject to certain conditions, and to make an early announcement.

The Board's announcement of 5 April 1963 recommended approval subject to the conditions (a) that the licensee, the CBC, would not commence transmission on Channel 8 prior to 1 October 1964; (b) that during the first two years of transmission on Channel 8 the CBC would refrain from engaging in either local or national selective business on Channel 8; (c) that the CBC would assist CJON-TV to obtain the use of microwave facilities, so that CJON-TV might be supplied with programs by this means; and (d) that the CBC would co-operate with CJON-TV in assuring the extension of alternative service in Newfoundland generally.[17]

The election occurred on 3 April 1963 and Mr. Pickersgill became Secretary of State. He was opposed to further production facilities for the CBC and was irate because the Board had announced its recommendations on the St. John's case in advance of the election. On 1 May, he announced he was seeking the views of the Chairman of the BBG, the President of the CBC, and the President of the CAB; thus, the "Troika" began its meetings.[18] The necessary order-in-council for the St. John's station was not immediately passed.

The Department of Transport was concerned about its role in enforcing the conditions. A letter of 17 April from the Deputy Minister requested further information, noting that the proposed conditions would be made by the Minister of Transport, pursuant to the authority of the Minister provided by Section 4(1)(d) of the Radio Act and the responsibility for their enforcement would rest with the Department. "It would, therefore, be appreciated if your Board would supply additional information, for this purpose, about the Board's intent with respect to the proposed conditions."[19]

Little progress was made in working out arrangements for the use of microwave facilities by CJON-TV and clarification of the conditions proposed in the St. John's case became involved in the more general discussions of the "Troika," on the principles governing extension of second television service. In August 1963 the Chairman wrote the Secretary of State with respect to the St. John's application. Mr. Ouimet, Mr. Jamieson, and the Chairman had agreed to recommend to the Governor-in-Council that the installation of transmission facilities by the CBC should proceed. The letter said, "We have had further discussions regarding the availability of microwave facilities to provide network service to CJON-TV after disaffiliation. While this matter has not been finally resolved, it is our view that a solution can be found, and that in the meantime the installation of the CBC transmitter might proceed."[20]

After further discussions and correspondence with the CBC, the Board wrote the Department of Transport on 24 September:

> With respect to the availability of microwave facilities it is our understanding that the Corporation is prepared to assist in two ways. First, within the period during which microwave facilities are under contract to the CBC, the Corporation is prepared to make available for the use of CTV network and CJON-TV such periods of time as the facilities are not required by the CBC. Second, if desired by CTV network and CJON-TV, the Corporation would be prepared to arrange for an extension of its contract period so that more time could be made available for use by CTV network and CJON-TV in this way.
>
> We are satisfied of the intention of the Corporation and CJON-TV to co-operate in planning the extension of service in Newfoundland.[21]

The St. John's licence was issued to the CBC in October 1963.[22] Mr. Pickersgill agreed that the method of dealing with the CBC applications was unsatisfactory and that a firm policy should be established by the Government.[23]

In spite of Mr. Pickergill's concern, little was done in the short run to enunciate clear cut policies or to alleviate the Board's problems, thus bearing out the Chairman's comment that the Liberals had no commitment to the Board or its decisions. While the Liberal Government sanctioned inquiry after inquiry, it took nearly another four years for more definitive policies to be put in place.

[9]

ALTERNATIVE TELEVISION SERVICE AND THE LIBERAL GOVERNMENT

THE SETTING

By 1963 the CBC appeared to favour a policy of applying for all second television licences and of opposing private applications for additional television in centres served by private affiliates of the CBC. An interim report from the "Troika" recommended in principle the expansion of alternative television service through the extension of transmission facilities of the CBC.[1] The Government applied a "freeze." The Board questioned the wisdom of a general freeze over an indefinite period of time; but the Committee on Broadcasting, 1965 (Fowler Committee) said the CBC had reached physical maturity and recommended that the Corporation should not receive additional licences for five years. This advice was not accepted by the Government. The White Paper[2] apparently supported the policy of at least one CBC station in each province, preferably the capital city. The BBG, commenting on the White Paper, added that further expansion should proceed by licensing CBC rebroadcasting stations. By 1967 the CBC, the "Troika," and the Board were all committed to a policy of extending the service through licensing of CBC outlets. There was no evidence of a firm government policy. Applications for licences in Saskatoon, Lethbridge and Brandon and demands for a station in Moncton were dealt with by the Board in a manner consistent with the policy it was supporting. By the end of the life of the BBG, however, Saskatoon, Brandon, and Moncton remained without second service.

The Board made repeated requests that a long-run policy for the extension of second television service should be determined as soon as possible. On 8 April 1963 the Chairman of the Board addressed a letter to the Prime Minister, stating that the members of the Board should "take this opportunity to urge on the Government of Canada the necessity of an early and comprehensive review of broadcasting policy and of the Broadcasting Act."[3] In a public address to the CAB, 3 May 1963, the Chairman said:

> Difficulties with respect to the allocation of frequencies and extension of the public service came to a head when it became known to the Board that the Directors of the Corporation were committed to a policy of applying for all "second television" licences, and of opposing private applications for additional television licences in centres now served by private affiliates of the CBC. The Corporation took the position that as the Directors considered these stations "necessary and desirable" [Section 29(1)(b)] the Board should recommend favourably on applications by the Corporation, leaving it to the Governor-in-Council to decide whether to provide the necessary funds and to pass the necessary order. The Board felt that, if it were committed to the procedure, and by inference to the policy, it should be on the basis of a statement of policy, and not as a result of a decision by the Directors of the Corporation . . . The Board believes, and has held this view for some time, that the only solution to this problem is a statement of public policy on the licensing of additional television stations to be owned and operated by the Corporation.[4]

Mr. Pickersgill was in agreement with the view that the method of dealing with CBC applications was unsatisfactory, and that a firm policy should be established by the Government. He was, however, vigorously opposed to additional "hardware" for the CBC.

In September 1963 the "Troika," in an interim report to the Minister, stated:

We have agreed to recommend that the Minister of Transport should not, during the remainder of 1963 and in the first six months of 1964, receive or under Section 12 of the Broadcasting Act forward to the Board applications for licences which would result in the extension of alternative Canadian television service. The effect of this would be that applications for television licences involving alternative service would not be heard earlier than the first public hearing after July 1, 1964.[5]

The Minister implemented the recommendation and a "freeze" was applied. The Committee on Broadcasting, 1965 recommended against the establishment of CBC facilities to provide alternative television services. The White Paper declared that the Government was ready to consider issuing second station licenses subject to reservation of channels for the CBC in Victoria, Saskatoon, Sudbury and Fredericton-Saint John. CBC services could be provided by repeater stations at first, as funds permitted. Private affiliates might want to disaffiliate from the CBC in order to join the CTV Network. In all cases, the BBG would have to satisfy the government that advertising revenue would be adequate to support a proper level of public service programming.[6]

The government had rejected the recommendation of the Committee on Broadcasting, 1965 specifically with respect to reservations for CBC stations in Saskatoon, Sudbury, and the Fredericton-Saint John area. However, in a memorandum reviewing the problem of extension of second service, the Chairman referred to the lack of precision in the White Paper statement:

The statement is singularly unclear. This has been commented on by the CBC, private broadcasters and consultants. As the issue of whether or not the CBC alone should extend second service must have been reviewed, the lack of clarity in the statement must be seen as intentional. . . . There is nothing in the White Paper to indicate that private applications may not be heard. There is nothing in the White Paper statement which would preclude the CBC from applying in other locations than the four in which channels are to be reserved; or from opposing private applications on the grounds that, although the Corporation is not prepared to move immediately, the private application would prevent the CBC from providing service through its own outlet . . . .

The Board may find itself in the position in which it will have to use its discretion in the recommendation to the Minister. As the Board has itself expressed a preference for extension of second service through outlets of the CBC, the White Paper may in fact imply that the Board is expected to make recommendations on the basis of this preference. At least the White Paper does not exclude a pattern of development which would move the system in the direction of two complete services.[7]

The Board reviewed the White Paper at its meeting in September 1966, and on 5 October on public announcement was issued outlining the Board's position on applications for extension of television service.[8] On the following day the Chairman wrote the Prime Minister:

The Board spent a considerable time discussing the emerging problems of dealing with applications for alternative television service, now that the "freeze" is off. The public demand for a second service exists and can be made vocal by prospective applicants; but the means by which the alternative service can be provided without jeopardizing the existing local service are by no means clear. I enclose a copy of an announcement approved by the Board, and call your attention to number four (4). The Board is apprehensive that in particular situations, in which demand for second service has already been stimulated by prospective applicants, there may be no practical solution without the intervention of the CBC. You will notice from the announcement that the Board propose a study of the markets involved, and some delay in hearing applications. The Board will be better informed on particular situations as the study progresses.[9]

In its confidential statement on the *Report* of the Committee on Broadcasting, requested by the Cabinet Committee on Broadcasting, the Board advised: "In principle, second television service should be extended through facilities of the CBC. The Corporation should have at least one station with production facilities in each province. Beyond this the service may be provided by rebroadcasting or network stations."

By 1967 the Board was publicly committed to a policy of extending alternative television service through the licensing of CBC outlets. The CBC had advanced the policy; the "Troika" had recommended it. The Board endorsed it in its comments on the White Paper. However, there was no indication that the Government would support the policy or indeed had any consistent policy for the CBC. The Committee on Broadcasting, 1965 had recommended against extension of the CBC facilities. The White Paper statement was ambiguous. The CBC did not know whether it would receive funds for expansion. The Board did not know whether the recommendations for the issue of licences to the CBC would be approved. Further, the Board realized that, if the existing local stations were to be disaffiliated from the CBC, they would have to receive network service from the only source possible—CTV Network—to enable them to survive and continue their local service. However, the Board had no authority to require CTV Network to extend it service into a small market.

SASKATOON-REGINA

After St. John's, Saskatoon and the Fredericton-Saint John area were the logical next centres for alternative service. The CBC decided to apply for Saskatoon. The Board was in favour of proceeding with the establishment of a CBC station in Saskatoon, but was concerned about the level of expenditures projected in the CBC application. The Board had lent its support for the extension of alternative television service through CBC outlets on its understanding that the CBC stations would, at least initially, be rebroadcasting—or repeater—stations; this was the condition under which the White Paper had supported CBC stations in four locations. The Board was therefore disturbed to find that the application for Saskatoon proposed facilities for a complete service, including local originations from substantial studio facilities. In its appearance before the Parliamentary Committee, the Board commented on the dilemma which the application presented.[10]

The Board had discussions with the CBC, and on 23 March the Chairman again wrote the Secretary of State noting the CBC's revised application containing considerably reduced capital expenditures.[11] The application was heard and recommended for approval. By March 1968 no action had been taken by the Liberal Government. The licence was finally granted, after a new hearing, in January of 1971.

CTV Network was prepared to provide network service to the Saskatoon station on its disaffiliation from the CBC. The Network had had extended negotiations with the licensee but had failed to reach agreement on the terms for provision of service. The Board, however, believed that once the CBC station was in operation agreement would be reached.

As the White Paper had approved a CBC station in Saskatoon, it is difficult to understand why the government did not proceed on the Board's recommendation. One complicating factor seemed to be the situation in Regina. In 1958 there was a private affiliate of the CBC operating in Regina and a private affiliate of the CBC operating in Moose Jaw. The Regina station, CKCK-TV, was owned by the Siftons, the Moose Jaw station, CHAB-TV, by the Moffat interests. In due course, by extending the coverage of both stations through rebroadcasting stations—including a high powered rebroadcasting station of CHAB-TV—and the affiliation of CHAB-TV with CTV Network, alternative service was brought to the area. The Regina-Moose Jaw area was seen as a single market. It was still a relatively small market in which to divide the audience. CKCK-TV Regina continued to attract the larger audience, but incurred heavy operating losses. Moose Jaw received substantial support from CTV Network but remained a marginal operation. It was part of the CBC's plan eventually to have its own outlet in the capital city of the province, but the conditions in the market in 1967 were not such as to justify a third station. Although the CBC would have preferred Regina to Saskatoon, it chose to apply for Saskatoon. The Siftons saw the way out of their problem through the CBC purchasing one of the stations in the area but they did not wish to sell their station. They therefore mounted a campaign to have the CBC purchase CHAB-TV and to dis-affiliate CKCK-TV, a move which would permit them to affiliate with CTV Network. They appeared to have some support from Premier Thatcher of Saskatchewan. Following the death of Frank Moffat, the owners of CHAB-TV became sympathetic to the sale of the station to the CBC if this were possible. Thus the Regina-Moose Jaw situation was probably a factor in the Government's failure to proceed with the CBC station in Saskatoon.

Pressure continued to build up for second service in a number of locations. Private stations, seeking extension of coverage through rebroadcasting stations, were directing public demand to the Board, directly and through local authorities and members of Parliament. On 27 February the Chairman wrote the Secretary of State seeking guid-ance. No directions were forthcoming.

SOUTHWESTERN ALBERTA

On 14 July 1967 the Board announced public hearings to be held on 14 November for applications from southwestern Manitoba, south-western Alberta, and the Maritime provinces. Following the hearings, the applications of CJCH-TV Halifax and CJAY-TV Winnipeg for rebroadcasting stations were recommended for denial, on the grounds that the local stations in Moncton and Brandon could not be expected to bear the costs of local service against the competition of a station covering both the larger city and the small market.

In January 1968, the Board was back to the Secretary of State:

It seems that the Governor-in-Council must give early considera-tion to the reservation of channels for the Canadian Broadcasting Corporation. Reservation of channels for the CBC, or at least a clear view of where the CBC may be going in the structure of the television system, is urgently needed if the Council [the then envis-aged new regulatory and licensing body] is to have any chance to deal efficiently with applications to provide "second" television service. In this connection we have prepared a memorandum "Alternative Service in Small Markets" setting out the views of the Board. A copy of this memorandum is attached.[12]

The memorandum contained an analysis of the costs of operating stations which were providing a local service in small markets, and of the effects alternative means of introducing a second service would probably have on revenues. It pointed out that although the CBC affiliates received 18% of their revenue from the CBC, this was *net* revenue. The stations did not pay anything for programs or their distribution. "It can be said categorically that if the stations were charged any significant part of the CBC costs of producing, purchasing or distributing the national network service, they could not survive and continue to offer the local service to audience and advertisers."[13] Further, as an additional 34% of revenues came from regional and national advertising, "the maintenance of local stations in small markets, their local program service, and their service to local advertisers, depended upon revenues generated outside the community and 'subsidy' by the network." The analysis of the effect of competition from a private rebroadcasting station was that because of the decline in the revenue of the local station, it would be necessary for the CBC to increase its payments to the station in order to maintain the distribution of the national service. "The local service would be maintained at the expense of the public purse." If the second service were provided by a rebroadcasting station of the CBC, there would be less effect on the revenue of the local station; but as the costs of operating a rebroadcasting station were no more than 40% of the costs of operating a local station, there was the possibility that the CBC could break even on the rebroadcasting operation. However, a local station would need CTV Network service. "As the local station will find its revenues from other sources reduced, it must expect no less *net* payment from CTV Network than it has previously received from the CBC. CTV Network will incur additional costs including the annual cost of providing facilities, the increases the network will have to pay for purchase of programs and some increase in other operating expenditures." The additional revenue which might be earned by the network was difficult to estimate "but there would appear to be no additional *net* to make payments to the local station." On the contrary, "CTV Network would incur a significant loss if it provided the network service and paid the local station the net amount the station is now receiving from the CBC. This would seem to be close to the minimum amount required to enable the local station to survive and continue its local service. The Board is not in a position to require the member stations comprising CTV Network to enter into such arrangements with the local station."[14]

Later, in January 1968, the Board sent a further memorandum, this time to the Under-Secretary of State, Mr. Steele, reaffirming the Board's position on the extension of second service by rebroadcasting stations of the CBC and pointing out the financial capacity of the CTV network to bear the cost of providing network service to smaller local stations. The Board failed to elicit any response, favourable or otherwise, from the Government. In 1958, the City of Lethbridge was served by a private affiliate of the CBC, as was the City of Calgary. The CBC did not apply for the second station in Calgary and the licence went to the Loves, the owners of Radio Station CFCN. CFCN-TV was affiliated with CTV Network. By 1967, CFCN-TV had been purchased by Maclean-Hunter and the controlling interests in the other Calgary station and CJLH-TV Lethbridge were owned by Selkirk Holdings. There was a third channel allocated to Calgary, and the CBC plans included eventual establishment of its own station there.

Earlier, when the Loves owned CFCN-TV, they applied for a rebroadcasting station to serve the Lethbridge area. The application was denied, basically on the grounds that CJLH-TV could not survive and continue its local service in competition with a rebroadcasting station; the balance between the two Calgary stations would be disturbed. However, the people of the area knew that CFCN-TV was prepared to offer them alternative service and they continued to campaign to get the service. The Mayor of Cardston was conducting a vigorous personal campaign to get alternative service for his community. On 3 March 1967, the Chairman wrote Mayor Burt pointing out that 25% of all Canadians still received only one Canadian channel. They all wanted second service too, but except for Saskatoon, no second service applications would likely be heard before the fall of 1967.[15]

Both Mr. Mackay of Selkirk Holdings and Mr. Campbell of Maclean-Hunter had a clear appreciation of the problem. Selkirk Holdings proposed a plan whereby CFCN-TV would be granted a rebroadcasting station in the Lethbridge area; CJLH-TV Lethbridge would operate as a rebroadcasting station of CHCT-TV Calgary and local programming for the Lethbridge area would be broadcast from CJLH-TV, but the costs of the local programming would be shared between the two organizations. Maclean-Hunter agreed, and the necessary applications were brought to the Board. The Board was happy that a solution had been found to the problem of providing alternative service in this area and endorsed the plan which, in due course, went into operation with the approval of the Canadian Radio-Television Commission.

BRANDON AND MONCTON

In 1958, Brandon was served by a local affiliate of the CBC, CKX-TV owned by H.A. Craig, who also owned the local radio station. The CBC had its English-language station in Winnipeg. In the ensuing years the Board received applications for competing radio stations in Brandon. These were denied, mainly because the Board believed that the establishment of a second AM radio station would make it more difficult to establish second television service in Brandon. Mr. Craig was, however, granted a licence to operate an FM station, which meant that he held a monopoly of the electronic media in Brandon. CJAY-TV in Winnipeg had received the second station licence and later applied for a rebroadcasting station in Brandon. This was denied for essentially the same reasons as the denial of the application for CFCN-TV to install a rebroadcasting station in Lethbridge. The CJAY-TV application for Brandon was reheard on information that a CATV system was proposed for Brandon. It was again denied.

The agitation for second service in Brandon continued; the Hon. Walter Dinsdale, Conservative M.P. for Brandon, was under constant pressure from his constituents and was frequently in touch with the Board. On 8 March 1967 the Chairman wrote to Mr. Dinsdale, "We appreciate receiving copies of the letters and resolutions you are receiving. The Board must take responsibility for any delay there is in getting at the provision of second television across Canada. It is, I know, not much comfort to say that we are working diligently on the development of a general policy, I hope the Board will be able to make an announcement soon."[16]

In 1958, Moncton was served by a private English-language affiliate of the CBC, owned by F.A. Lynds. Mr. Lynds was encouraged to extend first television service to northern New Brunswick and did so by establishing rebroadcasting stations. The second television licence in Halifax went to CJCH-TV, and was held by a company represented by Finlay MacDonald, the owner of the local radio station. The radio station was eventually sold to Alan Waters of CHUM Toronto. CJCH-TV applied for and was granted a licence to operate an unprotected 5-watt rebroadcasting station at Amherst, ostensibly for the purpose of extending the coverage of the in-school educational programs of the province of Nova Scotia. Later Mr. MacDonald indicated his intention to apply for a high powered station in Amherst, with extensive coverage, including coverage of Moncton. The Board was opposed to this on essentially the same grounds as it opposed the rebroadcasting station applications of CFCN-TV Calgary in the Lethbridge area, and of CJAY-TV for Brandon.

Again there was continuous agitation for second service in Moncton. By 1967, Margaret Rideout, Liberal M.P. for Moncton, was finding the pressure—particularly from the Mayor of Moncton— intolerable. In reply to a letter from Mrs. Rideout, the Chairman wrote: "The Board recently announced it would not be able to hear applications for alternative television service until after February, 1967. As I'm sure you will realize there are a large number of places in which alternative service is not now available; and there is an insistent demand in all of them."[17] He alluded to an economic survey of single station markets currently in progress, a study he hoped would enable the

Board to establish a general policy under which it could deal with particular situations.

At the same time, the Board wrote the Secretary of State referring to letters from viewers to the Prime Minister, copies of which had been forwarded to the Board:

> As the local members of Parliament know there is a persistent demand for second service in this area. People know it is technically possible to get second service by increasing the power of the Amherst rebroadcasting station. The operator of CJCH has publicized this well. It is the opinion of the Board that the extension of second service could better proceed through CBC outlets than by privately-owned outlets. The Board will not know whether this is possible without direction [from the Government] to the Board or to the CBC.[18]

Following the denial of applications for rebroadcasting stations, a series of meetings was arranged for the week of 11 December 1967. On Tuesday, 12 December, the full-time members met with H.A. Craig and R.C. Fraser of the CBC. On Wednesday, 13 December, there was a similar meeting with F.A. Lynds and the CBC. On Thursday, 14 December, the Board members met with Messrs. Keeble, Chercover and Campbell of CTV Network.

By recommending denial of the applications of CJAY-TV and CJCH-TV, the Board had removed them from the options to be considered in the search for solutions. The meeting with the local stations, the CBC, and CTV Networks were to explore alternatives. The meetings with the CBC were concerned with possible cooperation between the CBC and the local stations in the installation of facilities, with a view to reducing costs. The CBC agreed to send their representatives to Brandon and Moncton to explore the possibilities on the ground.

The meeting with CTV Network was involved with discussion of the possibilities of network service to the areas. The Network presented its analysis of the effects of a CBC rebroadcasting station and of CTV Network service to the local station. It was estimated that in

Brandon CKX-TV would lose about $140,000 from the CBC, and its annual cost of acquiring substitute service from CTV Network would be $180,000. Against this loss of $320,000 the station might expect revenues of $50,000 from CTV. There would thus be a loss of $270,000 to the station. It was argued that in Moncton, CTV Network would not be in a position to pay the local station any revenue and that the net cost to the local station of a shift from CBC affiliation to CTV affiliation would be $405,000. Generally the position of CTV Network was that it could afford to supply service in Saskatoon, Sudbury and St. John's, but the provision of service to other small centres—including Brandon and Moncton—on terms that would enable the local station to survive, would end in a net loss to the Network. If the Network were to enter into contracts more favourable than the formula applied to the minor market stations affiliated with the Network—St. John's, Halifax and Moose Jaw—it would be necessary to revise the formula at the expense of the other affiliates. The Board members noted that the combined revenues of the 11 member stations was increasing at the rate $5 million per year, and that the combined net income of the stations was $6.6 million in the previous year and might reach $8 million in the current year. The Board argued that it might be necessary for the private television system, comprising CTV Network, to accept responsibility for extension of the network in some orderly fashion, using the growing revenue in the expanding populous areas to facilitate the supplying of service to the smaller centres. It was agreed to have another meeting, and on 25 January 1968 a meeting was held with the full Board of Directors of CTV Network.

The 25th of January being Burns' Day, Dave Sim and the Chairman felt the occasion should not pass without recognition. The Chairman ordered a haggis and Sim provided the appropriate liquid for a toast. At the time that coffee would have been served, the haggis was marched in, copies of Burns' *Ode to the Haggis* were distributed and the verses were read by Dave Sim. This was the main accomplishment of the meeting.[19]

On 14 December 1967, the Board had again written to the Secretary of State as a result of receipt of correspondence between the Mayor of Moncton and the Prime Minister. The letter referred to the objectives of the meeting being held and again referred to the financial ability of the member stations of CTV network, operating in the major markets to subsidize local operations in smaller centres.[20] The Board was too optimistic.

Letters and telegrams received by the Board after its denial of the applications by CJCH-TV and CJAY-TV reflected the impatience of the people in the areas involved, and the continuing demand for action. There was increasing resentment directed against the local stations and the Board. After careful consideration, it was decided that the Chairman should visit both Brandon and Moncton. A letter was sent to the President of the Chamber of Commerce, Brandon, with a similar letter going to the President of the Board of Trade, Moncton. The presidents responded generously.

On 9 January 1968, the Chairman and Lorraine Sweatman, the Manitoba member of the Board, went to Brandon. In his address to the combined Kiwanis and Rotary Clubs, the Chairman said that the Board was as concerned as the people of the community to provide second service to them. He traced the development of television through the single station period to the introduction of the second service in 1960, and described the structure of the system in 1968. The immediate objectives were outlined—first service where not now available, minority language service, and educational television—and it was pointed out that these developments had to proceed within the framework of channels available, growth of wired systems, and the establishment of a domestic satellite. Reference was made to 28 markets with single stations, and to the special cases of Saskatoon, Sudbury, Saint John, Lethbridge and Charlottetown. With respect to the small markets generally, the Chairman said these markets would not from their own resources support one local station offering the variety of programs now available; it was obvious that the small markets could not support two local stations; what had been proposed was a rebroadcasting station operating against a local station. The proposals of rebroadcasting stations of metropolitan private stations had been rejected by the Board as this solution did not appear to be consistent with the maintenance of local service except through increased subsidization by the CBC or purchase of the station by the CBC. The

Board was pursuing the proposal of a rebroadcasting station of the CBC. The prejudicial effects on the local station would be less, the program alternatives better, and the CBC could break even. This method would mean some loss to CTV Network and to its member stations. The question of CBC financing required decisions by the Government; the Board was not in a position to require CTV Network to provide the network service. The Chairman asked for patience until the problems of extending second service into small markets could be resolved.

The meeting with representatives of local organizations was held in the afternoon. There were 30 people present, including representatives of the media and the Hon. Walter Dinsdale. The principal feature of the discussion was the difference between those who were in favour of maintaining the local station and the service it provided to audience and to advertisers, and the representatives of the Citizens' Committee who were critical of the local service being given and who were less concerned about protecting it. It was apparent both in this meeting and in a later meeting with the Citizens' Committee that those supporting the Committee did not all have the same objectives; some wanted a "full" CBC service, and some merely wanted a choice of service. However, spokesman for the Citizens' Committee said they were supporting the position of the Board as they understood it, and it appeared that this was also the case for others present.

In the evening there was a meeting with representatives of the Citizens' Committee. The Committee had held two public meetings at which resolutions had been passed. An analysis of a questionnaire and a list of comments made at the public meetings were presented to the Chairman of the Board, and it was arranged that copies of the resolutions passed at the public meeting on 8 January would be forwarded to the Board. After the Board's public hearing in the previous November, the Citizens' Committee had placed an announcement, with a coupon, in the local paper. The Board was informed that by 9 January, 2,133 coupons had been returned to the Committee.

The Moncton case was more complicated than the Brandon case. It involved problems of channel use in the Maritime provinces. On 22 January 1968 the Chairman and George Urquhart, the New

Brunswick member of the Board, were in Moncton. In the morning, accompanied by the President of the Moncton Board of Trade, they called on Mayor Jones. The Moncton City Council had taken a public position, and the Mayor was interested only in an assurance that the City would have a second service immediately. The Chairman addressed a Rotary Club luncheon and in the afternoon met with community representatives. There appeared to be less animosity to the local station than in Brandon, and the Board's position on a CBC rebroadcasting station appeared to be acceptable. The demand for immediate action on alternative service was pressed, particularly by the Council members, and it was indicated that political action would be taken if there were not immediate results. In the evening they met informally with the press at the Moncton Press Club. The headline in the *Moncton Transcript* of 23 January was "Looks Like More Waiting Before Alternate Viewing."

The meetings in Brandon and Moncton were almost the last functions Dr. Stewart performed as Chairman of the BBG; at the time of the Chairman's resignation, Mayor Jones was still waiting impatiently. The *Moncton Transcript* reporter had correctly summarized the situation: "Two main problems are holding up second service— lack of a commitment from the Federal Government to meet the costs required in setting up a CBC station in Moncton—CTV must approve Moncton Broadcasting Ltd.'s affiliation with the Network."

BASIC ISSUES UNRESOLVED

In addition to government support for the CBC, the role of CTV Network in the further expansion of second service was crucial. The CBC submitted its annual estimates to Treasury Board and Parliament, and its *Annual Report* to the Minister for tabling in Parliament. The Chairman of the Board never saw the form in which the CBC estimates were submitted; and the financial information in the *Annual Report* was presented in a more generalized way. Financial analysis of the operations of the Corporation was impossible on the basis of information available to the Board. The CBC claimed that the commercial programs it purchased in the United States generated enough revenues to cover the costs of acquiring them; and that, as far as the local operations of the "O & O" stations were concerned, the stations were profitable. The main costs related to the funds required from Parliament were therefore the costs of the network operations. The distribution costs of the widespread network service were substantial; but the major operating expenditures were incurred in the production of Canadian programs. The CBC had limited control over the costs of distributing the network service. The main controllable costs were therefore, the costs of producing Canadian programs for the national network service. These costs could be reduced either by reducing the amount of Canadian content in the service or by reducing expenditures on productions and perhaps lowering the quality of the productions.

The private affiliates, with few if any exceptions, could not have existed, and extension of the service could not have been achieved without the revenue obtained from the CBC. The arrangements with the stations were not ungenerous; and the rate at which extension of service occurred was a most creditable achievement. The CBC did not have the authority to require information on the financial position of the affiliates. The BBG was given this authority; and as information became available it was clear that the "basic" stations generally were in a healthy position. Some of the smaller stations were having hard sledging. Not unnaturally the affiliates would have been happy to modify the arrangements to their advantage—to secure more favourable rates, fewer sustaining programs and more commercially attractive programs in the network schedule, more flexibility in the timing of programs, and a greater opportunity to break into the network time when they could substitute more profitable programs. On the other hand, their costs in carrying the network service were minimal, and many of the programs they received through the network were highly desirable, and could not have been obtained in any other way. Outside of network time, the stations were relatively free to develop their local programming as they found best; although they were subject to regulations which limited the commercial revenue they could obtain. The CBC's relations with its television affiliates were generally good and the affiliates had little solid ground for complaint. Less generous arrangements would have restricted the extension of television service. Increasingly, however, extension became dependent on the ability and willingness of CTV Network to play a national role in Canadian broadcasting.

The White Paper proposed a new approach to the licensing and regulation of stations. Simply put, it was suggested that as the resources of stations varied from market to market, so too should the expectations placed upon each, most likely through conditions of licence.[21] Regulations affecting programming, specifically the Canadian content regulations, had been general in their formulation and application. Conditions affecting programming were now to be varied for individual stations or groups of stations, depending on the "profit potential." This could be done either by regulation or by conditions on the licence.

The new proposal appeared to present some administrative problems, the first being that of putting stations into categories on the basis of "profit potential." The White Paper distinguished between "larger and more profitable markets" in contrast to smaller and less profitable markets. Some stations in moderate-sized markets were able to show a substantial "profit" as a return on investment or proportion of gross revenues. On the other hand, the absolute "profits" of stations in the large metropolitan centres such as Toronto and Montreal were in part the consequence of limited outlets in relation to "reach." This "scarcity" profit was related to the scarcity of VHF channels. It was, apparently, the "scarcity profit" which stations would be expected to use in increasing the quantity and quality of their Canadian content, and it would be necessary to devise some means of measuring "scarcity profit." But "scarcity profit" could be significantly changed, if means could be found to increase the number of outlets. For example, the profits of CFTO-TV Toronto could be reduced by moving CKVR-TV Barrie to serve Toronto.

There were three possibilities in dealing with the profits of stations in the metropolitan centres. First, to license additional outlets, thus giving the viewers a wider range of choice of service. If this was difficult or impossible, the second possibility was to require, by regulation or conditions of the licence, that the station apply its profits to the improvement of service in the market. There was a third possibility, namely to use the profits of the metropolitan stations in such a way as to improve the service in the marginal locations in the smaller centres.

In an internal memorandum on the White Paper proposal, the Chairman wrote:

The policy reflected in Canadian content requirements is a national policy designed to serve national purposes. To accept the condition that because of the relative scarcity of channels (in relation to reach) in Toronto and Montreal, CFTO and CFTM should give exposure to more and better Canadian programs than CJON, Newfoundland or CHAB, Moose Jaw, seems to me wholly inconsistent with the national purposes behind the policy, and indeed behind the policy inherent in the operation of the CBC. The rationale of the Canadian policy on broadcasting is that the airways belong to the people of Canada—not the people of one province or of one city. Channel 9, Toronto, does not belong to the people of Toronto, and is to be used for national purposes.

The CBC operates a system. The stations are units in the system. Through the operation of its system the Corporation produces programs and originates material in various locations, and distributes its programs, through its network facilities, throughout the system. The CBC is a national entity; it was so designed. It is only because it is a national entity that it can serve the national purposes.

The Fowler Committee said: "We think there is need in Canada for a private national television network. . . . Major sports events . . . must be transmitted as they happen . . . news must be provided live, and the performance of any individual station would be totally inadequate if it failed to provide good coverage of national and international events. . . . the national responsibilities of private stations will not be fully discharged by providing a live news service nationally and carrying a number of sporting events. . . . In other types of programming—current events, drama, music, the interpretation of different regions to one another—the private stations have a national function to perform individually and by co-operative methods. They also have responsibility for some share in the development and use of Canadian talent." It has always been the view of the Board that the private stations had national responsibilities. It may well be that these responsibilities can best be met by recognizing the private sector as a system, in which the stations through a mutual network engage co-operatively in meeting their national responsibilities.

The principle of "equalization"—of requiring the "have" portions of the country to contribute to the "have not" portions—is built into the Canadian nation; and may be an essential condition of its survival. In the private system of broadcasting there is good reason why the "have" situations (in terms of financial and talent resources) should contribute to the "have not" situations (lacking in financial and talent resources). More should be expected from the stations in the "larger and more profitable markets;" but to help to enrich the program service in the smaller and less profitable markets. There seems to be no way of preventing the talent resources from gravitating to the larger centres.

There is a ready-made instrument for equalization in the mutual CTV Network.

The principle proposed in the White Paper would mean that CFTO would be required to plough substantial profits into production; but that this production would be exposed only in Toronto. No doubt CFTO would be prepared (as CFTM is doing with Chicoutimi) to deliver its productions to other stations, at a price. If the stations in the smaller centres were, by conditions on their licences, required to offer less Canadian content, they would have no incentive to acquire programs from CFTO, and the acquisition of programs, at a price, would be no significant assistance to them. It is probable also, under these conditions, that the productions of CFTO would be designed for the Toronto market rather than for a national audience. Theoretically, the "scarcity profit" in Toronto could be syphoned off and placed in a pool to support Canadian productions which could be distributed by the network. The same effect could be obtained by requiring member stations of the network to contribute to the operation of the network in proportion to their "profit potential." The mutual CTV Network has, in fact, moved in this direction. Although the control is exercised on the basis of one vote per station, the financing of the operation of the network is subject to a formula under which the larger stations contribute a larger proportion than the smaller stations do. This formula could be adjusted to fit more closely the "profit potentials" of the stations.

What is involved is the view that the private television stations constitute a system, and that the funds flowing into the system constitute a pool to support equalization of program service on the stations throughout the system. It follows that the funds flowing into the pool must be sufficient to support the level at which the service is to be maintained.

The Report, prepared by Dr. Firestone, which projects a trebling of television revenues over the next ten years, implies a substantial increase, in the revenue pool, although the increase will be unequally divided between the stations. Some part of it will be required to support new outlets, although it is unlikely that these new outlets and the availabilities they will offer will match the growth in demand for advertising time. Some of the new outlets will be second television stations. If the private sector (second stations) is to be seen as a system, the second television stations will have to be incorporated into the system. The difficulties of operating a mutual consisting of a large number of members can be appreciated; but a way could be found out of this difficulty. But it is essential that all second stations should be affiliated with the network, and to this extent part of the system. Unfortunately, the CBC has set a precedent with its supplementary affiliations. It would seem advisable to have the CBC discard the supplementary affiliation, and include all stations as basic affiliates; and to require CTV Network to affiliate all second stations on the same basis.

The important relations are those between the profitability of the major stations, the rate at which new stations in smaller markets are added to the network, and the level of service which is required across the system.[22]

Following the September meeting of the Board, the Chairman wrote to Miss LaMarsh saying that, while there seemed to be general support in the Board for the policies outlined in the White Paper, the Board was concerned about the future of the private television network.

> The Board shares the view that the private network is financially viable and can be made to serve an important function. But it appears to us that the authority of the Board must be extended if the desired results are to be secured. The Board is concerned lest, in the absence of the necessary authority, the network may break down by internal dissensions which cannot be resolved without the authority of the Board.

In January 1967 the Chairman received a request from the Prime Minister's office for his views on "dealing with private broadcasting licences on a 'public utility' basis." The objective would be to limit the profits of stations and to provide incentives to expend excess profits on Canadian talent and productions. The Chairman's views were set out in a lengthy memorandum to the Prime Minister. He argued against the "public utility" concept and instead argued in support of the Board's "equalization" policy whereby monopoly profits would be withdrawn from the private stations and placed in a pool to be used for the purposes of the network.[23]

The Board of Directors of CTV Network were able to hammer out an agreement on the formulae for allocating revenues and costs, and therefore net revenues between the member stations for the 1967-68 program year. Gross revenue was to be allocated in proportion to the rate cards of the stations which varied from $450 for CFTO-TV Toronto to $100 for CHAB-CHRE-TV Moose Jaw. Under this formula, CFTO-TV would be allocated 17.24% of gross revenues; CHAB-TV 3.82%. The same formula was to be applied to the allocation of the operating costs, other than the costs of producing and acquiring programs. The operating costs included administration and distribution costs. The formulae for allocation of the costs of producing and purchasing programs involved higher proportions for the larger stations and smaller proportions for the smaller stations. Under the formula applying to the costs of producing Canadian programs, CFTO-TV was to be charged 22.5%, CHAB-TV 2%. Under the formula for the allocation of the costs of acquiring non-Canadian programs, CFTO-TV was to be charged 25%, CHAB-TV 2.5%. In the application of the combined formulae the smallest share of the net revenue would go to CFTO-TV, viz., 16.2%. The composite formula—and therefore participation in the network—was of assistance to the small stations in St. John's, Halifax and Moose Jaw, each of which would obtain more net revenue than CFTO-TV. The distribution of net revenue between the larger stations did not appear to be entirely defensible, but there was a significant element of "equalization" built into the formula.

The study undertaken by Touche, Ross et al. indicated that after 1963, when in the aggregate the stations began to break even, the combined gross revenues of the affiliated stations and the network had increased at the rate of $4,800,000 a year, exceeding $35 million (11 stations) in 1966. Net income *after depreciation and taxes* was: 1961 (–$3,669,000); 1962 (–$1,984,000); 1963 (–$505); 1964 $1,484,000; 1965 $3,202,000; 1966 $3,298,000. In 1966 the network recorded a loss of $366,000; but the net income *before taxes* of the 11 stations exceeded $7 million, and that of the three stations in Montreal, Ottawa and Toronto exceeded $4.25 million. The net income *after taxes* of the three stations in the central provinces was more than $2.25 million. This represented a ratio of net to gross of 11% and a return on investment of 30%. Of these three stations, the net income *after taxes* in excess of 16% on invested capital or 8% of gross revenue, whichever was less, was $671,000; and each year the net income position of the stations was improving. The study confirmed the view that, provided net revenues were not seriously eroded by the licensing of additional stations in the same markets, e.g., CKVR-TV in Toronto, there was sufficient net revenue within the system of second stations to absorb some losses by affiliating stations in the smaller markets which were as yet without second service.[24]

There was no obvious enthusiasm on the part of the member stations of CTV Network to undertake the extension of service to new affiliates in small markets where losses in providing the service would be unavoidable. They did not volunteer to assume the responsibility, but they did not openly oppose it. The discussion at the meeting with the Directors of the Network on 25 January 1968 confirmed the Board's view that the implementation of a policy of extending second service and requiring the provision of network service to the local stations would necessitate the Board having authority to require the existing stations to remain in the network and to require the network to affiliate local stations in the smaller markets. Under these conditions there would be problems in the terms of affiliation of the new affiliates. One of the concerns expressed was that in working out affiliation agreements, the network—that is, the member stations—should not be expected to maintain some of the new affiliates in the affluence to which they had become accustomed. This point had considerable validity. At the time, the CBC had approval to establish stations in Saskatoon, Sudbury and Fredericton-Saint John. The return on invested capital of the local stations in the three markets (1966) ranged from 10% to 32%. The Board had announced hearings on second stations in southwestern Alberta, southwestern Manitoba, and the Maritimes (Moncton). Of the four stations whose position would be directly affected, the rates of return ranged from 10% to 20%. Although the Board was concerned to maintain the local broadcasting service already established, it was not prepared to support excess profits and, notwithstanding its rule that no member station was to hold shares in more than one station, the Board was sympathetic to the proposal that the network should share in the equity stock of additional stations.

The discussion of the structure of this system has been concerned heavily with the English-language service. In Quebec Province the problems of the French-language service were similar, although slightly less complicated. The public system consisted of the "mother" CBC station in Montreal with distribution of network service through private affiliates. The Montreal private stations clearly became the king-pins in any expansion of the private sector, but fragmentation of the audience in the smaller markets was again the problem. The Board dealt with applications for licences in markets outside Quebec (e.g.,

Northern Ontario and New Brunswick) in which there was a substantial minority of French-speaking people. Generally speaking, the minority audience was too small to support a second French-language station; and the Board had found no solution to this problem without substantial contributions from the federal Treasury.

Both public and private stations were part of the total broadcasting system in Canada; and the services which each provided together were the totality of service provided to Canadians from the Canadian system. But the Corporation which performed the public service was in a unique position. It was a direct creation of Parliament. Parliament should know what it expected the Corporation to do. If Parliament knew what the Corporation was intended to do, and articulated this in the legislation, the Corporation must do those things that Parliament intended; and Parliament must provide the means by which the Corporation could execute them. The private sector must then be seen as supplementing the public service in a manner consistent with the intended public service and the overall broadcasting objectives.

This was not a view that appealed to private broadcasters. From their position it seemed to give them a subservient position, a status of "second class citizens." As long as there was to be a public and a private sector, it was, however, the only view on which the supervision and regulation of broadcasting could proceed. The private broadcasters resented the situation in which development of the private sector was determined by the CBC. They welcomed the advent of the independent broadcasting authority; but in administering the broadcasting legislation the BBG found that, with respect to the total broadcasting service, unless there were some fixed points of reference, the problems of the relations between the public sector and the private sector were insoluble. The fixed points of reference must be found in the mandate of the public corporation. The difficulties encountered in the operation of the total system between 1959 and 1968 arose mainly because Parliament (or the successive Governments) was not clear on what it expected the CBC to do. The CBC did not want its mandate defined other than in terms of the broadest generalizations. When it became necessary to apply the broad working of the mandate in operating decisions and action, the CBC did not wish to share the decision-making role. Sometimes there was agreement between the CBC and the BBG, e.g., agreement was eventually reached on the question of extension of second television service. But this agreement was nullified by the failure of the governments to give it the required support. With respect to other matters, there was disagreement between the CBC and the BBG, but it was impossible to determine which position reflected the policy of the government or of Parliament. There were no adequate guidelines; the fixed points of reference were absent.

PRIMARY SERVICE

While the extension of second service consumed a great deal of time and energy, the extension of primary service proceeded continuously and by a variety of means between 1958 and 1968. The principal method was through the establishment of rebroadcasting stations relaying signals received by "off air" pickup. Some of the rebroadcasting stations were of substantial power; many were 5-watt stations covering small pockets of population. At March 1960 there were only 16 television rebroadcasting stations. Of these, five were owned by the CBC and 11 by private affiliates of the CBC. At March 1964 the number had increased to 99—15 CBC and 84 affiliates. At March 1967 the total was 173—29 CBC and 144 affiliates. The greatest increase in numbers was in British Columbia. In this province, in 1967, there were 70 rebroadcasting stations, 65 of them carrying the signals of affiliates of the CBC. There were 38 rebroadcasting stations in Quebec. Eighteen rebroadcasting stations of affiliates of the CTV were providing second service.

Extension of first service by rebroadcasting stations was mainly due to the activities of the private affiliates. The lesser participation of the CBC resulted from the location of its stations. The possibility of extension of coverage by rebroadcasting stations of the CBC without the use of costly microwave facilities was limited. The private affiliates were closer to unserved populations. The incentive to the private station lay in the increased coverage, but there were additional costs. Some more aggressive stations sought out opportunities to extend their service. Others responded more reluctantly to local pressures. The Board could not compel stations to install rebroadcasting facilities. Representations received by the Board were passed on to the local station and this, no doubt, had some effect on the outcome in particular situations. The cost of the added facilities, however, was the limiting factor.

The private affiliates distributed the national television service of the CBC. Consequently, increased coverage by their stations extended the distribution of the national service. It appeared to the Board that the Corporation could be of assistance and the possibility was raised with the CBC as early as 1963. It was proposed that where the establishment of a rebroadcasting station was clearly unprofitable to the affiliate, and the profit position of the affiliate was not such as to enable it to absorb the cost, the CBC should share in the cost of constructing the broadcasting facilities. Not without reason, the CBC was reluctant to become involved in this way. By May 1968, however, the CBC had embarked on a program of assistance to affiliates in circumstances which seemed to justify it. In remote northern communities, the CBC was providing a delayed kine-recording service.[25]

Andrew Stewart (front left) and Premier Daniel Johnson of Quebec (front right) with interested onlookers. *Photograph used with permission from the Archives of Ontario, #61—1165-1, C 109-2, Herb Nott Collection.*

[10]

EDUCATIONAL TELEVISION

FROM THE OUTSET, THE BOARD was sensitive to the jurisdictional problem involved in educational broadcasting; although anxious to facilitate the use of the medium for education purposes, the Board would have preferred to leave the initiative to educators. By 1962, however, the Board was willing to enunciate a policy. The interest of educators in the use of television continued to grow, and there was an effort to develop a national approach to the expanding use of the medium. The effort proved abortive. The provinces of Ontario and Alberta, by applying for licences to operate stations, forced the federal government to establish a position but the response was unbelievably slow. When the Government did declare a position, in the White Paper, its policy was subject to attack, even among the members of caucus. The problem remained unresolved within the lifetime of the BBG.

The first communications the Board received, early in 1959, about educational television were from universities. Dr. John Friesen, Director of Extension, University of British Columbia, requested information about applications for reservation of channels. Dr. Carleton Williams, Director, Department of Extension, University of Toronto, advised of his intention to marshal support for ETV. The Metropolitan Educational Television Association of Toronto (META) was formed in 1959. No organization did more to promote educational television in Canada. META presented a brief to the BBG at a public hearing in 1959. It was supported by a number of letters from universities and educational organizations. Before year end, the Province of Alberta, through Richard Morton, Supervisor of School Broadcasts, Department of Education, had also indicated interest in ETV, particularly school broadcasts. The Provinces of Ontario and Alberta, however, remained in the vanguard and by 1967 applications had been received from both provinces for licences to operate stations.

There was some early hope that the Board would reserve VHF channels for educational television rather than allocate them to second commercial stations. The Board did not encourage this expectation in situations in which VHF channels were scarce; in correspondence, further study was urged both of the services that ETV could provide to education and of the financial implications of operating the stations.

In an address to a conference on television, at Saskatchewan House, Regina, in April 1960, the Chairman referred to radio and expressed the view that the failure to use radio frequencies reserved for education was due to lack of financial support. "Educational authorities must be aware that television broadcasting is expensive. If they are not prepared to provide financial support, this can only be taken as evidence that they do not consider the medium as particularly valuable for their purposes."[1] It was suggested that educators explore the use of closed circuit systems in urban centres. This was represented as a relatively uncomplicated arrangement, offering greater flexibility, which could be developed wholly under the control of educational authorities and without reference to the federal authorities.

In February 1961, the Chairman was invited to speak to a workshop organized by the Ontario Teachers' Federation on "the general topic of the outlook for educational television in Ontario." In reply, the Chairman, noting that broadcasting was a responsibility of the Federal Government and education a responsibility of the provinces, said: "I would not wish to speak on the subject of the outlook for educational television in Ontario, particularly if the Minister of Education is to present his views on the subject. . . . I am prepared to concede that the topic is primarily "Education" and that is Mr. Robarts' territory. I would, however, be much interested in learning what the Minister has to say."[2]

In March 1961, the Board received an inquiry from the Separate School Board, Edmonton, about the reservation of a channel for its use. It was advised that the BBG "cannot at this stage recommend reservation of a number of channels in the same centre for educational purposes. There are two VHF channels allocated to Edmonton and not yet occupied. The Board has not stated any policy with respect to VHF channels for educational television, but might consider the reservation of one of the free channels."[3] The Metropolitan Edmonton Educational Television Association (MEETA) was later formed. Also, in 1961, META (Toronto) applied to the Board for reservation of Channel 19 (UHF) for educational television in Toronto. The Board recommended favourably to the Minister of Transport and was later advised that the reservation had been made.

Early in 1962 the Chairman was invited to address a Conference on Educational Television at the University of British Columbia. Because of Board meetings he was unable to attend, but he agreed to send a statement which could be read at the conference. This led to the publication of a "Statement of the Policies of the Board of Broadcast Governors with Respect to Educational Television, prepared for the ETV Conference, University of British Columbia, 31 March 1962." Some members of the Board took exception to the release of the statement before it had received the endorsement of the Board. It was, however, approved—with one amendment proposed by a member from the Province of Quebec. The amendment substituted "authorized" for "responsible" when used in reference to "educational bodies."[4]

In the meantime, developments were occurring which pointed to interprovincial cooperation among educators. The underlying reasons appeared to be: a growing interest and concern among educators, the expansion of television broadcasting with the introduction of alternative service, the relatively unsuccessful efforts to obtain time on private stations, some restiveness among educators with the association with the CBC in school broadcasting, and the growing feeling that the general broadcasting system would prove incapable of meeting the needs of educators.

A National Conference of Educational Television was arranged by the School Broadcasts Department of the CBC with the support of the Canadian Education Association. The conference, which was held in Toronto, 25–26 May 1961, was presided over by Dr. W.H. Swift, Deputy Minister of Education for Alberta. It was widely representative of professional broadcasters and educators. The conference established a management committee. The committee met with the Chairman of the BBG in January 1962 to urge the BBG to call a meeting for the purpose of determining the degree of interest there might be in establishing a national group to coordinate activities in educational television. This was reported to the BBG at its meeting in Quebec City in February 1962.

Members of the Board were concerned about any involvement by the Board which would bring it into conflict with the provinces, and particularly with the Province of Quebec. As the Board was in Quebec City, it was agreed that a meeting should be held with the Quebec Minister of Youth. A group of members had lunch with the Minister. As Mr. Gerin-Lajoie saw no good reason for the traditional policy of not granting licences to provincial governments or agencies of provincial governments, the attempt to discuss with him how the Board might operate within this policy was not particularly productive.

The Chairman reported to the Board that, at the meeting of the National Conference Management Committee, he had said the Board would not take a hand in setting up a more widely representative committee or council without first obtaining the views of the educational authorities. This decision was approved by the Board.

Later in February the Chairman wrote Dr. Swift, asking him to initiate action through Mr. Freeman Stewart of the Canadian Education Association which might result in an invitation to the Chairman of the Board to attend the spring meeting of the CEA Standing Committee of Ministers. An invitation resulted, but the meeting with the Ministers did not occur until September 1962 in Edmonton. The Board was later advised that the Committee had agreed it would give support to the convening of a meeting to determine the degree of interest there might be in establishing some national group to coordinate action in the field of educational television "should the Board of Broadcast Governors undertake to convene it." No immediate action was taken by the Board. In February 1963, a resolution was received from the CBC National Advisory Council on School Broadcasting. In reply the Board wrote, "I confess we have been 'dragging our heels' on the calling of a meeting to consider whether or not a National Committee on Educational Television should be established. We have had some reasons for our hesitation. The resolution of the National Advisory Council, however, indicating that the NAC is in favour of early action to call a meeting will certainly encourage the Board to move on this."[5] The Chairman then wrote the CEA suggesting a meeting in either May or September when the CEA would be meeting in Quebec City. This suggestion was not followed up, and after the annual meeting of the CEA the Board received an inquiry as to its intentions. The Board then decided to act to convene a meeting, and one was eventually held in Toronto on 4–5 March 1964.

The minutes of the meeting record:

Dr. Andrew Stewart, Chairman of the BBG, was in the chair for this meeting. Dr. Stewart welcomed the delegates to the meeting and in his opening remarks he made it clear that the Board of Broadcast Governors did not intend to support the idea of an organization that was the creature of the Board. He suggested that these sessions were a meeting of educators rather than of broadcasters, and that the BBG had, in fact, done all that it was asked to do, that is to convene a meeting to discuss educational broadcasting. He suggested that whatever the meeting decided to do would be entirely of its own volition and he emphasized that he did not expect the meeting to set up any body which would be in an official sense advisory to the BBG. Dr. Stewart indicated he was prepared to remain in the chair until such time as the meeting decided that it wished to set up a specific organization. If this decision was taken, Dr. Stewart would turn over the chair to the person elected by the meeting.[6]

The meeting on 4 March passed two resolutions:

1) That we go on record as favouring the existence of a national body concerned with Educational Broadcasting at all levels having interests broader than those currently applicable to the National Advisory Council on School Broadcasting as it is presently constituted; and
2) That a committee of five people giving due consideration to English and French representation be nominated by the Chair to be known as a provisional committee to explore the means of establishing an organization in Canada of the character envisaged by the motion passed previously and to discuss these matters with the ad hoc committee of the Standing Committee of Ministers and other appropriate bodies.[7]

Another meeting was to be called as soon as possible to which the provisional committee should report back.

The members of the provisional committee were Maurice Gosselin (Chairman), Department de l'Instruction Publique, Quebec; Gerald Nason, Canadian Teachers' Federation, Ottawa; H.M. Nason, Department of Education, Nova Scotia; Arthur Knowles, University of Toronto and META; and Madeline Joubert, Institut d'Education des Adultes, Quebec. At the meeting held on 5 March and presided over by Mr. Gosselin, there was further discussion of the objects and purposes of a national body.

Immediately following the meetings the Chairman wrote to Mr. Gosselin assuring him of the Board's desire to be of help to him as Chairman of the Provisional Committee and offering the Board's facilities for any meeting in Ottawa. He added the hope that he would "have an early opportunity to report to our Minister, The Honourable Maurice Lamontagne, Secretary of State, on the Board's part in organizing the meeting in Toronto."[8] A meeting of the provisional committee was subsequently held in the board room of the BBG, and in July 1964 the Board received a report on the meeting from Mr. Gosselin. This was the last the Board heard from the Provisional Committee.

During 1964 the governments of Alberta and Ontario moved in directions which would force the issue of educational television with the federal government. In May 1964 the Alberta Government Telephones lodged an inquiry with the Department of Transport concerning an application for a licence. The Board then inquired of the Minister's office whether any thought had been given to licensing stations for educational purposes by provinces or provincial agencies. In a brief memorandum, the Board wrote: "The policy in effect is a government policy rather than a policy devised by the BBG, and I think it should be so. It seems unnecessary for the purposes of this memorandum to express views on the policy. We are, of course, at the disposal of the Minister."[9] The Province of Ontario was also preparing to apply for a licence, and on 21 December 1964 the following letter was sent to the Secretary of State:

At the request of the Minister of Education, Province of Ontario, I met with the Honourable W.G. Davis and a number of his advisers in Toronto on Friday, December 18.

The Minister informed me that the Department of Education had decided to apply for a licence to operate an educational television station on a UHF channel.

I reminded Mr. Davis of the standing policy that broadcasting licences should not be issued to Provincial Governments or their agencies. I also informed the Minister that some months ago I had reported to the Secretary of State that an application by a Province for educational television seemed imminent. I added that the reaction of the Secretary of State seemed favourable.

Mr. Davis agreed that I should report our meeting to the Secretary of State, and said that representations would be made by the Province of Ontario. In the meantime, the officers of the Department of Education will proceed with the preparation of a technical brief for submission to the Department.

I pointed out that if the standing policy were changed it might be necessary to determine a new policy with respect to applications by Provincial Departments of Education for licences to operate educational television stations.

As I indicated to the Secretary of State in my earlier conversation, I would not be prepared to recommend against the issue of licences to Provincial Departments for educational television; indeed I would consider it desirable as a means of assisting in the development of educational television. The matter has not, however, been referred to the Board.

If the principle of licensing Departments of Education were approved, I would think it desirable to lay down certain terms of policy and procedures, in advance of any application being received, with the object of ensuring that, subject only to its technical acceptability and to its effect on existing stations, the application as submitted would be likely to proceed and be recommended for approval.

The Secretary of State may wish the Board to make some proposals with respect to acceptable conditions. As other provinces are likely in due course to follow the lead set by the Province of Ontario, if it proves to be the initial applicant, the Secretary of State might consider it desirable to have some discussion with other Provinces, either directly or through the Board, before conditions governing educational television stations are prescribed. Changes in the regulations under the Broadcasting Act may be necessary to meet the particular conditions of ETV. These would have to go to a public meeting.[10]

In the meantime, the federal government had appointed the Committee on Broadcasting. The report of the Committee recommended "as a matter of urgency" an evaluation of the needs of educational TV and of the means to satisfy them.

Early in 1966, the Board was made aware of consideration being given to educational television policy by a Cabinet committee and was drawn into preparation of material for the committee. The matter was discussed at the April 1966 meeting of the BBG. The Chairman reported that he had made a commitment to have the subject aired at a public hearing in September. There was some discussion of a proposal that the federal government retain ownership of the physical facilities to be used for educational television. The full-time members were authorized to submit a paper to the Minister and the Cabinet committee. A memorandum was forwarded to Miss LaMarsh on 12 May 1966.

The idea that the federal government retain ownership of the physical facilities to be used by educational authorities originated in the BBG. In the early days of the Board, before second television licences were issued, Edward Dunlop had shown interest in the system of independent television in the United Kingdom under which the broadcasting facilities were owned by the Crown but were used for broadcasting by program contractors. It was his interest in this arrangement that led to the inclusion of Section 6(6) on the Radio (TV) Broadcasting Regulations. However, no thought had been given to the application of the principle to licensing of education television stations until the suggestion was made to the Chairman of the Board early in 1966, in an informal session with a few private broadcasters during a convention in Montreal.

The memorandum of 12 May to the Secretary of State referred to the application of the Department of Education, Province of Ontario, for a licence to operate an educational television station on Channel 19 in Toronto and to the plans of the Department for the establishment of 30 educational stations in Ontario over ten years. "The question is, who should be licensed to own broadcasting stations or networks in the educational field?"[11] The Board had considered three broad possibilities: first, the licensing of provincial departments; second, the licensing of local or provincial corporations or other entities; and third, the provision of broadcasting facilities under federal legislation—programming being provided by program contractors, including the Department of Education of the province. The Board thought the third proposal to be preferable. This proposal envisaged the establishment of a public corporation under federal legislation, with authority to construct and maintain facilities for educational broadcasting. The corporation would lease time to educational organizations including provincial departments of education. Such a solution would safeguard the principle of provincial authority over education, since the provincial authority would have complete responsibility for programming and production time within the broadcasting time available. Regulatory policy would be established by the proper federal authority and would have to be taken into account in the negotiation of contracts for rental of facilities. "If this proposal were adopted there would remain the problem of answering the need of the Ontario Department of Education, which seems to be anxious to start operating as soon as possible, namely in the fall of 1967. The Board feels that, if necessary, an ad hoc solution could be found to this question until the Government has been able to work out a general solution."[12]

The Board had further conversations with the Hon. W.G. Davis who showed a desire to be cooperative in working out a solution. An application had been submitted by MEETA with the support of the Government of Alberta, and there was evidence of interest in New Brunswick.

The Government published its White Paper in July 1966. With respect to educational television it stated that the Government was prepared to give immediate consideration to the creation of a new federal organization licensed to operate public service broadcasting facilities and empowered to enter into agreements with any province to meet the needs of the provincial educational system as determined by the responsible provincial authorities. The new organization would be subject to the authority of the BBG in all matters affecting general broadcasting policy in Canada. It also noted the imminent availability of ultra-high-frequency channels which would be adequate for the needs of education, thereby precluding the need to proceed with the recommendations of the Committee on Broadcasting that very high-frequency channels should be pre-empted for educational purposes.[13]

Following the publication of the White Paper, the Board was advised it would be expected to take action to develop the policy with respect to educational television, the focus of the responsibility resting on Pierre Juneau, the Vice-Chairman of the Board. Mr. Juneau applied himself diligently to the problem.

Pressure was being exerted by both Ontario and Alberta for decisions and action which would enable them to proceed with their plans, and both the BBG and the Department of the Secretary of State were aware of the problems which would be created by unnecessary delay. At the end of August 1966, after further representations from Alberta, the Chairman wrote the Secretary of State:

As you know the Department of Education, Province of Ontario, and the Metropolitan Edmonton Educational Television Association have both submitted applications for licences to operate stations. They have both received from the Department of Transport the same advice, viz. that in view of the policy considerations involved there will be delay in dealing with the applications.

Both organizations have spent much time and effort in preparing their applications which are based on a timetable of operations. Delay in dealing with the applications would, itself, make it impossible to proceed under the time table proposed.

We believe that the Minister of Education, Ontario, and the Government of Alberta, which is involved in the MEETA application, would be disposed to be cooperative with the federal authority in finding solutions to the problems of ETV. However, we very much fear that goodwill will be lost by more delay in dealing with their applications.

In a brief conversation I had with the Prime Minister on August-18, I referred to the advantage, as it appeared to me, in obtaining a working arrangement with at least one of the provinces as quickly as possible.[14]

Obviously, although charged with the responsibility of developing the policy set out under the White Paper, the Board could not complete any arrangements with the provinces which would be unacceptable to the federal Government, and conversations with the provinces were becoming increasingly embarrassing and frustrating. On 2 September 1966 the Chairman addressed a memorandum to the Department of the Secretary of State seeking "guidelines" on the following points: (a) Was the Board correct in understanding that the licences would not be issued to either the Department of Education, Ontario, or the Metropolitan Edmonton Educational Television Association? (b) Might it be assumed that any recommendations on the use of channels for ETV stations made by the Board following a public hearing in October would be approved by the Government? (c) Was the Board correct in understanding that the Government of Canada was prepared or was giving some consideration to financing transmission facilities through a new federal organization? (d) Could the Board assume there would be a maximum amount or proportion of "straight cultural programming" which must not be exceeded, using the facilities licensed for the purposes of educational television, and that the Board would have the authority to determine and apply the criteria?[15]

The response received indicated that licences would not be issued to provincial agencies and that, in order to proceed without waiting for the establishment of the "new" federal organization, the CBC would be the interim licensee. The Government would not be prepared, as suggested by the provinces, to allow the provinces to proceed with construction, subject to later compensation by the federal government. The CBC would have to be provided with funds. The Government, notwithstanding an application from Alberta for a VHF channel, favoured the use of UHF channels for ETV. It also favoured a strict limitation of educational material to material of a "curriculum nature."

Following the public hearing in October, at which wide-ranging representations were made with respect to the need for educational television, the Board issued a public announcement. Most of the briefs by educational authorities had proposed extensive reservations of channels for ETV. The announcement said the Board felt it would be unwise to adopt such a policy. In addition to the prospective demands for general broadcasting, the Board enunciated other reasons:

1) There is still considerable uncertainty regarding the most effective electronic means to serve the purposes of the educational authorities. Evidence of interest on the part of educators in the use of coaxial cable and of other parts of the spectrum, e.g.: the 2500 M c/s band, to distribute programs to educational institutions indicates that these means of distribution may predominate, and significantly limit the dependence, for educational purposes, on broadcast channels.[16]

2) None of the provinces has, at this time, submitted plans for the use of broadcasting facilities which justify the immediate reservation of the two best assigned channels in any location for educational television. In some provinces there seem to be no plans at all. In the opinion of the Board, reservation of channels for educational

purposes should follow rather than precede substantial evidence on the part of educational authorities of commitment to the use of television facilities as an effective means of advancing their purpose.[17]

The Board said it would welcome proposals from the provinces as to the channels which should be reserved in relation to a considered plan for the development of the use of television in the educational system.

The announcement included a section on "The Use of VHF or UHF Channels for Educational Television." The point was made that in some centres VHF channels were still available. In others, resort would have to be made to UHF channels. Under these conditions it seemed to the Board to be indefensible to apply a policy that ETV must proceed only on channels in the UHF band.

A general policy of confining educational television to the UHF band implied a consistent preference for a third or fourth channel for general commercial broadcasting over a first educational outlet. The Board believed it would be inadvisable to build this preference into the policy respecting educational outlets.[18]

Although the Government appeared to be opposed to the use of any VHF channels for educational stations, the position taken by the Board led to a request that the Board submit to the Cabinet committee a proposed policy for the use of VHF channels; a proposal was submitted in December 1966. It was recommended that a VHF channel be reserved for ETV in centres to which four VHF channels were allocated under the Canadian Television Channel Allocation Plan, 1966, of the Department of Transport, and in centres in which three VHF channels were allocated, and only one station had been licensed prior to 1967; that, for the time being, only one UHF channel be reserved for ETV in any other centre and that all reservations should be subject to review at the end of three years. The Board noted that, under the conditions proposed, only two locations would qualify for a VHF channel, viz., Winnipeg and Edmonton, but if the conditions were broadened so as to allow for "drop in" channels at various centres, the availabilities would then, in addition, include Calgary,

Regina, Saskatoon, Yorkton, Lloydminster and Prince Albert. In view of the need for rebroadcasting stations for expansion of general broadcasting, the Board recommended against committing "drop in" channels for ETV.

There were, of course, many locations in which there were only two allocated VHF channels, one of them being occupied by an affiliate of the CBC. In Ontario this included, for example, Fort William-Port Arthur. The Board believed that in these situations the remaining channels should be held for second general broadcasting stations, but educators were anxious to get access to them. The concern to obtain the use of VHF channels where these were available was related to the emphasis on the need to reach the public for the purposes of adult education.

The Board cooperated with the Department of Education of Newfoundland and with Memorial University in organizing an International Conference on Educational Broadcasting which was held in St. John's in September 1966. The conference was attended by some 100 educators and ETV specialists from Newfoundland and other provinces and by about 15 ETV specialists from the United States, United Kingdom, Japan and Italy.

In November 1966 Mr. Juneau submitted to the Government a memorandum recommending an action to implement governmental policy as outlined in the White Paper. The memorandum dealt with the need for legislative authority and for an interim agency. The Government decided to seek approval of the creation of a company under Part II of the Canadian Corporations Act with power to construct, operate and hold licences for transmission facilities for ETV. The attempt to introduce the necessary expenditure item raised opposition in the House, and it was withdrawn by the Government.[19] The Standing Committee on Broadcasting, Films and Assistance to the Arts was already meeting on the White Paper and was displaying a considerable interest in educational television. The Government was unwilling to proceed further in defining its position until the Committee had reported. However, educators were concerned about the direction in which some things were moving.

In October 1966, Dr. Alan Thomas, Director of the Canadian Association for Adult Education, had submitted to the Under-Secretary of State a proposal for a seminar on ETV. Early in January 1967, Mr. Steele referred Dr. Thomas to the BBG. The Board saw no reason to oppose the seminar and agreed to participate in it. A date was set for the second week in April.[20] In the meantime, the CBC issued a statement implying that it should be the agency referred to in the White Paper and outlining what the CBC proposed to do to assist the provinces.[21] This statement was seen as contrary to the policy of the Government and the policy supported by the BBG. Consequently the Cabinet intervened to designate the BBG as the authority responsible for the coordination of federal representation at the proposed seminar, and the Board was authorized to advise all representatives of the federal government on the Government's policy, so as to ensure that their participation would conform to the policy. It was a firm plank in the policy, one approved by the Cabinet Committee on Broadcasting, that a new federal agency would be set up.

A meeting of federal officials—including Eugene Hallman, who represented the CBC—was convened by the Board, and an outline of the policy as approved by the Cabinet was presented. In the meantime the Secretary of State had written the President of the CBC a sharp letter, pointing out that the CBC was challenging Government policy in a matter in which the CBC had no clear mandate from Parliament and expressing the view that it would be inappropriate for the CBC to provoke controversy before an open conference.[22] The reprimand from the Secretary of State did nothing to change the position of the CBC and, indeed, in an appearance before the Senate Committee early in 1968, the new President of the CBC, Mr. George Davidson reconfirmed the view of the Corporation that it should be the agency to develop ETV.[23] The controversy placed Mr. Hallman in an awkward position both at the meeting of officials and at the seminar. Those attending the seminar were fully aware of the position of the CBC but Mr. Hallman did not take the occasion to promote it.

Mr. Juneau presented a paper on the "Federal Approach to Educational Television," in which he outlined the policy with respect to the special agency. The paper dealt, also, with the problem of defining educational broadcasting.[24]

The seminar also heard, via recording, a statement by the Secretary of State. The statement left with the delegates the impression that educational television would be confined to the UHF band; they were conscious of the implications of this for adult education. The discussion of the definition of educational broadcasting helped to illuminate the problems and disclosed potentially significant differences, without achieving a consensus.

In a memorandum of November 1966, the Board had elaborated its views on the definition of educational broadcasting (television):

The Content of Material to be Broadcast Over Facilities Committed to Educational Purposes.

If approved educational bodies wish on-air time on educational television stations for programs in which participation does not lead to some form of certification (and indeed even in relation to these programs) there should be arrangements to identify the numbers of the public desiring to participate, i.e. by registration; arrangements for communication between registrants and the institution or instructor sponsoring the program; arrangements, where a series of programs is being offered, to provide registrants with an outline of the content of the series; arrangements to provide registrants with other and supporting means, e.g. reading material, of assisting in the learning process; and arrangements for assessing the results of the program in educational terms.

Time should not be made available on facilities committed to educational purposes unless these conditions are met with respect to particular programs.[25]

It appeared to be the intention of the Government to implement its proposals for educational television under a separate part of the general Broadcasting Act, and Mr. Juneau had been engaged in drafting this part of the legislation. The proposals for educational television, however, were meeting with opposition in the Standing Committee on

Broadcasting. The principal concern was the involvement of the provincial Department of Education.[26] In May 1967 the Chairman prepared another memorandum, including a proposal to meet this problem. He noted that the provincial Department of Education might appropriately be associated with broadcasts of material related to educational curriculum broadcast during school hours. For broadcasting outside of school hours of programs related to educational needs other than those of the schools, the Department of Education of the province might be prepared to agree to the establishment of a different agency, within the province, for this purpose. "The form of this agency could be a matter of negotiation between the Federal and Provincial authorities."[27]

When Bill C-163 appeared, it did not contain the specific provisions necessary to develop educational television. The Standing Committee, in reporting on the White Paper, had indicated that it wished further opportunity to consider educational television.[28] In introducing the Broadcasting Act (Bill C-163) on 17 October 1967 the Secretary of State, Miss LaMarsh, said:

> While the legislation which the Government is now seeking permission to introduce will declare that facilities for educational broadcasting are to be provided within the framework of the single broadcasting system, and therefore subject to the regulatory authority like all other broadcasting undertakings, the bill will not make specific reference to the provision of these facilities. I think most honourable members will understand it is our intention to bring forward a separate bill for this purpose, which will be drafted in its final form only after the subject has been thoroughly considered and carefully examined by the Standing Committee whose recommendations, needless to say, will be taken into full and careful consideration after the Committee has heard witnesses and has reported to the House.[29]

On 17 November the House of Commons passed a resolution referring the subject of educational television to the Committee.[30] The Committee's hearings on ETV began in February 1968.

[11]

TECHNOLOGY AND
TELEVISION SERVICE

EXISTING TECHNOLOGY EMERGED as a factor facilitating improvement and expansion of television. The introduction of colour television, which added a new dimension to viewing, occurred before 1968. Cable systems and new UHF channels eased the problem of the limited number of VHF channels. Cable systems came into being in the 1950s, but public policy with respect to them was declared only in the 1968 Act. Expansion into the UHF channels had hardly begun by 1968. Satellites in the service of television were only appearing on the horizon.

COLOUR

The possibility of colour television was drawn to the attention of the Board before action was taken on the licensing of second television stations. As the result of negative representations from the CBC and the absence of any marked enthusiasm on the part of the private stations, the Board on 3 September 1960 issued a statement that it was not yet willing to recommend the introduction of colour. In January 1963, at the request of the Electronics Industry Association (EIA), the Board devoted the first day of its public hearings to the presentation of information on the topic of colour television. The Board concluded that, because of the great cost involved, the lack of appreciable public demand and the absence of support from the CBC and CTV networks, the time to introduce colour had not yet arrived.[1] By 1964 the Board noticed a significant increase in sales of colour sets and in the volume of colour programming in the U.S.; but in an address to the EIA in June the Chairman defended the lack of action.[2] The Committee on Broadcasting, 1965 became involved in the issue but before it reported the CBC sought approval to broadcast from EXPO '67 in colour. The Government asked for an interim report from the Committee. The Committee although noting that the effect would be to add further cost burden to broadcasting gave qualified approval. On 15 June 1965 the Secretary of State announced the decision of the Government to permit the introduction of colour transmission not earlier than 1 January 1967 and to allow the CBC to install colour at EXPO '67.[3]

On 18 November 1965 the Board announced that, as the next meeting would not occur until February 1966, the full-time members had been authorized to deal with applications.[4]

In a further announcement of 28 January 1966 the Board defined the categories of licences it planned to recommend. Category A would permit only transmission of colour programs received through a network; Category B would permit network programs and the production and transmission of colour films; Category C would be the same as B plus the installation of colour videotape equipment; and, Category D would permit production and transmission of colour programs by all means available. It was estimated that the cost to stations to introduce colour would be approximately: Category A, $60-70,000; Category B, $160,000; Category C, $250,000; and, Category D, up to $1-1.5 million.[5]

By March 1968 the Board has recommended for approval 34 applications in Category A; 12 in Category B; 20 for Category C; and, 11 for Category D; no applications had been denied.[6] Colour proved a remarkable technical advance, greatly enriching the television service.

COMMUNITY ANTENNA TELEVISION SYSTEMS (CABLE)

Wire systems or cable systems, sometimes called Community Antenna Television Systems (CATV), involved the installation of powerful receiving antenna to pick up distant signals and to distribute the signals to home receiving sets by cable. The effect was to extend the range of signals which would be received by viewers and generally to improve reception. The Board's concern centred on the extension of service from U.S. stations and the possible consequences to the national broadcasting policy. It was reluctant to oppose CATVs but by 1963 the increased flow of capital into wire systems led to the expression of concern. The government was uncertain how to proceed. Finally in the new legislation, CATVs were placed under the control of the CRTC.

By 1960, some two hundred systems were in existence in Canada, about half of them in the Province of Quebec. The CAB advised that it would not be adverse to bringing CATVs under the jurisdiction of the Board.[7] The CBC refused to provide programming to CATVs and also favoured regulation.[8] In May 1960 the Board received a letter from the Minister suggesting a meeting of the BBG, DOT, CAB and CBC to discuss possible regulations and to make recommendations. Four meetings were held. The report to the Minister said that the growth of broadcasting suggested that the policies designed to advance the national purposes had not been unduly inhibited by the emergence of wired systems, but that the Board should be kept informed and, if necessary, report to the Minister on the impact on television broadcasting.[9]

Early in 1963, the Board's concern was strengthened by the developing situation. There were proposals for the use of translator stations south of the border for the purpose of extending the range of reception in Canada. There was evidence of a substantial movement of U.S. capital into the extension of wired systems in Canada, but information on wired systems was generally inadequate. The Board finally came to the conclusion that the wired services should be subject to its control.[10]

After the election of April 1963, the Board held a public hearing at which representations on wired systems were presented. A summary of the evidence was forwarded to the Minister. In December 1963 the Board was asked by the Secretary of State and the Minister of Transport to inquire into and recommend any legislative action which might be required to ensure that, as far as the constitutional jurisdiction of Parliament would permit, the use of community antenna television was subject to similar regulation to that applied to direct broadcasting. In undertaking this inquiry the Board was to consult with the Department of Transport. A report was made to the Minister in March 1964. The report said:

> The Board should regulate the Commercial Broadcasting Receiving Stations and Land Stations as defined in such a manner to ensure that, consistent with the public interest in the reception of a varied and comprehensive service, the Board should to the greatest extent practicable maintain the Canadian identity and character of service available to the public and further the purposes of broadcasting as set out in Section 10 of the Act. The Board should also regulate the relationship between licensees and provide for the final determination of all matters and questions in relation thereto.[11]

On 18 March 1964, the Board forwarded to the Special Assistant to the Secretary of State a lengthy document dealing with "Regulation of CATV Systems," "Legislative Authority to Regulate CATV Systems," and "The Case for Further Regulations of CATV Systems."[12]

Mr. Pickersgill, as Minister of Transport, had announced a "freeze" on CATV applications. He was prepared to take a tough line on further extension of U.S. signals into Canada. There was, however, considerable opposition to the "freeze" and it appeared that some of Mr. Pickersgill's colleagues did not share his views. In July the Minister lifted the "freeze" and asked the Board to examine applications and advise on the possible effect on broadcasting. Late in 1964 the Minister proposed to introduce an item of $1 in the estimates of his department in order to clothe the Board with authority to recommend on CATVs. The attempt met with vigorous opposition and the Minister hastily withdrew.[13] The Government seemed to be having difficulties in its caucus on the subject of CATVs, with Ralph Cowan (Liberal, York-Humber) providing the focus of the opposition. The Chairman was invited to a meeting of the CATV Study Group of the Liberal Caucus. He left the meeting, which was dominated by Mr. Cowan, feeling he had not made much impression.

The Committee on Broadcasting, 1965 was given terms of reference which specifically excluded CATVs. The Committee in its report, however, said: "It is not possible to do more than stress the need for prompt action and the exercise of some judgement in laying down rules to regulate the orderly growth of this new television technique while pursuing the objectives of Canadian broadcasting policy."[14]

In 1965–66, the Board received from the Minister of Transport 82 applications and found 72 of them "unlikely to make the operation of existing TV stations uneconomical or to inhibit the progression of alternative service." In 1966-67 the numbers were 92 and 84.[15]

The White Paper said: "The new legislation will provide that community antenna systems will be treated as components of the national broadcasting system; subject to licensing, regulation and control by the Board of Broadcast Governors."[16]

In early 1967, there was a significant increase in the number of applications for CATVs. There seemed to be a deliberate move to challenge existing controls before new controls might be introduced. The Minister of Transport favoured a "freeze" until the legislation was enacted. This idea was dropped in favour of a study proposed by the BBG. The Board engaged the services of Communications Associates to make an inventory of CATV systems.

Bill C-163, although offering little guidance as to the nature of the regulations to apply to "broadcasting receiving undertakings" placed them under the control of the CRTC. There appeared to be general agreement that the CRTC would have sufficient authority to control closed circuit television as undertaken by CATV operators, and it appeared likely that, for some time at least, closed circuit television as a separate operation would not be significant. However, there was continuing concern that, with the rapid changes in techniques, conventional transmitters might become redundant. At March 1968, the

Department of Justice was examining the legal position with respect to closed circuit television.

THE UHF BAND

At the time of the introduction of television, the state of the technology determined the use of channels in the Very High Frequency band. Technically, the VHF band suffers from relatively high attenuation of signals beyond the horizon and from the effect of obstructions. A higher signal level (power) is needed for a particular picture. This means higher costs. Otherwise VHF channels can provide a satisfactory service. Originally, home television receiving sets were made to receive VHF channels only, although it was possible to buy a converter which would enable the sets to show UHF channels.

At 3 January 1966, the Canadian Television Allocation Plan provided third unoccupied VHF channels in centres with two channels already occupied, basically only in cities in the Western provinces and in Quebec City and St. John's. Thus service in the major metropolitan areas could be provided only by the use of UHF channels.

In 1964, the Department of Transport held a licence application to operate on a UHF channel. The application was by Jack Tietolman of CKVL-TV, Verdun. It was made contingent on a relaxation of the TV regulations. The Board wrote the Minister, Mr. Pickersgill, advising that, before the UHF band was opened up in the metropolitan centres, there should be a public hearing to establish general policy.[17] The Department of Transport set up a study of the allocation plan to ensure that relocation would not make additional VHF channels available. When the study was completed the Board announced a public hearing for 25 October 1966. The announcement of 22 August 1966 invited representations on possible allocations other than those found by the DOT. It also called for regulations on other demands for channels and on the means by which the number of all-channel sets could be increased.[18]

In August 1967, the Chairman had, at the request of the Prime Minister, submitted a memorandum on "Toronto Television." The choice was between approving the application by CKVR-TV, Barrie to move its transmitter to Palgrave, thus providing an additional VHF channel to serve Toronto, or to discontinue the search for a VHF channel for Toronto and establish a policy of support for the use of UHF channels. The Chairman recommended the latter and urged the government to require the manufacturing and distribution of all-channel receiving sets.[19]

On 6 September, the Minister of Transport issued an announcement under the heading "Television Station Licences Extended One Year Pending Review of Allocations." The announcement requested a review of channel applications in Southern Ontario. It soon became evident that this was a device on the part of the Government to avoid declaring a position on the CATV applications.

Early in October 1967, the Chairman received a call from an officer of the Privy Council asking him to put together a list of questions that would be involved in considering the utilization of television channels in the UHF band. The Chairman replied with a list of seven questions. On 12 October the Chairman received a letter from the Prime Minister, saying that the immediate opening up of the UHF band was essential, but it was important that the development of the band proceed in a planned fashion. The Government requested the Board to give its views on the seven questions previously submitted by the Chairman.[20]

On 12 January 1968, the Chairman forwarded to the Prime Minister a report of the Committee on Review of TV Channel Allocations in Southern Ontario and a copy of a "Report on UHF Broadcasting."[21] The Chairman's "Report on UHF Broadcasting" was returned to him for his signature and with a request for the comments of the Board members on it. After the Board's meeting of 16 February the Chairman sent a lengthy memorandum to the Prime Minister.

The memorandum concluded:

a) It should be declared that with the exception of London, no more VHF channels will be assigned to the major centres in the central provinces. . . . There are three reasons for taking this position, first the inherent defects in the cases which have been considered. These are analyzed in detail in the Report on the Review of Channel Allocations in Southern Ontario. Second, the introduction of another VHF station in Toronto would impede the extension of CTV network service and the establishment of second general broadcasting service in small centres across Canada. Third, the immediate establishment of UHF outlets in the major metropolitan centres would assist in extending ETV service.

b) There are significant relations between the establishment of third service, eg: in Toronto, and the capacity to introduce third service in small centres, eg: Brandon; and the establishment of UHF service in, eg: Toronto and the development of ETV service. These relations have been developed in the body of the report. Consideration of these leads to the conclusion that action should be taken to establish UHF commercial outlets in the major metropolitan centres as soon as possible.

c) A policy of establishing UHF commercial outlets in the major metropolitan centres is unrealistic in the absence of legislation requiring the distribution of receiving sets with capacity to receive UHF signals; and of favourable policies to be implemented by the licensing authority. It is, therefore recommended that immediate action be taken by the Governor-in-Council under Section 50 (1) (b) (ii) of the amended Radio Act; and that the licensing and regulatory authority be directed to pursue policies favourable to the establishment of UHF broadcasting."[22]

At the public hearing of 25 October 1966, the Board received a presentation which involved the use of a space satellite. The presentation was made by Kenneth Soble, Niagara Television, Hamilton, in association with Power Corporation of Canada. The proposal, which created consternation in the industry, involved first the operation of a space satellite (CANSAT) to be functioning by the end of 1970; and second a broadcasting network (NTV) which would transmit programmes originating in three centres (Vancouver, Toronto, Montreal) through 97 outlets using UHF channels. The estimated cost of the related projects was in excess of $83 million. Because of the satellite proposal the Board felt obliged to bring the matter to the attention of the government. The letter said the Board realized that satellites lay outside the jurisdiction of the Board.[23]

The Board called a hearing on the network portion of the proposal for 7 March 1967.[24] The applicants outlined the proposal in considerable detail and representations from other parties were received. The full-time members of the Board were delegated to meet with the Cabinet committee to express the Board's views. However, on 29 March 1967 the Board received a letter from the Under Secretary of State saying that it would be untimely for the Board to make any public announcement of its views on the Power Corporation application until the government study was complete.[25] At a meeting on 27 April 1967 the Board considered the network part of the proposal. They found it bold and imaginative. However, there were too many uncertainties to permit the Board to make a commitment. The Cabinet committee was so advised.

The introduction of colour television made viewing more pleasurable. The effect of the CATV systems, the expansion of the UHF band and eventually the use of space satellites would be to increase the range of signals received by Canadian viewers. One inevitable consequence of this would be further fragmentation of the viewing audience.

[12]

CHANNEL 3 BARRIE AND THE TORONTO MARKET

THE ORIGINAL ALLOCATION PLAN for the scarce VHF channels provided three channels for Toronto. Under the original single station policy, the CBC was licensed to operate CBLT-TV on Channel 6. Channel 11 was subsequently moved to Hamilton, and was used by CHCH-TV. CHCH-TV was eventually disaffiliated from the CBC on grounds of substantial overlapping of signals. When the second station policy was announced there was one remaining VHF channel for Toronto—Channel 9. Even before television was introduced into Canada, Toronto was receiving television from U.S. stations, and by 1960 at least two Buffalo stations had substantial audiences. Nonetheless, the licence to broadcast on the last available VHF channel was seen as a real prize, and there were nine applicants for it. The Board recommended in favour of the application by Baton, Aldred, Rogers. The principal shareholder in this company was *The Telegram,* of which John Bassett was the proprietor. Mr. Bassett's allegiance to the Progressive Conservative Party was well-known, and following the recommendation of the Board, Joseph Sedgwick, in a letter to *The Globe and Mail,* accused the Board of political partisanship.[1]

The original licensee of CKVR-TV Barrie, operating on Channel 3, was Ralph Snelgrove. Sometime before the application was made to move the CKVR-TV transmitter to Palgrave, Geoff Stirling and Alan Waters each purchased a one-third interest in the station, at a substantial price. Mr. Snelgrove had declared his political sympathies by running, unsuccessfully, as a Liberal candidate.[2] Mr. Waters did not appear to have been active politically. Mr. Stirling was known to have been a supporter of the Liberals, and of Mr. Smallwood and Mr. Pickersgill, in Newfoundland.[3]

In January 1966, in reply to a question in the House, Mr. Pickersgill, then Minister of Transport, advised that the Department had received an application for a change in the transmitter site of CKVR-TV.[4] The Board began to receive letters of protest. The Toronto *Star* and *The Globe and Mail*—particularly the former—mounted opposition to the proposal. The principal target was Mr. Stirling.

Apart from the political aspects of the case, the main grounds for opposition was the potential interference with the reception of the signals of the two Buffalo stations operating on Channels 2 and 4. This was not the first time the Board had become involved in the problem of adjacent channel interference with the signals of U.S. stations. In 1960, the Board had approved the relocation of the transmitter of CHEK-TV Victoria to a site on Saturna Island. When the new facilities went into operation, there was significant interference with the reception of at least one American station in Vancouver. The public protested vigorously, and were supported by the local MPs, most of whom were supporters of the Conservative Government. It became necessary to hold a special hearing in Vancouver to deal with the protests. The Board discussed with Mr. Nowlan the principle the Board believed was involved, that was the principle of limiting the development of the use of Canada's broadcasting resources in order to protect the reception of already-established U.S. stations. Mr. Nowlan agreed that this principle was unacceptable.[5] The Board confirmed its earlier decision, and the opposition quickly subsided. The CHEK-TV case, although involving the same principle, was not identical to the CKVR-TV case in all relevant respects. In the CHEK-TV case, the opposition developed only after the event, and the audience of the U.S. stations affected was relatively small. Further, the CHEK-TV case was not involved, to the same extent, in the broad policy of development of television service.

The Barrie case had to be considered within the framework of the emerging policy with respect to the expansion of second television service, additional television services (including educational television) and the use of UHF channels. In March 1966, the Board wrote the Minister of Transport proposing a study of possible reallocation of channels and, following this, a public hearing on the opening of the UHF band. The Minister approved.[6] The Technical Advisory Committee of the DOT began a study of channels, and in July the Board announced a public hearing on the UHF band for 25 October 1966.[7] On the same date as the Board wrote the Minister of Transport, a letter was sent to the Secretary of State saying, inter alia, that the CKVR-TV application appeared to provide for a third Toronto station and was, therefore, inconsistent with the policy in effect.[8] It was at this time that differences between the ministers became apparent.

The Board's support for a study of possible reallocations proved to be a mistake. It stimulated considerable activity but, with respect to Ontario, disclosed only two proposals which were technically acceptable. The Technical Advisory Committee noted that by changing CBLT-TV Toronto from Channel 6 to Channel 5, Channel 6 could be made available for use in London and in Kingston-Belleville area. Radio Station CFRB found what appeared to be a technically acceptable arrangement for an exchange of channels with a station in Rochester, N.Y.

The Department of Transport eventually forwarded the Barrie application as an application for a change of facilities and it was announced as an agenda item for the regular hearing of the Board in November 1966. At the *in-camera* meeting preceding these hearings, the Chairman explained to the Board why it had been decided to put the CKVR-TV application on the agenda. He pointed out that the Department was, in his opinion, acting properly in sending the application forward to the Board as a change of facilities. Although it appeared that the effect of the application would be to establish another Toronto station, this was a decision the Board would have to make and, it seemed to the Chairman, would properly make after a public hearing at which all aspects of the application had been exposed. The Chairman referred to the announcement, dealing with the special hearing of 25 October on the UHF band, which had been drafted and was being presented for Board approval. The announcement recorded the decision that the Board would be prepared to hear applications for "third" stations in Montreal and Toronto after February 1967. If the CKVR-TV application was found to be an application for a Toronto station, it could be reheard at that time. The meeting agreed that the question of whether the application was a Toronto application was the main issue before the Board, and Counsel was instructed to direct his examination of witnesses to this issue.

At the public hearing CFRB appeared with its proposal. The proposal required that CBLT-TV change from Channel 6 to Channel 5. CFRB was, at considerable expense, contracting with a Rochester station occupying Channel 13, for the exchange of Channel 6 for Channel 13, subject to the necessary approvals. In order to make Channel 13 useable in Toronto, it would be necessary to change the site of the Kitchener station, and the Kitchener station was willing to enter into a contract to assure this. As Channel 6 was at the time occupied by CBLT-TV, the DOT could not accept an application from CFRB predicated on its transfer; but the plan was a bold and ingenious one, and CFRB was given the opportunity to present it publicly.

On Wednesday afternoon, 16 November, the Board considered the application by CKVR-TV and the evidence received at the public hearing. In introducing the discussion, the Chairman referred to the meeting on Monday and asked if there was anyone who felt the application did not provide an additional service in Toronto. A member immediately moved that the application be recommended for approval. The motion was seconded. There was prolonged and vigorous debate. The question was eventually put. The Chairman counted seven in favour of the motion, and then counted six contrary votes. One member had abstained. The Chairman then said that he cast his vote against the motion, and recorded a tied vote. He ruled that a tied vote had the effect of defeating the motion. The Board then proceeded to other business.

Unfortunately there was no by-law on the voting powers of the Chairman. Some members, although not disputing the decision, had found the Chairman's actions arbitrary; it was later agreed that Counsel should be instructed to advise the Board on an appropriate by-law. Counsel recommended that the Chairman have the right to vote on all motions and, in the case of a tied vote, to cast the deciding vote. Some members found the principle of allowing the Chairman two votes to be objectionable and no decision was ever reached by the Board on the matter.

On Wednesday evening the mover of the motion called the Chairman to review the consequences of the defeat of the motion. The Chairman said that by defeating the motion on the application for a change of facilities it appeared that the Board had taken the view that the application had the effect of providing an additional service in Toronto; and by approving the announcement stating that the Board would, after February 1967, recommend on applications for additional service in Toronto, it followed that the CKVR-TV application could be resubmitted and dealt with at that time. The Chairman undertook to have for the Board on the following morning a draft of the Board's announcement on the application.

On Thursday morning the following statement was put before the Board:

This application proposed that the transmitter of Station CKVR-TV be moved from its present site to Palgrave, Ontario, and that the height of the antenna be increased from 820 feet to 1,267 feet. The application was, properly, forwarded to the Board by the Department of Transport as a change in facilities.

The evidence before the Board at the public hearings on November 15 indicated that the proposed change in facilities would:

(1) reduce the strength of the signal received by viewers to the north of the present site, and increase signal to the south;

(2) make the station's signal effectively available to a greatly increased number of viewers in metropolitan Toronto.

The prospective coverage figures supplied to the Board by the Department of Transport showed:

population in the "A" contour: 2,134,137

population in the "B" contour: 3,434,748.

On the basis of the evidence before it, the Board concluded that the effect of the proposed change would be to establish CKVR-TV as a Toronto station.

In a recent public announcement, the Board reaffirmed its policy, which had been in effect since 1961, of not recommending licences for additional television stations in centres already served by two Canadian stations. Having concluded from the evidence at the Public Hearing that the effect of the application of CKVR-TV would be to create an additional Toronto station, the Board had no option but to recommend the denial of the application. The Board is preparing an announcement dealing with applications for "third" stations. This will be released shortly. When it has been publicly announced that the policy is changed so that applications for additional stations for Toronto may be recommended, this application may be re-submitted and re-heard.

The mover of the original motion said he was satisfied with the draft statement. There was discussion, particularly with reference to the last paragraph, and amendments were approved. It was agreed that only the population in the "A" contour should be used. The words "had no option" were removed from the penultimate paragraph. The last paragraph was amended to read: "The Board is releasing an announcement dealing with applications for additional television service. In accordance with the policy now being announced, applications for additional service to the Toronto Metropolitan area may be submitted and will be heard."[9] The announcement as approved was released, as was the change in policy which would permit receipt of applications for third channels in Toronto and Montreal.[10]

Stirling, Snelgrove and Waters met with the full-time members. The members indicated to them that the application would be heard in June. This was taken by Stirling as a commitment. Later, there was some doubt that the Board would be able to proceed with the hearing of Toronto applications as early as June. It came to the attention of Stirling that the hearing of the CKVR-TV application might be delayed. He took strong exception to any delay, which he charged would be a breach of a commitment made to him by the Board. The reason he gave for an early hearing was that there might be an election in the fall, the Liberals could be defeated, and his chance of getting a television licence would be gone.

The application of CKVR-TV was on the agenda for the public hearing of 20–21 June 1967. Prior to the meeting of the Board two documents had been distributed. The Technical Advisor to the Board had been charged with preparing a report on potential adjacent channel interference. In the course of preparing his report he had looked at experiences in the United States. His report confirmed a report made by officers of the DOT to the Minister, that interference with reception of Channels 2 and 4 would be substantial. Notes by the Chairman referring to affiliation with the CBC and to the CFRB plan were also distributed.

At the public hearing, spokesmen for the applicant presented evidence in support of their contention that interference would be minimal, and defended the proposal to continue affiliation with the CBC for a time. CFRB produced a remarkable colour film illustrating the kind of programming their station might be expected to provide.

The composition of the Board had changed since the earlier occasion on which the application was before it, by the appointment of Ian Stott of Sydney to replace Dr. Woodfine. Miss LaMarsh later told the Chairman she had nothing to do with Mr. Stott's appointment and, in referring to attacks later directed against him, the Prime Minister said Stott was appointed to the Board for reasons that had nothing to do with CKVR-TV. Ian Stott himself expressed surprise that he had been labelled as a supporter of the Liberal party.[11]

At the meeting of the Board following the public hearing, the same member of the Board who moved the approval of the application in November 1966 moved for approval. The discussion which followed indicated a majority in support of the motion. The motion to recommend for approval, subject to certain conditions respecting CBC affiliation was passed by a vote of 8 to 7. The Chairman voted against the motion.

On 5 July the Board received a letter from the CBC, registering with the Board and the Minister of Transport opposition to the decision. On 13 July a message from the Minister of Transport was relayed to the Chairman from the DOT. The substance of the message was that there would be no ministerial approval until "the CBC problem was resolved." The newspapers became more virulent in their attacks and Stirling was goaded into defending himself in the media.[12]

During July, the Chairman prepared two memoranda analyzing the alternatives. On 26 July he wrote the Prime Minister:

I am writing to you as Chairman of the Cabinet Committee on Broadcasting. It seemed preferable to me to approach you directly rather than through either the Secretary of State or the Minister of Transport.

Approval of the application by CKVR to move its transmission facilities to Palgrave, and thus to provide a Grade "A" signal to metropolitan Toronto, has been recommended by the Board. The application presents problems related to probable interference and to affiliation with the CBC.

The Board has taken the position that, before moving into the UHF band for commercial broadcasting, it would be wise to be sure that no opportunities remain for further use of VHF channels by re-allocation. The two opportunities which have been presented are the proposals by CKVR and CFRB; although it seems probable that the licensee of CHLT-TV Sherbrooke (Power Corporation) will apply to move Channel 7 so as to give Grade "A" coverage to Montreal.

Because of the problems created by the proposed moves it might appear desirable, negatively, to take the position that, in the central provinces, at least, no re-allocation of channels can be approved. Positively, the position would be that it is now necessary to move into the UHF band, both for commercial broadcasting and for educational television. The government could announce that the necessary steps are being taken to ensure the distribution of all-channel receiving sets.[13]

The Chairman outlined in greater detail the strengths and weaknesses of the proposal and put himself at the service of the Committee. At Mr. Pearson's request, the Chairman prepared an extended memorandum on the alternatives. Alternative A was to allow CKVR-TV to proceed, require disaffiliation from the CBC, and face the problem of interference. Alternative B, which it was indicated the Chairman favoured, was to discontinue the search for VHF channels, deny the CKVR-TV application and the CFRB proposal, and establish a policy in support of UHF channels. The Chairman undertook to have the Board reconsider its CKVR-TV recommendation at the September meeting and to declare itself in favour of the UHF policy. "I am sure that some of the members who voted in support did not appreciate some of the implications, and must have had second thoughts."[14] The evidence that the Cabinet was having a problem in dealing with the CKVR-TV case continued. Prior to the meeting of the Board in June, Mr. Pickersgill phoned the Chairman to say that although of course he did not wish in any way to influence the decision of the Board, he hoped that in view of the attacks on the applicants the Board would deal kindly with them. This was probably the least he could do for his friends. On the other hand, following the Board's announcement, when the Chairman encountered Miss LaMarsh at the Governor-General's Garden Party, she registered her disgust. Later, at a luncheon for Russia's representative to the Centennial, Paul Martin told the Chairman that he could not understand how some of the Board members could be so stupid. At the September meeting of the Board, the supporters of the CKVR-TV application agreed that it was a dead issue.

The Government did not follow the advise of reference back to the Board. Instead the Board was requested to make a study of UHF and to make recommendations. The report recommended in favour of opening up the UHF band, and denying CKVR-TV and CFRB. The Government moved to establish broadcasting on UHF channels.

It was a mistake to recommend the CKVR-TV application for approval because, as the full-time members recognized, it did not fit into a sensible policy for the development of television service. The accusations that the Board's decision was influenced by the political affiliation of the successful applicant stuck.

Miss LaMarsh, in her book, *Memoirs of a Bird in a Gilded Cage*, provides an extended discussion of the Barrie case, and there is confirmation that, within the ranks of the Liberal Party, there was some feeling that the award of the second Toronto television licence to Bas-

sett entitled the Liberals to an outlet favourable to them. This propo-
sition appears to have been discussed in a meeting in Mr. Pickersgill's
office. It was, however, effectively disputed by Ralph Cowan, the
renegade Liberal member from Toronto, on grounds that ownership
had little political influence. He pointed out that Barrie, served by a
station owned by a Liberal remained in the centre of Tory representation in Ontario; whereas in Toronto, where the private station was
owned by a Tory, there were no Conservative members at all.

Although charging interference in the Barrie case, Miss LaMarsh
claims she had no proof of direct interference by any of her colleagues
in the Government, and that those she charged denied it. She records
that a part-time Member of the Board told her that one of Paul Martin's assistants had advised members of the Board that the Government would be pleased to see the application approved; and claimed
that to her sure knowledge this led to one Board member changing his
vote. Involvement by Paul Martin's assistant seems credible although
it would be consistent with Mr. Martin's remarks to the Chairman
only if either he did not know what his assistant was up to, or did not
wish the Chairman to know that he knew. Miss LaMarsh goes on to
say that she finally found the guilty party. This was one Pat "Leaky"
Lavelle. According to her account, Lavelle who has been an Executive
Assistant to Allan MacEachen, had been hired by CKVR-TV applicants to lobby for them; and she concludes that Lavelle had earned his
salary by ensuring that all the representatives from the Maritime
provinces voted for the application.

The Chairman did not recall having heard of Lavelle or having met
him. Many of the rumours current at the time came from the staff of
the Toronto *Star* who interviewed the Chairman on the case. One of
the rumours was that MacEachen's assistant had been responsible for
the appointment of Ian Stott from Sydney, primarily for the purpose
of securing approval. Miss LaMarsh says she was informed that the
representatives of the Maritime Provinces (not the Atlantic Provinces)
voted for the application. The sources of her information were
unknown to the Chairman as was knowledge of any contact between
Lavelle and the Maritime members, indeed any members of the Board.

Miss LaMarsh had some interesting comments on the actions of the Cabinet. She referred to the difference between an application for a change of facilities and an application for a licence. Under the Act and the regulations, while both required a recommendation from the Board, a change of facilities needed only the approval of the Minister of Transport, the issue of a licence needed an order-in-council. Miss LaMarsh seemed to imply that Pickersgill would have wished to have the application dealt with as a change of facilities, because with a favourable recommendation from the Board he could then have permitted it to proceed without consulting his colleagues. By the time the application reached the Board the possibility of action by the Minister without reference to his colleagues seemed remote.[15]

Miss LaMarsh said that the Cabinet eventually reversed the decision of the Board, and pointed out that this had happened only once before in the history of the Board. The other instance referred to was the application for a private French-language radio station in Hull, Quebec in which Jack Tietolman of CKVL, Verdun, was the principal. This application was heard and recommended by the Board prior to the April 1963 election. It was dealt with by the new Cabinet, and the Cabinet did not pass the required order-in-council. The Board was so advised. There had been some differences of opinion within the Board and the Board accepted the decision of the Cabinet without comment. The Chairman had always believed that the Cabinet's decision had been influenced by the opposition of the Oblate Fathers, who through the ownership of *Le Droit,* were the owners of the French-language station in Hull. In any case, the representative of the Order had made it clear to the Board that they thought a new private station would have serious consequences for the Hull station. Some members of the Board, including the Chairman, felt that competition would be good for the service to the French-speaking residents of Ottawa and Hull.[16]

Miss LaMarsh incorrectly referred to the "reversal" of the decision of the Board in the Barrie case. This implied that the Cabinet, even if the Board should recommend against a licence, could issue a licence. The legislation provided that, after a recommendation from the Board, a licence could be issued only after an order-in-council was passed. It was the Board's understanding that if it did not recommend an application for a licence for approval, the application could not go forward. In any event, Miss LaMarsh's statements that the Cabinet "reversed" the decision of the Board and held the licence in abeyance for a study of channel availabilities were inconsistent. She went on to say that she was not aware of any reaction by the Board to the Cabinet's action. The Board was certainly never advised that the Cabinet had "reversed" its decision. Instead, the Board was asked to undertake the study of channel availabilities.

Miss LaMarsh established that the Barrie case was responsible for the inclusion in the new Broadcasting Act of an appeal to the Cabinet against a decision of the CRTC on licence applications. The White Paper, the Committee on Broadcasting, 1965 and Bill C-163 as drafted at the time made no provision for appeal. Later drafts of Bill C-163 provided for appeal.

Miss LaMarsh concluded that it was impossible to provide for an impartial board, by legislation, where its membership is appointed by the Cabinet, and that the Cabinet would always bear the brunt of public blame.[17] In the matter of the issue of new licences, involving the use of part of the public domain, the Chairman had always thought that the government should be in a position to prevent action which they might feel would be against the public interest. In political terms, it was inescapable that the government should be held responsible; and delegated authority must be limited to allow the government to intervene when it considered that it must do so. The government would not do this unless it sensed that it had public support. If the government were frequently to find that the decisions of the authority were unacceptable, it should move to change the legislation or to replace the authority.[18]

III

THE END RESULTS

[13]

THE BOARD AS A REGULATORY BODY:

A CASE STUDY

THE EXPERIENCES OF THE BBG over the ten years, 1958–1968, test the hypotheses postulated in the Doern analysis. For instance, it seems clear that the Board regarded itself much more in the Vickers's tradition viewing regulation as "a continuing transaction between the governors and the governed."[1] Instead of relying on the narrower concept of regulation as a rule of conduct backed by the force of law, the Board became amply involved in the mutual transactions which Vickers envisages as involving elements of persuasion, authority, bargain and threat which flow back and forth between the governed and the governors. In addition to these two interpretations of regulation, Doern underscores a third potential aspect of the life of regulatory agencies, the Bernstein thesis, which suggests that regulatory agencies tend to be captured by the industries that they were intended to regulate.[2]

As Doern rightly points out, an understanding, analysis or adaptation of any of these concepts requires the drawing of a sharp distinction between the theory and the practice of regulatory agencies, between the process and the performance. In search of this distinction, Doern first analyzes seven factors which affect the environment of Canadian regulatory agencies.

THE ENVIRONMENT OF CANADIAN REGULATORY AGENCIES

LIBERALISM, PLURALISM AND CORPORATISM: THE ROLE OF THE STATE

Because the hinterland nature of the early Canadian economy with its primary resources base necessitated significant areas of state intervention, Canada did not succumb totally to the philosophy of laissez-faire liberalism of nineteenth century Britain or America. Canadians did, however, evolve a political style with "a high degree of individual freedom and market activity" in a democratic framework and involving "benevolent competition among interest groups, with the state as independent referee removing the excesses of the marketplace."[3] A challenge to this brokerage concept of Canadian political life in the 1960s revealed the existence of more enduring regional, class and ideological cleavages than heretofore had been acknowledged. A more organic view of the state gave the state a more significant role in relation to social values than that of mere referee.

Doern suggests that from liberalism the Canadian regulatory process acquired a concern for individual rights, including rights to public goods and property which are objects of public regulation and allocation. As well, Canadians have acquired the "myth" that private enterprise opposes state regulation where in fact it often actively seeks it.[4]

From pluralism, Doern suggests the derivation of the concepts of the regulatory agency as being representative of those interests with a stake in the regulatory process and of the regulatory agency as an independent tribunal. This latter concept of independence is considered misleading by some.

Finally, from the concept of corporatism, the notion—and practice—of the curtailment of agency independence by the regular use of state enterprise is derived. Thus the government is part regulator of itself as well as of the private sector. The presence of the CBC in broadcasting field is a case in point. This latter phenomenon, of course, gives rise to concern about the personnel of the agencies and the implications of development of career patterns between the regulatory and operational sides of public enterprise. There appear to be, from the vantage point of the Board, elements of all three factors mentioned, liberalism, pluralism and corporatism.

LIBERALISM: Dr. Stewart gives evidence of concern for individual rights and a concept of the free flow of ideas and of consumer choice which would have made John Stuart Mill proud. At the same time, he recognized the rightness of parliamentary action directing the use of the broadcast media to further public purposes such as the enhancing of national unity or subjecting the media to regulation purporting to make them "essentially Canadian in content and character," even at the expense of limiting the unfettered free flow of ideas or consumer choice of programming. Mr. Nowlan quoted as justification for the creation of the BBG Donald Creighton's support of "national policies devised to strengthen our unity from ocean to ocean and to maintain our separatism in North America" and was cited approvingly by Dr. Stewart. The Board's Canadian content regulations provide a concrete manifestation of such policies. So too did the concept of equalization in which the Board envisaged the more profitable private stations providing funds to subsidize the less economically viable stations of the second network. The private stations were seen as having a definite role to play in fulfilling national goals.

Prophetically, it is noteworthy that Dr. Stewart expressed doubt as to the effectiveness of broadcasting in achieving political and cultural ends. He suggested that, in a political democracy, a number of factors were necessary for any success not the least of which was what he termed "the disposition of the public to support the [political or cultural] purposes."

Clearly, once the private stations were freed from the threat of nationalization, there was to be a role for private enterprise in the realm of broadcasting although no property rights were ever considered to adhere to a broadcasting licence. At first, the forces of the market place were to be subordinated to the needs of national public service broadcasting, but, especially after 1958, the political and economic power of the private sector were forces to be reckoned with. Yet the role envisaged by Parliament and the Board for the private sector was not without its restrictions or public purposes as well. Entry into the field was always restricted by the licensing process. Some private stations performed a public service as affiliates of the CBC providing a means for the national distribution of its programs. Later, the BBG sought to achieve certain public goals through the private sector. For example, the Board aspired to ensure that the private stations did not earn unconscionable monopoly profits and that the scarcity profits of some be utilized through the equalization scheme. At no time were the private elements of the system not subject to the dictates of public policy as expressed through the democratically-elected Parliament and made manifest in the Broadcasting Act and subsequent regulations. In order to achieve a fully recognized equalization concept, however, Parliament had to be willing to amend the Act in order to give the BBG the necessary regulatory power.

Adherence to a concern for individual rights in terms of this liberal concept of the free flow of ideas and to the belief in the efficacy of the market economy is evident. This adherence, of course, is limited by the dictates of public policy. We also see evidence of what Trebilcock terms the myth of liberalism, that private enterprise opposes state regulation.[5] On one hand, the private stations opposed the regulatory functions of the Board of the CBC and campaigned for the creation of a separate regulatory agency. The creation of the BBG was welcomed by the President of the CAB as action which "corrects many of the anomalies of the past and represents a major step forward toward the full development of Canada's great broadcasting potential."[6] The Chairman reported to the Minister, however, that the private broadcasters would claim that any regulation restricted the freedom of action of broadcasters, that each was undesirable and that broadcasting should not be subject to any regulations not applied to other mass media. He suggested to the Minister that any regulations would likely be met with a show of opposition by the CAB.

PLURALISM: Of the three concepts Doern poses, pluralism seems the least well manifested, if by pluralism we mean "a benevolent competition among interest groups, with the state acting as independent referee removing the excesses of the market place."[7] The Board seemed to act in a much more positive way than such a concept suggests. This could be perhaps because of the very lack of competition in the system. Only in a few major markets did broadcasters, especially in television, seriously compete with each other, and the voice of nonbroadcasting elements of society were at best imperfectly represented. The impression is left that the Board took the positive stance that it did on a number of occasions as a surrogate for other groups not present to challenge the broadcasters. Challenges of a more formal institutional approach were not to appear in great numbers until the 1970s.

The period 1958–1968 is an on-going study of the problem of uncertain relationships between the two public boards. From the beginning, the CBC asserted the responsibility of its Board to Parliament, not the BBG, and refused at first to recognize, for instance, the need to go to the BBG to alter its agreements with its network affiliates—as evidenced in the Grey Cup controversy of 1962. The BBG was often put in an uncomfortable position when faced with hearing conflicting applications from the CBC and private interests for a single licence. Similarly, in attempting to carry out parliamentary mandates, the Board found itself at times in the position of having to make invidious decisions about the proper course to follow affecting the two sectors, one financed basically by public means, the other dependent upon commercial revenues. The Canadian content policies and the principle of equalization reflect the problems involved and indicate most clearly of all that the Board was much more than an independent referee amongst conflicting private interests. Through the regulatory process, the Board implemented public policy and indeed supplemented it where the government or Parliament had been deficient in their own acts of creation.

CORPORATISM: We also have clear evidence of the corporatist element perhaps more in the meaning of Rae and McLeod rather than Prethus.[8] That element has been, of course, circumscribed as Doern suggests by the presence of a crown corporation, the CBC. The fact that the CBC held its own unique view of the broadcasting system and that it felt free to enunciate policy in many areas as though it were still the prime mover of the system complicated the BBG's life immeasurably. The relationship between the public and private sectors of the broadcasting system became increasingly competitive rather than complimentary and the BBG became, as has already been suggested, something more than an independent referee removing the excesses of the market place.[9] It, of course, was the main gatekeeper into a regulated industry and, as well, acted on a number of occasions in a very positive fashion, encouraging, persuading, cajoling and sometimes ordering the various elements of the system to move in particular directions in pursuit of public policies. The processes by which these were accomplished were varied, but one at least reflects the process of elite accommodation of which Prethus spoke. The concern of the Board for the extension of the second television service and the visits of the Chairman to Brandon and Moncton illustrate the process.

ECONOMICS OF REGULATION: RATIONALE AND CONSEQUENCES

The regulatory process can obviously affect many aspects of the economic life of an industry. Doern identifies seven factors as being of prime significance. One would expect some if not all of them to come within the purview of the agency regulating broadcasting.

ACCESS TO THE INDUSTRY: It has often been said that the BBG acted to protect the economic interests of the private sector. The evidence suggests that such an assessment is overly simplistic and unfair to the Board. The Board did consciously limit entry to the industry during periods such as the 1963–64 freeze when governmental clarification of policy ambiguities was sought or on occasions when it was believed that local markets conditions did not merit a new station of the type of service sought. While the financial condition of the existing licensee had to be considered, clearly it was not the only factor in question. The Board was under a parliamentary mandate to introduce a second television network and to extend primary television service to all Canadians while at the same time enhancing the distribution of the CBC national service. These goals almost contradict each other. It could not and did not close off entry to the industry. In fact, in the eight years, 1960–68, at a time when television was supposedly having a negative effect on radio, the number of private radio stations increased by 30%.[10] The number of private television stations increased by 62% and the number of privately-owned satellite television stations increased by over 1400%. It is also true to say, however, that bankruptcies in the broadcasting field during this period were minimal. It must not be forgotten, however, that the Board had its promoting and planning functions to fulfil.

As far as the second television network was concerned, the Board initially envisaged only five centres large enough to justify a second station. It had some doubts about the sixth, Halifax. Before applications were heard, the Board announced a number of criteria by which applicants would be judged. The Board was dealing with a scarce commodity, the granting of the single licence in essence creating an oligopolistic situation. Destructive competition was not a concern. To ensure some order in the arena, the ground-rules were laid down and entry granted accordingly. The fact that two of the licensees had to be refinanced and the programming commitments were varied through time indicates the frailty of human judgement and the impact of changing circumstance.

In the expansion of the primary service, where the cost per capita figure was the overriding factor, and in the extension of television service to encompass the development of second and third stations, the Board had to ensure the continued provision of existing services as well as the introduction of the new services at a level at least comparable to the existing fare. To have done other than to proceed in their cautious fashion would have run counter to the mandate. A bankrupt station provides no service. How the system would have developed without any parliamentary direction or regulatory activity will never be known. One can only surmise that the earlier tendency exhibited in radio to concentrate service in the large centres of population would have been repeated. The pressures to affiliate with American networks might well have been enhanced as well. Yet the policies followed by the Board required in effect the subsidization of the less affluent by the more affluent in order to extend services to the less populated areas.

The Board was also faced with a dilemma posed by the CBC and the chronic uncertainty concerning the adequacy of the funding to support its application for new stations. In some instances, the Board probably could have licensed a second private station with the expenditure of much less time and energy than was required for the CBC licence. To have done so, however, would have led to exclusion of a CBC "O & O" station from many areas because of the limitation on a number of channels.

PRICE: The Board was not unaware of the problems of price (rate cards) especially as reflected in the rates charged by the CBC relative to those of the private sector. Practices which the CBC looked upon as protecting its commercial revenues were regarded as unfair competition by the private stations. As the Board was not specifically empowered to set rates, there was little it could do formally. At best, it could consult the CBC and urge restraint. On occasion, the Board did engineer agreements between the CBC and a private station whereby the CBC agreed to limit its local commercial operations during an initial phase-in period of the new licensee.

RATE OF RETURN: As with pricing, there can be a concern that the licensing authority may favour existing licensees in order to protect their rate of return. One of the crucial issues to be faced in analyzing such a question is the matter of what constitutes undue protection. It could mean maintaining an inordinately high rate of return; it could mean ensuring a minimum profit in order to keep the licensee in operation.

The Board clearly did take the profitability of stations into consideration when formulating its regulations. Generally speaking, the whole movement toward content regulation was circumscribed by a concern for the impact of the policy on station finances—or put the other way around—on the stations' ability to generate sufficient revenue to produce adequate Canadian programs. The policy had within it a highly redistributive element, in effect asking the stations to bear to cost of a particular public policy. The impact on the stations' profitability was twofold. Canadian programming tended to be more expensive than comparable or better foreign programming and it tended to be less popular, therefore less profitable than the imports.

The extension of service, both primary and secondary, forced the Board to look at the profitability of stations. The development of CTV and the concern for the principle of equalization of station profits and for the possible application of the "public utility" analogy to such profits gives indication of the Board's and the government's willingness to consider both the adequacy and the distribution of profits in the private sector. One of the prime issues involved in the potential move of CKVR-TV, Barrie into the Toronto market was the concern for the impact of the new channel on the scarcity profits of the existing stations. The reduction of those profits would reduce the funds thought necessary to absorb some of the losses incurred by stations affiliating with the new network from smaller markets still without second service.

The extension of primary service was also a very cost-conscious operation and one which in large measure might logically have fallen on the shoulders of the licensees in the private sector because of their proximity to the unserviced areas. The installation of rebroadcasting stations was one possible way to extend service, but the Board could not order such installations. It could only cajole stations into cooperation, usually only when the profit prospects appeared adequate to justify such a move.

The arrival of cable television was a prime threat to the profitability of the on-air broadcasters. The Board was called upon by the Department of Transport to comment upon applications for cable licences in terms of the potential impact on the economic viability of existing stations and on the plans for the development of the second service. The Board, while expressing concern, showed no inclination to reject many applications and reported favourably on all but 17 of 173. It demurred only on those which it thought would have negative implications in areas where second service was imminent.

The White Paper in its concern for the quality of service suggested that the Board be required to satisfy government of the adequacy of advertising support whenever it recommended the granting of a second licence in an area. The White Paper also suggested that stations be grouped according to profit potential and according to the size of the centre in which they were located. The Board was rightly cognizant, however, of the fact that stations in medium and small centres might well produce profits greater than those in larger centres, at least when measured as a rate of return.

The CBC/CTV aspect was raised early in the period by Spencer Caldwell of CTV Network who pointed to the limited drawing power of the private network and commended to the Board the desirability of adding some CBC affiliates to CTV Network in order to enhance the size of the audience it could deliver to the advertiser. The Board seemed lukewarm to the proposal as it was committed to extending the national service to those not presently receiving it, not withdrawing it from taxpayers currently receiving it. Similarly CTV's idea of cross-programming between networks brought open hostility from the CBC and no positive action from the BBG.

The Board sought on a number of occasions to placate impatient viewer groups seeking alternative service by stressing that markets possessed limited resources and that merely wishing them into existence would not create new resources. As the Chairman wrote to Prime Minister Pearson: "The public demand for a second service exists and can be made vocal by prospective applicants, but the means by which the alternative service can be provided without jeopardizing the existing local services are by no means clear."

As was so often the case, one of the intentions of a Board letter to the Prime Minister was to seek clarification of the government's position with regard to CBC expansion. CTV Network coveted CBC affiliates to enhance its selling power. The CBC wanted more "O & O" stations, especially in each of the provincial capitals. It could achieve such a goal only with capital financing from the government. Hence CTV's efforts to gain former CBC affiliates and a larger share of the market were in part inhibited by governmental inactivity. The BBG was also curtailed in its range of actions by its inability to require a station to accept network affiliation except with the CBC. Ultimately, of course, as more and more private stations and cable undertakings were licensed the CBC's share of the market did decline.

TECHNOLOGY: The Board was caught up in a number of matters related to changing technology, especially cable television, colour television and the use of UHF channels. How did the Board react to these? Did its activities hasten or inhibit the introduction of the new phenomena?

In the matter of cable, one can say that the Board did little or nothing to retard the development of cable, in spite of its expressed concern over the impact of the growing importation of more American signals on the Board's Canadian content regulations and on the general intentions of the Broadcasting Act. While in the early 1960s the Board could declare that it felt that cable had not been "significantly detrimental to the national purpose" and that it did not wish to oppose CATVs, the Board did become increasingly alarmed over the growing number of cable undertakings and of the changing means of relaying signals. Whatever its concerns, the Board was helpless as it had no regulatory authority over cable and, in spite of requests for amendments to the Broadcasting Act, the government delayed and no concrete action was taken to integrate cable into the regulatory authority of the Board.

Colour television provides an example of the Board's becoming embroiled in a conflict of economic interests of two competing groups, the CBC and the Electronic Industry Association. The latter was anxious for the introduction of colour, the former opposed to it; both were motivated by financial considerations. The CBC's stance changed, however, once Expo '67 became imminent and the Government was prepared to provide additional capital financing. The Board proceeded to create the necessary standards and received applications for colour telecasting. As the Chairman said, "although colour was introduced during the period of the BBG, the Board could hardly take credit for this."

The move to utilize UHF channels seemed much like the cable issue, that is to be held up by governmental inability or unwillingness to reach firm policies on the subject. The Soble application for a new network provided ample opportunity to review policy concerning both UHF channels and satellite technology. The Board prepared recommendations, the government delayed. Certainly the Board could not be criticized for significantly delaying the move to UHF channels or satellite services. In fact, the Board's drawing the Soble application to the attention of the government held out some hope of hastening the government's consideration of the policy implications of the new technologies.

OWNERSHIP: The Broadcasting Act set down limitations on non-Canadian interests. The Board could not recommend the issuance of a licence to or grant permission for the operation of a network to anyone who was not a Canadian citizen or corporation, the chairman and two-thirds of the directors of which were Canadian citizens and of which at least three-quarters of the stock was held by Canadian citizens. The Governor-in-Council could grant exceptions. The Act was silent on matters of cross-media ownership.

The Board made no statement on non-Canadian interests believing that the Act was explicit enough on the subject. No American broadcasting interests were significantly associated with any applications for a second licence. Two British companies were involved. The Cabinet granted exemption to the Marconi Company for its involvement in the Montreal English channel. Granada TV was involved as a minority faction in the Ottawa licence as was NTA, an American film distributor. The Board made clear its negative views towards the involvement of American networks in Canadian television in its stance on the CFTO-TV Toronto reorganization.

On the matter of cross-media ownership, the Board seemed to take a pragmatic stance. Of the eight second licences granted, two (Calgary and Halifax) went to owners of radio stations and a radio station was involved in the ownership of a third (Winnipeg). Two radio applicants were unsuccessful. Film distributors were licensed or involved in three licences (Montreal French, Ottawa, and Toronto). Newspapers were involved in at least six applications but were successful in only one (Toronto). The Board took no action against existing cases of cross-media ownership, London, for instance, where the cable revolution began and where the Board did, of course, license additional radio stations.

Cabinet-Parliamentary Government and Federalism

The dictates of cabinet government and of the principles of ministerial responsibility create situations in the Canadian context in which the concept of the independent regulatory agency idealized in American literature is inapplicable. In a system of responsible government, the Cabinet is to retain control over and be held responsible for all public policy. On occasion the Cabinet or a minister is the agent officially designated as the regulatory authority, with the actual function merely delegated to the regulatory agency. Often the minister is empowered to issue binding directions to the agency. At times the agency is faced with regulating a crown corporation which reports to the same minister as the agency. Often the agency is dependent upon the administrative and political support or just plain goodwill of other ministers or departments. Hence the Canadian circumstance might be more accurately characterized as one of interdependence rather than independence.

Federalism, of course, imposes another set of pressures and constraints. Matters of divided or uncertain jurisdiction, of differing priorities, of differing and at times conflicting standards, are typical of the problem created by the existence of the two levels of government. Equally important are concerns over the standing of the other jurisdiction before the agencies of the first jurisdiction and over the matter of the appointment of individuals to the regulating agencies, federal or provincial. Finally, for the democratic parliamentary process of both levels, the evolution of the practice of "executive federalism" becomes increasingly significant.

LICENSING: The Minister of Transport was the licensing authority, although all licences required the approval of the Governor-in-Council. The Board's role was to inquire and recommend.

On only three occasions did ministers express their displeasure or desire for reversal of a licensing recommendation (Edmonton, Quebec City, St. John's). In each instance, the Board's recommendation stood. Given the number of licensing recommendations made during the period, the experience would seem to indicate a considerable congruence in thinking between the minister and the Board on licensing matters. Board recommendations were forwarded to the minister before being made public. Covert attempts to change them may have been made through individual members. Overt attempts were limited. As Dr. Stewart has suggested, members voted their individual consciences and he as Chairman had no way of determining whether or not their judgement was influenced by partisan political considerations. Perhaps ministers, regardless of political stripe, were content to let the Board's recommendations stand by themselves thus avoiding potential political flack.[11]

There was little concern expressed over the other subjects involved in Section 12 of the Act such as changes in power or transmitter sites except, of course, for the famous Barrie relocation case, where the Cabinet ignored the Board's recommendation.

MINISTERIAL DIRECTIVES: The minister had no directive power and one wonders if he had whether it would have been used. There seems to have been a tendency for ministers to shy away from communicating with the Board, even to the point of failing to respond to dozens of requests for policy guidelines on a range of subjects most of which involved in some way the CBC or the CBC-government relationship.

The reverse could be argued. Had the ministers possessed a directive power, they might have used it to inform the Board and the public of the government's attitude on particular policy matters. The Board's attempts at openness might have been undermined, however, if the industry turned to lobbying the minister behind closed doors. Regardless of the motivation, the issuing of the directive would make evident the direct political responsibility.

BOARD INDEPENDENCE: The matter of Board independence seems to have been achieved "de facto" almost against the Board's wishes. In discussing the phenomenon, two facets come to mind, licensing and policy-making. Policy-making is perhaps the more controversial issue. Is policy-making properly the function of the regulatory agency? Brown-John lists four functions of a regulatory agency, policy-making not amongst them.[12] Janisch and Baldwin argue that the regulatory agency should want and should have policy-making independence.[13] It would appear that the BBG was loathe to take unto itself independent policy-making functions. On a number of occasions, it made recommendations to the minister suggesting modifications of existing policies or new policy initiatives, but only after undue delay and frustration did it venture to develop its own policy statements and then not entirely happily. The ultimate enunciation of a policy statement concerning "The Extension of Alternative Television Services" was issued by the Board on 20 December 1962.

The Board's statement was finally issued after the Quebec City decision, but it did nothing to flush out a government policy, to make the St. John's decision any easier, or even to convince the minister to respond to the Board's query as to the Board's responsibilities to comment on the financial aspects of the CBC's applications.

At one point in time, the Secretary of the Treasury Board replied to a query about a particular policy area by stating that "although the matters which you now raise are important, they are matters which the Board of Broadcast Governors should more properly pursue in its examination of the Canadian Broadcasting Corporation's request for licenses."[14] A perfect Catch 22 situation!

Shortcomings in the Act were made all too evident. As CTV Network grew, so too did the problems arising out of the shortcomings. Yet no remedies were provided by either Conservative or Liberal Governments. The Board had no taxing power, it could not provide capital grants for the CBC nor could it require private stations to join CTV Network. These matters—finance and amendments to the Act—were beyond its competence. Only the government could take definitive action. In other areas, the development of policy for educational television for instance, the Board was also hampered by governmental inactivity or indecision.

SUPPORT FROM OTHER MINISTERS AND DEPARTMENTS: Overall, it would appear that governments wanted to keep clear of the controversies of broadcasting matters. A Conservative minister once admitted that "we set up the BBG to look after broadcasting; now it is up to them to do it."[15] The minister was asked to announce the new television regulations in 1959; he declined the honour, presumably wanting to distance himself from the substance of the regulations. The minister suggested that the Board draft an amendment to the Act to bring loan and management agreements under the Board's jurisdiction. The Board did as requested, but the minister did not follow through.

The Conservative attitude could perhaps be attributed to some or all of these attitudes:

1) We created the regulatory agency to look after broadcasting. Pride of parenthood precludes admitting deficiencies in our creation.

2) We created the regulatory agency to look after broadcasting. Let it get on with the job regardless of the difficulties in the Act.

3) We created the regulatory agency to look after broadcasting. We have enough political problems elsewhere. Let us not get into more at the moment by tampering with the Act now.

One can only speculate as to what the Conservatives might have done had they been returned to power in 1963.

The Liberals were not committed to the Board or to any of its decisions. At best, they were perplexed by the situation and caught in the cross currents of several politically sensitive circumstances.[16] There were some protestations by ministers that aspects of the Act or particular procedures had to be improved. Rather than take short-run measures, however, the Liberals seemed content to leave the Board in limbo while they worked on more permanent solutions—from the "Troika" of 1963 through the Committee on Broadcasting, 1965 and the White Paper, 1966 to the 1968 Act—a five year hiatus for the Board.

In terms of the Baldwin hypothesis concerning regulatory boards fighting for their survival, the BBG was in a difficult position, especially in relation to the Liberal Government. The Board made decisions which annoyed the Government; governmental supporters in the broadcasting community still turned to the Government on broadcasting matters expecting the Government to intervene; the Government could not issue formal directives to the Board; the Board had few inducements to offer those whom it was regulating. Perhaps it was too independent, or neglected; certainly it would appear to have been more independent or bereft of governmental direction or policy initiatives than it might have wished.

If an attempt was made to put broadcasting matters beyond the realm of "politics," the arrangements were perhaps backwards. The Board's powers in licensing matters were only of recommendation; the ultimate decision rested with the minister and the Governor-in-Council. Even in 1968, while the CRTC was empowered to grant licences, a power to review, set aside or refer back was retained by the Governor-in-Council. In the matter of public policy, however, a vacuum seemed to have developed in several areas in which the Board was more often than not left to fend for itself.

Finally, the tentative conclusion can be drawn here that appointments to the Board and to the senior staff of the Board had little direct impact on the independence of the Board.[17] Conservative governments appointed known Conservatives to the Board and Liberal governments appointed known Liberals, yet it seem impossible to associate this fact conclusively with the outcome of particular decisions. Other compelling factors can always be produced to support a particular decision. Political consanguinity, however, did not help the Board in its times of need.

As Doern suggests, if an agency or its actions are not subject to parliamentary review, there can be no guarantee that the agency is carrying out Parliament's will.[18] Overall, the Board was subject to several reviews in its ten-year life span—five parliamentary committees, the Committee on Broadcasting, 1965 and the self-analysis of the "Troika." While it is not our task to judge the quality of these various reviews, it seems fair to suggest that Parliament and/or the government had ample opportunity to study broadcasting and to alter the system as deemed appropriate. The BBG did operate in a glass house. It held no secrets from government; government ultimately controlled its independence, real or illusory. Clearly the Board needed independence from daily partisan pressures to build and preserve its credibility; equally it was to the government's advantage to appear to remove at least some matters from "politics." But Doern states:

That politics (in the sense of making value-laden choices) is not in fact removed by such steps, or that the appointed bureaucrats who take the elected politicians' place are *not* inherently more trustworthy or less subject to their own forms of professional and occupational "partisanship," will not, at such times, be likely to dissuade or impress those who advocate the need for independence. Nor should one underestimate the desire, and the need, of politicians at different times to escape the obligation to make "regulatory" choices (especially those which impose penalties as opposed to inducements) and hence their willingness to give such choices to others.[19]

In matters related to the federal system, the Board was again at the mercy of government. In the issues of educational television, cable and the extension of primary service, several aspects of public policy required discussions on the part of the federal government with the provinces, singly or collectively. The Board could not act independently; in each instance its actions were strained by existing policies or by the absence of clearly enunciated federal stands. In these three instances, little had been resolved by 1968.

Provincial premiers did become involved in the licensing process such as the interest displayed by Premier Thatcher in the CBC Saskatoon application or the appeals to Premier Smallwood in the CBC St. John's applications. These interventions by provincial authorities in licensing matters appear to be rare and of limited consequence.

THE CONCEPT OF GOVERNING INSTRUMENTS

Ideology, institutional forms and economic rationales form only part of the environment in which regulation takes place. Regulation itself implies the choice of one instrument from amongst a field of many.

> A regulation can be viewed politically as a rule of behaviour backed up more directly by the legitimate sanctions of the state. It is a more directly coercive way of achieving objectives and can be distinguished in part from somewhat more pleasant ways of governing such as spending (offering an incentive) or exhortation (soliciting voluntary compliance).[20]

The selection of a particular governing instrument can be exceedingly important politically as can be the amount of support provided for that chosen form once the decision has been made. "Subtle and not so subtle degrees of legitimate coercion are important."[21]

Doern suggests three ways in which the concept of governing instruments can aid in understanding the regulatory process. First is the relationship of the governing instrument to the annual priority-setting process of government. The second relates to the degree of harshness of regulatory instruments and the contention of Doern and Wilson that politicians tend to move in a continuum from the least coercive governing instruments to the most coercive. The third envisages a market place for the three types of governing instruments in which limitations on one will lead to an increased use of the other. Of the three types, for instance, a period of governmental financial restraint such as that of the early 1960s should enhance the use of regulation and/or exhortation as opposed to expenditure.

As Doern suggests, the government's priorities will give rise to differing regulatory responses—the fight against inflation, the Anti-Inflation Board; the reduction of regional disparity, transportation subsidies; the encouragement of second language training, increased transfer payments to the provinces; the encouragement of competition in the economy, the appointment of a royal commission; deficit reduction, budgetary cutbacks. Each response has varying impacts upon the federal budget, provincial budgets, federal-provincial relations, public-private sector relations, and the legislative process. The permutations and combinations are infinite. What of the implications of a policy for a broadcasting system essentially Canadian in content and character?

The various types of governing instruments can be differentiated by the degrees of directness or indirectness in applying legitimate coercion and by the size of the unit to which the coercion is applied.

In the market place of instruments, during a period in which high rates of government expenditures are being heavily criticized, one would expect greater reliance on instruments of exhortation and regulation than say increased governmental subsidies or financing for crown corporations.

Governing parties have particular goals in mind when seeking public office and, having achieved office, in choosing the specific instruments deemed most appropriate for implementing those goals. The basic goal, of course, is to retain power and to do so, to choose instruments which will "magnify the gain and depreciate the pain."[22] At the same time, given the fact that information and understanding are imperfect on all sides, it is likely that the politicians will seek instruments which will provide both reversibility and flexibility.[23]

Both major parties saw advantage in putting distance between themselves and broadcasting matters by choosing or supporting the use of the public corporation as both the regulatory and operating agency. Yet neither was willing to give up too much direct political control. The administration of the broadcast band still remained within departmental control under the direct authority of the Minister of Transport and the awarding of broadcasting licences, radio and television, remained, until 1968, the prerogative of the Governor-in-Council, on recommendation of the regulatory agency. The appearance of agency independence was fostered, for instance, by the refusal of either party to consider the inclusion in the 1936 or 1958 Broadcasting Acts of anything resembling the ministerial directive power possessed by British or Australian counterparts or by the continual refusal of ministers to answer questions in the House concerning matters not only of day to day administration but also of matters of broad policy. Further, successive governments refused to grant the CBC the form of financing thought appropriate to an independent agency and recommended by numerous investigative bodies. Government, however, was seldom unaware of the Board's thinking, if for no other reason than because of the policy vacuums created by government, it was necessary for the Board constantly to seek clarification of government attitudes.

The political parties did finally show differences of opinion over the nature and shape of the regulatory process, the Conservatives arguing that the goals of national unity and cultural development could better be served through a freer play of market forces and the separation of the regulatory and operating functions earlier amalgamated by the Liberals in the CBC.

With the BBG as the new regulatory agency, however, great differences between the parties did not develop with regard to the governing instruments to be used by the Board. Throughout the ten-year period, these instruments remained essentially unchanged. They were contained in the Broadcasting Act and the Act was not altered by either party. The Board was given extensive responsibilities under the Broadcasting Act, especially those growing out of Section 10, and it had a number of specific powers related to those responsibilities (Sect. 11, 12, 13 and 14). It recommended to the minister the granting of licences, radio and television (Section 12); it granted permission to operate networks (Section 12); it could require stations to affiliate with the CBC networks (Section 13); it enforced the new station ownership provisions (Section 14); it exercised control over program standards (Section 11b), the character of commercials (Section 11c), and the time devoted to advertising (Section 11c); it sanctioned affiliation agreements (Section 13); it could compel stations to broadcast network programs considered of public interest; it could make regulations about the employment of Canadian talent (Section 11e); and, it possessed the authority to scrutinize all operations, including finance and programs as its regulations might specify (Section 11(i)).

By way of penalizing those who transgressed its conditions of licence or affiliation agreements, the Board could, after a public hearing, suspend a licence for a period of up to three months (Section 15(1)). The licensee could appeal to the courts on any question of law (Section 15(3)). The Board could also seek summary conviction for violations of other provisions of the Act or its subsequent regulations.

In terms of Doern's three ways of analyzing the concept of governing instruments, we note first that the broadcasting field seemed to rank low in terms of the annual priority-setting process of government. The Conservatives came to power committed to bring change to the broadcasting scene and did so in short order by creating the BBG and by sanctioning the licensing of the second television network and the creation of the Canadian content regulations. It achieved its goals with relatively inexpensive instruments—the licensing and regulatory powers. The Government restrained expenditures on the CBC, however, and gave to the BBG no power to offer financial inducements to the public or private sectors and questionably useful punitive powers to be used against those who transgressed the Act or its regulations. While the impact of the policies on the public treasury was limited, the impact on individual stations or groups of stations could be significant in light of possibly increased competition and increased production costs.

The Liberals returned to power perplexed by the new situation and unsure of their own commitment to the single system. Hence they turned to the traditional delay tactic, the appointment of investigative bodies to recommend changes while at the same time retaining for the next five years the regulatory structure and priorities which they had inherited.

In terms of a continuum of governing instruments running from lenient to coercive, the Board's arsenal was skewed to the lenient end. Looked at in terms of Lowi's fourfold classification of policy outputs, some of the Board's activities were distributive, others redistributive, still others regulative and finally, some constituent.[24] Each genre carried with it varying degrees of coercion. Recommendations of a licence or the creation of a network were distributive and obviously the least coercive. Content regulations and others carrying criminal penalties were more coercive. The Board distributed licences; it attempted to redistribute profits from station to station, region to region; it regulated ownership and Canadian content; and it created networks. Its use of instruments varied in each case.

Even if the Board chose to be coercive in enforcing its regulations, its options were limited. Suspension of a licence for a minor infraction of a regulation was recognized as heavy-handed. Seeking summary conviction under the Criminal Code was time-consuming, expensive and of limited utility. From 1959 to mid-1965, 20 prosecutions were pressed for infringements of its regulations. Of these, one brought a $5.00 fine, seven $25.00 fines, three fines of $150.00, $340.00 and $380.00 respectively, three withdrawals and four in which counsel had been instructed or judgement was pending. The punishments were hardly draconian.[25] Could the Board have appealed the courts' decisions?

As Doern suggests, the market for governing instruments implies shifts in policy between regulation, expenditure and exhortation, the last being the least coercive, the first being the most. The Board at no time had opportunity to offer direct financial inducements, although it could offer them indirectly by modifying or relaxing its regulations. It did so with regard to the content regulations in the summers of 1962, 1963 and 1964 and by the granting of extra advertising time in programs classified as Canadian. Only the government could offer direct financial inducements and, especially during periods of restraint, it was loathe to do so.

The Board's main method of operating was through exhortation. This was so in part because of its limited powers with regard to the private stations and its uncertain powers with regard to the CBC, in part because of the conciliatory personality of its Chairman. It was in his nature to seek amicable solutions to problems on the assumption that reasonable people, given a reasonable amount of time, could reach reasonable solutions.

POLICY, ORGANIZATIONAL FORMS AND ADMINISTRATION
The day-to-day regulatory process can involve more detailed choices than suggested by broad categories of regulation, expenditure and exhortation. This is true both in terms of the finer range of regulatory instruments available and in terms of the kinds of organizations through which these instruments might be utilized. The regulatory process may include, for example, sanctions such as imprisonment, fines, suspension or revocation of licences and reporting requirements. Spending instruments could include grants, subsidies, transfer payments, conditional or shared grants and research support. Information programs, research and consultative or advisory committees could be possible amongst the exhortatory instruments.

As Doern points out, even those finer delineations need further examination to be understood fully as part of the regulatory process. Policy objectives, for instances, may be derailed if the regulatory function is housed in one government organization and the expenditure function in another. One may not always know what the other is doing or be supportive even if it does know. As well, the so-called regulatory agencies may do more than just regulate and their willingness or ability to be aggressive regulators may well depend upon their relations vis-à-vis the regulated in regard to adjudication of disputes, research, distribution of subsidies or policy advice.

It is important to stress that the regulatory processes are not confined to regulatory activity precisely because the specific organizations that regulate are not usually just performing regulatory functions, nor can the resolution of the policy problems, or the implementation of policy objectives, usually be achieved only by regulatory means.[26]

Three subsidiary issues flow from these observations. The first deals with the extent of discretion held by the agency both over the interpretation of the policy mandate and over procedures. The second concerns the differences in organizational forms between regular departments and independent boards or commissions. The third issue involves the relationship between regulation-making and compliance within the regulating organization.

Agencies do hold and exercise discretion as to which aspects of the mandate will be emphasized and with what degree of openness the mandate will be pursued. Who will be consulted, and at what point in the regulatory process? What monitoring will be done or reporting required and what results of monitoring or reporting will be made public and to whom? Doern contends that the more closed the process, the more likely that the affected groups will consider themselves to be the objects of arbitrary power.[27]

The multi-functionary nature of some boards may make them more negotiating tribunals than regulatory agencies and the representational virtue of some multi-member boards or commissions may raise expectations of greater consultation with affected interests.

As to the organizational form, Doern notes that the distinction between the departmental and agency form may be illusory. On the surface of it, the regulatory department is more susceptible to ministerial and cabinet control than the quasi-independent board yet myriad factors may affect the operation of each to nullify the apparent differences. Is there a difference in legitimacy of powers exercised by elected politicians as opposed to those exercised by collective boards appointed by the elected politicians? Both are, in theory, subject to being captured by the interests they are intended to regulate. Both must develop good relations with these same interests or regulation becomes nearly impossible. Effective implementation of regulation obviously requires a considerable amount of voluntary compliance on the part of those being regulated. This must be accomplished by either type without too many enforcers being necessary.

Hence we come to the third issue of regulation versus compliance. Most Canadian agencies tend to be understaffed. The staff necessary to develop and maintain monitoring and compliance procedures and technology has often been sparsely provided. The tendency has developed on occasion to "piggy-back" compliance needs, that is to service the needs of one agency with the staff of another agency already in the field. Such activities are popular with politicians and Treasury officials in times of financial restraint.

PRACTICE VS. THEORY: In theory, the range of instruments can vary from the regulatory with coercive sanctions through the spending with monetary or other inducements to the exhortatory. The first category could include sanctions such as fines, suspension or revocation of licences and reporting requirements. In the Board's case, suspension of licence was provided for in the Act as the penalty for failure to abide by conditions of licence or of affiliation agreements and stations were required to report information to the Board at regular intervals—program logs monthly and financial statements annually. The Board had complete discretion in enforcing these regulations and seldom extracted the ultimate penalty.

Information collection was a necessity for the Board even though some stations did consider the reporting procedures to be a nuisance. The task was not a terribly burdensome one, when compared with what was to follow under the aegis of the CRTC.

The White Paper did recommend a more complicated form of content regulation and minimum public service programming to be determined on an individual basis taking into account the circumstances of the licensee or groups of licensees.[28] These standards were to be incorporated as conditions of licence of individual licensees. The Board envisioned in the White Paper was to be empowered to inflict monetary penalties for breaches of regulation or failure to comply with the conditions of licence. In the latter case, there would also be the power to suspend or revoke the licence.[29] The BBG did not have this flexibility although such was granted to the CRTC.

In the second category, that of spending instruments, the Board had no powers to dispense grants, subsidies or transfer payments. It did, however, have a number of inducements at its disposal which it could offer its clientele. At one end of the scale, it could offer meeting space and facilities as it did to the Provisional Committee on Educational Television. At the opposite extreme, it could vary conditions of licence as it did with the CBC licence in St. John's to the benefit of CJON-TV or alter capital financing plans as it did in the CFTO-TV reorganization. It could affect whole industries as it did the television set manufacturers with regard to the introduction of colour telecasting or the move to the UHF band. In these instances, of course, final responsibility lay with the government. The Board could, however, approve domestic or foreign network affiliations and declined to approve any foreign affiliation. It monitored the purchase of individual programs or program packages from foreign sources and could, although it never did, refuse any such arrangements. It could and did vary the Canadian content regulations in the summers of 1962, 1963 and 1964. It attempted to use regulations, without success, to foster an animated cartoon industry in Canada. It declined the opportunity to vary its content regulation to help foster the making of television commercials in Canada although it did offer extra advertising time in Canadian programs. In sum, the Board had a number of inducements with monetary implications which it could and did use, primarily, it would seem, to sustain the system as inherited and to attempt to expand it, without cost of quality, to provide greater coverage and variety for the Canadian viewer and listener.

The third area was clearly the one in which most of the Board's efforts lay—that of exhortation. Where it lacked regulatory or expenditure powers, the Board could only exhort those it hoped to move in a particular direction. The Board could work through its two committees on Public and Private Broadcasting, it could provide all manner of information concerning market capacity or industry profits, its Chairman could visit the localities involved in a form of elite accommodation but it could not force the various elements of the system to accept its vision of the bright new day. Given its limited regulatory powers and heavy reliance on exhortatory techniques, it would seem correct to characterize the Board as more of a negotiating than a regulatory tribunal.[30]

As the Board needed the co-operation of those whom it was designed to regulate to give effect to concepts such as equalization, it could not alienate them by overly draconian regulation, nor could it offer direct economic benefits to win them over. It would seem that governments of both political persuasions, which could not help but be aware of the situation, did not want to lose friends in the media world or alienate those not enthralled with Canadian programming by enhancing the Board's regulatory powers. In essence, governments were indulging in symbolic politics.

The Board was also faced with what might be termed a split between the regulatory and expenditure functions. While some of its actions could affect the financial status of the public and private sectors, it was powerless to have any effect upon one of the main expenditure areas, that of the capital financing of the CBC. As well it had no direct control over the broadcast band and decisions such as the opening of the UHF segment.

In terms of the amount of discretion exercised in interpreting its mandate and procedures, the Board seemed to exercise a reasonably free hand, but only within the serious constraints of government policy or non policy. For instance, it chose to emphasize the "basically Canadian in content and character" aspect of Section 10 of the Act, but it did not enforce rigorously the ownership provisions of Section 14. Even in enforcing the content regulations, it was restrained in part by the limited range of sanctions available under the Act. In its pursuit of another major priority, that of the development of the second network and of the extension of primary service, it was constantly bedeviled by the lack of clarity in the governments' policies toward the CBC.

The Broadcasting Act laid down certain procedures which the Board had to follow as for instance in the holding of a public hearing on an application for a licence before making a recommendation to the minister. In most other matters relating to procedures, the Board held complete discretion and decided on its own initiative, for instance, what matters not required by the Act to go to a public hearing should do so. The frequency, length and rules of procedure of public hearings were at the Board's discretion as well, as was the choice as to whom the Board would consult in reaching its decisions. The Board tried to be as open as possible with the industry, with affected and interested pressure groups and with the general public.

The two consultive committees provided regular means of communication with the CBC and the CAB. While their use tended to diminish after 1964, so too had passed the most creative period of the Board wherein new waters were being charted, new problems created and the need for consultation the greatest.

While the bulk of public hearings were held in Ottawa, a significant number were held in various parts of the country, usually at a place near the major focus of attention of the particular hearing. The Board had no branch offices, so documentation was available only from Ottawa. The Chairman tried to keep hearings as informal as possible and encouraged applicants to appear in person rather than be represented by counsel. The Chairman and other full-time members of the Board spoke regularly across the country, often, as Dr. Stewart evidenced in speaking to the Electronic Industries Association Annual Meeting in 1964 or the service clubs in Brandon and Moncton, carrying the message into the lion's den and, of course, receiving feedback therefrom. The Board did guard cautiously some of the data provided to it, especially matters dealing with the financial standing of individual stations. Such action was necessary to maintain the confidence of the organizations providing the data. Overall, however, the Board seemed to maintain a general openness which could hardly lead any of its affected groups to "consider themselves to be objects of arbitrary power."[31]

The Board was not only multi-functional, it was also multi-membered and one gets the impression that this representational role put stresses and strains on the Board in fulfilling its regulatory function. Not only in the period of mixed-partisan membership when Liberal appointees were supplanting Conservative appointees, but also in periods where the bulk of the Board membership was of the persuasion of the governing party, there were splits (regional, ideological, personality) in the Board which led to deep divisions (e.g., Quebec City, Barrie) and to at least two members of the Board seeking to make contact with members of the Cabinet. Such circumstances strained the collegiality of the Board and made life much more difficult for its Chairman. In point of fact, however, he was able to conduct the Board's meetings with sufficient consensus so that as late as 1966, the need for a procedural by-law had not been encountered.

The structural form of the Board seemed to have considerable bearing on its operations. In some circumstances, interested parties seemed to think of the Board as a department and of going to the minister to affect policy as one would in a regular department. The Board was able to treat ensuing ministerial reaction with impunity, although the Cabinet's reactions to particular decisions in the long run helped shape the new legislation.[32]

Doern suggests that most Canadian regulatory agencies are understaffed and short of personnel to maintain monitoring and compliance procedures. The BBG is perceived to have been no exception to this generalization. While its budget was underspent each year, the amount underspent averaged about only $20,000 per annum.[33] That would not buy many competent people. With greater personnel resources, more monitoring could have been undertaken and greater research and enforcement possibly achieved. Historically, the industry saw the Board to be understaffed and thus not a terribly ferocious policeman.

Also, in terms of what Doern refers to as "piggy-backing," certain functions performed by the broadcasting regulatory agencies in the United Kingdom and Australia lay not with the BBG but with the Department of Transport. The prime example in question was that the control of the broadcast band. While the Board had its own technical advisor, ultimate jurisdiction over the band and most technical matters lay with the Department which, of course, was subject to direct ministerial control. Contrary to Doern's suggestion that such piggy-backing might be undertaken for financial reasons during periods of financial restraint, at no time had any Canadian broadcasting regulatory agency been entrusted with control of the broadcast portion of the radio spectrum. The relationship with the Department of Transport was not without its complications.

Legal and Procedural Determinants

The regulatory process has become surrounded by a conflict between formality and informality, between public and private interests, between what has been termed lawyers' values and civil servants' values.[34] The right of the individual to be heard before a regulatory agency plus concern for the costs of such a hearing must always be balanced against the fact that, especially where the economic stakes are great, expert will be pitted against expert and matters both procedural and substantive will be constantly challenged. The reconciliation of the conflicting claims of openness and informal ease of access over and against those of expertise and formal proceedings is clearly difficult to obtain.

It was the Board's custom to strive for as great informality as possible. While the Board initially questioned intervenors at public hearings through counsel, members then posed their own questions less formally. The Board encouraged applicants to appear in support of their applications so that it could judge in person the mark of the potential licensee. The more complex the subject matter of the hearing, or the greater the economic stakes, the greater the likelihood that counsel would appear on behalf of clients, but the Board did always insist on cross-examining the applicant personally. The Board did try to downplay lawyers' values.

The Regulators

A knowledge of the background of those who make up the regulatory boards and commissions may lead to a clearer understanding of their behaviour. Career patterns and relationships to the regulated interests or associated groups may help explain behaviour as may a knowledge of any distinctions between the chairman and full-time members and these and the part-time members. The Doern work looks at the regulators in terms of their professional experience, education, francophone representation, age and sex.

THE BOARD: In the matter of appointments, 40 appointments were made to the BBG, 21 by the Conservatives and 19 by the Liberals. The number includes the appointment of six full-time members (Stewart, Duhamel, Allison, Goulet, Juneau and Sim)[35] and 33 part-time appointments, including Messrs. Brown and Gagnon who appear twice having been appointed by the Conservatives and reappointed by the Liberals.

Perhaps the most noteworthy feature of the appointments of either party as far as occupation is concerned is the almost total absence of anyone with broadcasting knowledge or experience. The Act, of course, precluded the appointment of anyone "engaged in the business of broadcasting." Mr. Goulet through his Radio and Television Productions firm was the only appointee with any sustained experience in the entertainment or broadcasting world. Mr. Juneau had held a number of appointments in the National Film Board.

The Conservative appointments were fairly evenly spread through people with backgrounds in business, the law, journalism, education and social service work (three each) but with two drawn from other professions and one each from the civil service, agriculture and labour. One person, not included in the figures, resigned on the day of his appointment.

The Liberal appointees were much more oriented toward business (seven), law or other professions (four) and education (four) for a total of 15 out of 19. The other four were associated with the civil service (two), agriculture or social service work.[36]

In a socio-economic sense, the appointments were representative of a cross section of middle-class Canada but with few names which had anything but an Anglo-Saxon or Francophone ring to them or which would have received national recognition. Most were prominent in their regions. In a geographic sense, the Board was well representative of the country, each province being represented by at least one appointee until the Liberals failed to appoint someone to represent Saskatchewan. Each party appointed two women. The Conservatives appointed a slightly higher percentage of Francophones than did the Liberals but, at an average of 23.01% of appointments during the ten-year period, both were below the percentage of Francophones in the overall population.

There appeared to be no great career patterns evident amongst the members, full-time or part-time. Dr. Stewart evidenced his willingness to make way for a successor from 1963 onward. Mr. Allison would apparently have liked a reappointment, but partisan considerations precluded that although they did not seem to justify the scurrilous treatment bestowed upon him. Mr. Duhamel left to become the Queen's Printer. Mr. Goulet died in office and Mr. Sim's was clearly a stop-gap appointment. Mr. Juneau had expectations, later to be fulfilled, with regard to the successor body.

What can be said about both the process and the outcome of the process of appointment? Clearly, Dr. Stewart was not impressed with the process. He had to live with what the partisan process threw up, and as he says, while that was geographically representative, there was nothing to lead one to believe that their collective views were reflective of public opinion or of what Parliament would have done in any particular circumstance. While admitting that partisan pressures were not openly noted in Board proceedings (votes were taken by secret ballot), Dr. Stewart suggested that the perceptions of partisan favouritism inherent in the appointments helped diminish the credibility of the Board. Especially after the patronage issue in the 1984 federal election campaign, it is perhaps wise to heed his suggestion that there must be a better way of appointing persons to quasi-judicial national agencies. One wonders if the appearance of prospective appointees before parliamentary committees could improve the process. Yet the positions must be filled. The media's penchant for labelling all such appointments as "patronage" in a pejorative sense does not help to create a positive image.[37]

THE SENIOR STAFF: The senior staff came to the Board after incredible delays as a result of Civil Service Commission procedures. Again they seemed not to be career oriented in the broadcasting world. This phenomenon bears out another Doern observation that, to a significant extent, Canadian regulators are drawn from bureaucratic careers as

opposed to the industry regulated.[38] They came from diverse bureaucratic quarters and went in equally diverse ways. A few remained with
the CRTC. Fewer went into activities in the broadcasting world. They
were, almost without exception, civil servants, not broadcasters and
had little to gain by way of career advancement through currying
favour with the regulated industry.

Evidence is also presented of the Board's dependence upon another
department of government, the Department of Transport, both for
much data and for the initial approval of applications which the
Board would later consider. As well, we see signs of the Board's multi-
functional role not only as regulator, but also as adjudicator, consultant and advisor and of its obvious need to rely on a number of governing instruments, not just the regulatory. Clearly exhortation would
play an important role in the Board's activities, in part, because of the
gaps in policy and the impasses in the policy-making process with
which it had to live. Relations with the Civil Service Commission were
at times frustrating and with the Treasury Board, businesslike.

Overall, there were few experts in the ranks of the Board or its
staff. This phenomenon could not help but make it more dependent
upon groups outside itself for information, opinions and advice. This
very dependence and the ensuing consultation in turn in the eyes of
some justified the accusations of agency capture.

DAY-TO-DAY FACTORS INFLUENCING REGULATORY
AGENCY BEHAVIOUR

THE SCOPE OF THE LEGISLATIVE MANDATE AND THE DEGREES OF
CONFLICT AMONG THE GOALS THE AGENCY IS EXPECTED TO PURSUE
The scope of the Board's legislative mandate was fairly considerable
particularly in the light of the broad strokes of Section 10 of the Act—
the purpose of ensuring the continued existence and efficient operation of a national broadcasting system—the provision of a varied and
comprehensive broadcasting service of a high standard that is basically Canadian in content and character—the regulation of the estab-

lishment and operation of networks of broadcasting stations, the activities of public and private broadcasting stations in Canada and the relationship between them and, finally—the provision for the final determination of all matters and questions in relation thereto.

The mandate was there but its goals, if not in conflict, were somewhat ambiguous and the powers necessary to achieve them clearly lacking. What was "a national broadcasting system"? What was a "varied and comprehensive" service? What was a high standard of programming? What constituted a network? What was to be the appropriate relationship between the public and private sectors? The Act was silent on these and many other issues. The Board, on a trial and error basis had, from day-to-day, to seek out answers with powers not always equal to the task. The Board was faced with possibly conflicting legislative goals, a legislative mandate supported by inadequate or inappropriate powers and governments which delayed interminably in coming to grips with the situation.

The Board inherited the results of the single station policy and was expected to implement a two stations or alternative service policy. Yet, as a throwback to the past, it could direct private stations to affiliate only with the CBC network. It could not direct a station to add a rebroadcasting station and it questioned its own authority to become involved in rate setting. All three factors greatly complicated the Board's efforts to extend alternate service, even to the point where the Board feared that CTV Network might collapse through internal dissention over the implications of the Board's equalization policies. The Board in its attempts to limit the profits of some stations had to cajole the Network into spreading these profits around. The Board could not direct such a move and some network members were not enthusiastic about being asked to subsidize the development of alternative services. Did this equalization policy in itself not conflict with the Canadian content policies? Some were even unhappy about the Board's definition of a network and threatened a legal challenge of it. The Board regretted the absence of an appropriate definition in the Act. Coupled with its inadequate powers vis-à-vis the private sector were, of course, the forbidding uncertainties concerning the CBC, its role in the development of alternative services, its financing and its relations with the Board.

The Board despaired of the Conservatives ever making changes, so it pressed on with its own tentative policy statements regarding the CBC. After the 1963 election, the Board explained at great length to the new Prime Minister and Secretary of State the nature of the situation, even requesting an early and comprehensive review of broadcasting policy and of the Broadcasting Act. Reviews continued for nearly five years.

Similar situations existed in other areas. In educational television, cable, colour and the UHF Band, the Board was dependent upon policy decisions, the taking of which rested with the government. Often the decision-making process was protracted. But such was the day-to-day life of a pioneer—faced with new challenges, uncertainties and frustrations.

THE DEGREE OF MULTI-FUNCTIONALITY OF THE AGENCY

In Doern's terms, the Board was indeed multi-functional. He suggests at least six functions, the regulative, the adjudicative, the expenditure, the consultative, the advisory and the research functions. As evidenced by the Canadian content regulations and the ownership provisions, the Board did regulate, even if not as rigorously as some might have wished. As well, it did play an adjudicative role in recommending amongst competing applicants for licences, in settling differences over affiliation agreements and in handling disputes between the networks such as the Grey Cup affair. While it had no direct expenditure function, its actions did have financial implications for the industry, individually or collectively. The consultative role was on-going through the two standing committees and through ad hoc committees, conferences and public hearings. So too was the advisory role as government and other interested parties constantly sought the Board's advice, especially after the review process was started in 1963. The research function was perhaps the one least stressed although the senior staff of the Board did produce research papers for the Board in the technical, cultural and economic fields. As well private firms such as

Touche, Ross and Communications Associates and academics from the university community were hired on contract to undertake research on specific topics.

It is doubtful if the Board saw its functions divided into such neat compartments. As Dr. Stewart suggests, he was there to preside over "the administration of broadcasting" and saw the Board's main functions as related to licensing and regulation.

Opportunities for and Modes of Cabinet and Ministerial Intervention

Meetings with the Prime Ministers of the day were few in number and seemed largely related to Dr. Stewart's future as Chairman. Conversations with ministers responsible were more numerous, but not necessarily more productive than that when Miss LaMarsh chastised the Board for not being tough enough on the private broadcasters. As a portent of things to come, we are told of Dr. Stewart's feeling that after the 1963 election the Liberal Government was not committed to the Board or to any of its decisions.

The opportunities for the Cabinet collectively or ministers individually to review the Board's activities seem extensive. In addition to such normal procedures as the annual report to Parliament and the almost regular reviews such as the "Troika," the Committee on Broadcasting, 1965, the White Paper review and the Cabinet Committee on Broadcasting, numerous other review opportunities were provided.

The Chairman's personal interviews with the minister were not uncommon.[39] The Chairman was also called before Cabinet and parliamentary committees. The Board presented draft material to the minister on a number of occasions beginning with the initial regulations to be used in the introduction of the second stations and continuing through to the proposals for opening of the UHF band. Included were draft statements for responses to questions asked in the House of Commons and for use in press statements related to Board recommendations such as the recommendation that the licence of CJOR Vancouver not be renewed. The Chairman sat with the minister during discussions of the Board's estimates in the House of Commons. The minister was made aware of the Board's views on a wide range of subjects varying from CBC licences through cable policy and the Barrie affair to the UHF problem. Some ministers had confidential knowledge of and tried to postpone or revise at least three Board decisions. The Chairman knew of other occasions on which members of the government of the day sought to influence members of the Board on particular cases. At one time, he wrote to the minister deploring the discussion of political considerations by members of the Board outside of Board meetings. The minister sought regular advice on the potential impact of CATV applications. As well, the Prime Minister sought advice with regard to the UHF band. On two occasions, the Cabinet directed the Board to do specific things—to co-ordinate federal policy in educational television and to undertake a study of CATV. While there were appeals possible from other quarters to the minister, the only one mentioned is that of Mr. Stirling in the Barrie case.

Overall, with regard to Cabinet and minister, the impression derived is more one of opportunities lost than of heavy hands being exercised upon the Board. For example, the minister sought amendments to the Act to give the Board powers over corporate loans but nothing was done with the drafts presented to him. Another time, no comment was made on the Board's oversight in failing to consider the CBC as a second station applicant in drafting the network regulations. As well, no advice was given to the BBG as to what to expect or how to handle CBC applications for second stations. Nor was advice given on extension of second service to less populated areas. A final example, no understanding of or support for the principle the Board saw in the Grey Cup issue was given.

On balance relations with the minister and Cabinet were not constructive. To the extent that the system as it evolved was increasing viewer choice through the introduction of alternative service and the extension of primary service, the Cabinet, in its hands-off attitude, was perhaps reflecting public opinion, happy with the wider choice even at the expense of CBC hegemony.

AGENCY DEPENDENCE ON ITS CLIENTELE

The Board's dependence on its clientele for research and information seemed to vary from subject to subject. In terms of the operations of the stations being regulated, the Board was largely dependent on information provided by the industry through regular reports from program logs and from financial reports submitted annually. It did, however, at a later point in time have doubts about the validity of this data as it commissioned Touche, Ross to audit the accounts of all television stations to ensure the Board had adequate information on station profits and to develop a reporting system which would enable the Board to be well-informed on a continuing basis about revenues and costs in the private sector.

On industry-wide matters, the Board seemed less well informed and in many instances had to rely upon or, as a matter of courtesy, canvass opinion from the industry in order to formulate recommendations.

ROLE OF AGENCY LEADERS AND SENIOR STAFF

Obviously, in a body the size and nature of the BBG, the Chairman will set the tone of the organization. This tone was one of caution, reason and hard work tempered with a quiet sense of humour. As has been suggested on more than one occasion, the Chairman held to the belief that full, frank and reasonable discussion could lead to a fitting solution of almost any problem. He was to be disappointed more than once in dealing with the CBC, CTV and particularly the government of the day. Still, he retained his sense of balance and he continued to try to give leadership under difficult circumstances, first in the creation of the new network, in the extension of the second services and in the attempted implementation of the concept of equalization as a means of expanding service and reducing oligopoly profits. There was always the desire on his part to see both sides of the story and to search for a fair and dispassionate assessment directed toward just and reasonable solutions. The Board's actions were not, however, always in like spirit.

That the Board was perceived by some to be lenient toward the private broadcasters is perhaps more a result of the Chairman's mode of operation than of actual fact. The Board went to considerable length to explain its predicament concerning the expansion of both the CBC and the private network, but it did not, or more likely could not, explain this in meaningful terms to the public. So it had to hope that the government would take heed and bestow upon the Board greater powers—powers eventually granted to the successor body. If the Board had had the power to order affiliation with CTV Network, what a different picture it would have been. Better still, what if it could have offered subsidies to CTV Network to go into unprofitable areas as the Canadian Transportation Commission could then do with railways? Then surely, the nature of the problem would have been more clear and the image of leniency would have been less likely.

The senior staff came to the Board after incredible delays as a result of Civil Service Commission procedures. Again they seemed not to be oriented to broadcasting careers. Their prime contribution was in keeping the Board well entrenched within the bureaucratic structure vis-à-vis the Department of Transport, the Treasury Board, the Queen's Printer, the Civil Service Commission and the other empires within the governmental labyrinth. They laboured long and hard in the vineyard.

THE NATURE AND EVOLUTION OF CLIENTELE PRESSURE

Pressure from the industry on the Board came in a variety of forms: through the industry association, the CAB; through the network collective, CTV; or through individual stations. The legitimacy of such pressure was recognized almost from the beginning by the formation of the Consultative Committee on Private Broadcasting. The meetings with the Committee to discuss the proposed TV regulations provide an example of it as a forum for the exchange of views and information between the Board and the industry.

Pressure from CTV Network varied. In the first instance it came largely from one person, Spencer Caldwell. At times there were countervailing views expressed by the stations associated with the Network, the ITO. When the Network was mutualized, the two groups in effect became one, but the need to press views on the Board did not diminish. The Board also needed the Network's and stations' views to ascertain the impact of its regulations and where amendments might be in order. Also, it had to be recognized that the members of the Network did not necessarily speak with a single voice, and that the Board had its views, welcome or unwelcome, to get across to the Network and stations.

Pressures from individual stations obviously varied according to the circumstances. The reports of their dire financial plights lead to a reduction of the summer content quotas. Their own interests lead them to oppose certain proposals such as a second CBC network or the continued expansion of wired systems. Some worked as lobby groups, stirring up support amongst the public for second stations. CFTO-TV favoured the introduction of colour while most other private stations were ambivalent on the subject.

State enterprise, in the form of the CBC, also had strong views to present on many subjects. Again the formation of the Consultative Committee on Public Broadcasting provided a vehicle for regular exchanges of views. As with the private network, however, views of the private affiliates sometimes differed from those of the CBC itself. The affiliates, for instance, believed themselves disadvantaged by a proposal which would allow the other private stations to use CBC material in nonprime time while, as part of their affiliation agreement, they would have to use it in prime time. Similarly, they opposed private rebroadcasting stations and instead proposed the "twin-sticking" principle. The Corporation had views on virtually every subject of interest to the Board. Some of the most notable spectacles came in licence applications when the CBC opposed the applications of private stations and vice versa. Such circumstances also brought out endless numbers of groups in support of the CBC or the private application. The CBC brought particular pressure to bear in matters such as its opposition to proposals of the private broadcasters and in the development of educational television.

Not unnaturally, pressure came from related industries as well. The animated cartoon producers appeared early on the scene to seek protection—to no avail—as did church groups seeking to gain Canadian content quotas for American educational material—again to no avail. The community antenna interests were active early in the period arguing against any further regulation and expressing opposition to any freeze on cable development. The Electronic Industry Association was keenly interested in the introduction of colour. Adult education associations were active in encouraging educational television and the opening of the UHF band.

The provinces appeared in a number of instances—in the attempt to foster primary service in remote areas or in the field of educational television. Alberta and Ontario were particularly active in this area. Some provinces, frustrated by federal delays, threatened to set up their own systems and import American programs directly.

Pressure also came from the mass media, largely the newspapers in the form of editorials and letters to the editor. Local licence applications brought out local comment and events such as the 1962 Grey Cup game brought national reaction.

The views of various publics were represented by private organizations which appeared at Board hearings such as the CBL, the Canadian Federation of Agriculture, ACTRA and Canadian Association for Adult Education. Less well organized voices were not as fully represented before the BBG as before the CRTC in a later era when the CRTC, with more generous funding, was able to subsidize interveners to appear before it.

The ultimate pressure came from the viewers in the form of complaints to the Board about the quality of Canadian programming or in the form of audience rating figures which showed Canadians voting against Canadian programming. As with election polls, one wonders if they were an accurate reflection of the public taste and public interest.

[14]

"CAPTURE THEORY" AND THE BOARD'S EFFECTIVENESS

THE BBG WAS NOT WITHOUT its critics. Many argued, especially with what was perceived to be the Board's "soft" attitude on the Canadian content regulations, that it had surrendered to or been captured by those whom it was supposed to regulate. This line of criticism was based largely on the "capture theory" developed by Marver Bernstein. A set of more specific criticisms was contained in the *Report* of the Committee on Broadcasting, 1965, dealing with the Board's effectiveness and the stewardship of its resources.

BERNSTEIN'S CAPTURE THEORY

Bernstein developed the capture theory out of an analysis of American regulatory experience.[1] It suggests that a regulatory agency goes through a predictable life-cycle. Initially, it is vigorous and regulates aggressively, having behind it the initial popular support of that group which influenced the legislature to establish the agency. As the agency matures, however, that popular support falls away and the agency stands along dealing largely with its clientele, those whom it was created to regulate. As its support group diminishes, the agency's range of interests also diminishes to the point where it comes to think like those it is regulating. In effect, it becomes captured by them.

259

Bernstein's theory has been questioned on several grounds. First of all, as a theory it is subject to the fact of nonfalsifiability. Secondly, many agencies are given a positive, quasi-promotional role to play and hence the "captivity" is built in. Thirdly, it is argued that the very lack of statutory precision makes it necessary for the agency to use day-by-day, case-by-case methods of conduct that require amicable relations with the regulated if they are to succeed.

Two further qualifications not present in the American scene from which Bernstein derived his theory are present in the Canadian context. Canada's major regulatory agencies have historically been given a larger managerial role over the policy field than their American counterparts. They are something more than merely regulatory policemen. "If captivity exists, it is more of a governmental or state captivity, rather than a clientele captivity as such."[2] Secondly, in the Canadian context there already exist and probably will continue to do so, countervailing forces (e.g., provincial governments; public-interest groups, some even funded by the Crown) which act as counter-balances to the activities of the agency and lessen the possibility of its capture.

In the application of this thesis to the BBG, five areas of alleged capture (Canadian content, the structure and development of CTV, extension of second television stations, cable policy and the introduction of colour) have been examined in detail and the following conclusions reached.

The Board's interest in and contacts with the private sector were considerable and varied. Formal contacts took place on a regular basis through the public hearing process and through the workings of the Consultative Committee on Private Broadcasting, as they did with the CBC through the Consultative Committee on Public Broadcasting. Activities within the former Committee were particularly great during the time of the formation and ultimate reorganization of the CTV Network. More informally, numerous contacts took place through correspondence, through telephone calls, through personal meetings and through appearances of Board members at meetings of various industry associations. On several occasions, the Board sought out informed industry reactions to particular scenarios; conversely, the industry had legitimate concerns that it wanted to get across to the Board. Such is a necessary and healthy aspect of our system of government.

After initial financial difficulties, the private sector did begin to make money. Undoubtedly, the industry would favour many things which the Board did—e.g., reducing the summer Canadian content quota, extending the Commonwealth quota, postponing applications for second stations, failing to enforce more rigorously than it did some of its own regulations. Yet, private interests were not the only or even the determining factor in the decision-making process.

The Board had clear evidence that the content regulations could threaten the existence of the network and some of the second stations it was trying to foster as part of the broadcasting policy it was mandated to implement.

The doubling of the Commonwealth quota maintained a market for Canadian programming in the United Kingdom and at the same time provided a wider variety of program fare for the Canadian viewer. The problem of the entry of second stations into a market was one with which the Board dealt at great length and depth. It made no bones of the fact that entry into a regulated industry was not free but it also wrestled at length with a definition of "necessary" profit for the first station. The Board was not there to protect monopoly profits, but it did have to protect the standard of service expected of the system. Sadly, it had no power to force a station or network to move into an area so interminable negotiations were at times necessary when, for instance, a private station was to be disaffiliated from the CBC and possibly become a CTV affiliate. As well, the Board's powers to enforce its regulations were limited. For minor infringements of content or advertising regulations, the suspension of a licence or the costs of a court case looked a great deal like using an elephant gun to catch a flea. Hence a tendency developed to try to keep the stations in line by moral suasion, not always an effective tool in a competitive market place. One notes that the CRTC was granted more flexible enforcement powers. All in all, the BBG's course was not any easy one. In Sabatier's terms, the Board was much more the manager or coordinator than the policeman, seeking accommodation rather than all-out battle.[3]

Relations with the minister constituted another cross to bear. Clearly the 1958 Act had many deficiencies and only the minister or the government of the day could overcome them. Yet time and time again, appeals to ministers of both political stripes fell on deaf ears. They seem to believe that the agency, once established, relieved the minister of responsibility for all policy decisions in this field, especially if the decisions might be politically difficult.

Obviously with regard to the deficiencies in the legislation, but more particularly with regard to the CBC and its financing, the government could not avoid making policy decisions. It was not up to the Board to dictate CBC expansion plans; neither the Board nor even the CBC could do that without governmental direction. By and large, that was lacking and the Board's life was made all the more complicated as a result. One of the more difficult aspects of the BBG's life span to assess is the basis of and extent of its popular and political support. There was general support for the concept of regulation, technical and cultural, as evidenced by submissions to the Massey and Fowler Commissions from organizations such as the Canadian Broadcasting League, the Canadian Federation of Agriculture and dozens of cultural and educational organizations. The major thrust of such support was to underpin the need for national broadcasting policies and support of public service broadcasting such as that provided by the CBC. It tended to distrust the impact of the free play of market forces. Primary support for the creation of the separate regulatory agency, however, came from no great popular outpouring but from private broadcasting industry itself. It is therefore perhaps inappropriate to talk of "decay" setting in as popular support fell away from the Board. Suffice it to say that the Board seemed to lose political support as time passed. While the Conservatives established the Board with certain purposes in mind and were, in its initial stages, prepared to support it, eventually neither Conservative nor Liberal regimes seemed anxious to heed the Board's requests for remedial actions, be they with regard to CBC finances or to legislative lacunae.

The 1958 Broadcasting Act was inadequate in a number of ways. It was silent on issue such as cross and/or multiple ownership, it lacked an appropriate definition of "network," one of its key definitions precluded the Board from regulating cable, it did not allow the Board to effect network-affiliate relations except in the case of the CBC, the enforcement powers given to the Board were too limited. Not until the Board was about to pass out of existence were most of these issues finally addressed in the 1968 Act. It took the Conservatives some time to realize the problem which the 1958 Act had created, but before constructive action could be taken, they were out of office. It took the Liberals five years and three major inquiries to unravel the problems and to pass the 1968 Act. The second of Sabatier's concerns was in effect fulfilled.[4] In the meantime, the Board was expected to carry on making day-to-day decisions while the government called upon a variety of experts to try to solve the policy problems with which it was faced. Such a circumstance should earn the Board commendation, not condemnation.

It is hoped that it has been satisfactorily demonstrated that Bernstein's law has at best only limited application to the BBG.[5] The interests of the private sector could not help but be in the minds of the Board, but attention to such interests does not constitute surrender or capture. The Board had clear concerns for other elements in society as well and, if anything, it was precluded from serving its constituency as well as it might have wished by indifferent ministerial support, vacillating government policy, uncertain financial commitments, inadequate legislation and a schizophrenic public. In truth the Board was victim rather than captive.

Having dismissed one aspect of Bernstein's analysis, it is perhaps fitting to conclude with another. Amongst the requirements he lists for effective regulation are the following: firm political leadership; solid popular support; a clear legislative mandate and policy integration.[6] Had the BBG been blessed with all of these, how much its considerable effectiveness might have been enhanced.

THE FOWLER CRITIQUE

The Committee on Broadcasting, 1965 questioned the effectiveness of the Board, its perceived lack of resources—human and technical—and its alleged failure to use "the full powers it undoubtedly [had] been given under the. . . . Broadcasting Act."[7] It attributed the alleged inadequacies of staff and facilities to a failure on the part of the BBG to discharge its duties under the Broadcasting Act 1958. The full-time members of the Board were said to have spent much of their time on detailed work that could have been done by a better qualified and more expert staff; and that, as a consequence they had insufficient time to give to the regulation of private and public broadcasting. With proper organization and staff, the Committee concluded, "there should not be sufficient work for more than one full-time member to do."[8] The BBG had tried to avoid conflict with the "sometime belligerent Management and Board of the CBC"[9] and had not exercised its authority over the CBC. With respect to the private sector, in the opinion of the Committee, the BBG had failed to exercise sufficient control over private broadcasting, because of inadequate staff and facilities. "It has received many performance reports from the private stations, but has not had the staff and processing equipment to analyze them."[10] This was the responsibility of the Board, and the "lack of real status" resulted from the choice of the Board not to exert the "quite extensive powers" it had under the Act. Presumably this is what Miss LaMarsh meant when she said the Board was not "tough" enough.

The Chairman would argue that the Committee on Broadcasting, 1965 was wrong in asserting that the full-time members had insufficient time to devote to the regulation of broadcasting. The record of the extensive consideration given to the roles of the CBC and private broadcasting, particularly through the Consultative Committees, disproves this. The recommendation of the Committee that there should be only one full-time member of the proposed Authority received more attention than any other recommendation; the recommendation was universally rejected as ridiculous. On the other hand, no one connected with the Board believed that it was either necessary or desirable in terms of organization or work load, to increase the number of full-time members to five as was done under the 1968 Act.

The Committee believed that the Board lacked sufficient information to exercise effective control and did not have enough staff to analyze the information available. This criticism is more difficult to answer. It would be foolhardy to take the position that more and better information would not have been helpful. Better data assembling and processing techniques were coming into use during the life of the BBG. It would be argued, however, that inadequate information was not the principal problem of the Board. The real problem was to decide what information was relevant, and what to do on the basis of information available. The problem was agreement on goals, and it will not be known whether more personnel or more sophisticated information would have reduced this problem significantly.

The Committee concluded that the BBG should have exercised more control over the CBC. Certainly larger involvement in the activities of the CBC would have required more information and more staff—perhaps as much information and as many staff as the CBC itself had in its management information service. The main criticisms of CBC, and therefore perhaps the main areas in which control by the BBG might have made a difference, were directed to the efficiency of the Corporation's operations and the nature of some of its programming. To have become involved in the efficiency of the CBC's operations, the Board would have required a much larger staff, and would have found it necessary to require a much larger flow of information from the CBC. The Board did not believe, however, that it was responsible for the efficiency of the CBC, and found no disposition on the part of the government to place this responsibility on the Board. The Board members probably knew as much about the programs aired by the CBC as the Directors of the Corporation did. What they did not know as much about were the financial data and the internal disputes within the Corporation on programming. There were obvious differences of judgement and the same differences were apparent within the BBG. More information would not have resolved these differences.

Under both the Conservative and Liberal Governments, members of Parliament and of the Government referred to the CBC as a "monster" which was out of control in respect of both expenditures and programming. These were both highly important matters; and there is no doubt that the agitation about them contributed to the inability of the governments to come to grips with other problems.

As was required of private broadcasters, in submitting its applications for licences through the Board, the CBC had to provide estimates of its capital expenditures and projections of its operating expenditures and revenues. In this way the Board had some knowledge of levels of costs and some basis of comparison of the costs of the CBC and of private stations. The expenditures proposed by the CBC often appeared high in comparison with the level of expenditures proposed by private applicants. All members of the BBG were well aware of what was being said among parliamentarians, in the press and elsewhere about the inefficiency of the CBC. There were some differences within the Board about the responsibility of the BBG for the levels of expenditure of the CBC, particularly the expenditures on station facilities. The Chairman adhered to the position that the efficiency of the CBC was a management problem for which the Directors were, and must be, directly and solely responsible to Parliament. The Board could not be responsible unless it were to become the Board of the CBC. The Board had no mandate under the legislation to investigate the expenditures of the CBC and had no expertise in the management of networks and stations. Governments apparently shared this view. Notwithstanding the mounting criticisms of the CBC for inefficiency neither government gave any indication that it saw the efficiency of the CBC as a direct concern of the BBG.

Throughout the discussions in the "Troika," which extended over a year, Mr. Ouimet and Mr. Jamieson debated the comparative costs of the public and private services and the efficiency of the CBC. Mr. Jamieson was convinced that the CBC was inefficient. Mr. Ouimet did not deny that in the large organization and sprawling operation of the Corporation there was some inefficiency. He argued that this was not unique to the CBC, nor a major factor in determining the budget required to carry out the functions of the CBC. He claimed that the valid comparison was not with the operations of private broadcasters but with other networks, such as the BBC in the United Kingdom and the major networks in the United States. He produced evidence that, in comparison with other networks, the CBC unit costs of providing service were relatively low.[11]

The Chairman was not in a position to know how inefficient the CBC was, or whether any other management could have reduced the expenditures without affecting the quality of the service. He was not convinced the possible reductions were of a magnitude which would have eliminated the criticism that the CBC was costing the taxpayers a lot of money. To a considerable extent the attack on inefficiency was a response to the criticism that the public service was costly; but the cost of services rendered, however it was met, involved much more than efficiency. If it had not been for mounting criticism of the service provided, much less would have been heard about inefficiency.

In the matter of programming, the Directors and management of the CBC were, of course, fully aware of the criticism of "bias and of lack of good taste" in some of their programming. Publicly they tended to defend their programming against both changes, although occasionally they admitted to a mistake. Privately they agreed they had a problem; they were conscious of it, and were endeavouring to contain it. The problem was with the producers. Whose judgement was to have effect—the judgement of the Directors or the judgement of the producers? This was essentially a management problem. The Directors did not wish the Board to become involved in any manner which would weaken their capacity to deal directly with it. In the opinion of the Chairman, if the Board had moved in to impose its judgement, it would have undermined the authority of those in the CBC who were appointed by the government and were accountable to Parliament.

Additionally, even though the Board did have general regulations which applied to all broadcasters, the penalties which the Board could apply—prosecution, suspension of licence and revocation of licence—were generally inapplicable to the CBC.

The Board did not have a regulation on bias in the treatment of controversial issues. It did have a statement of policy endorsing the fairness doctrine; and, occasionally, on complaints being lodged with the Board, directions were given to private broadcasters. On one occasion, the Board asked the CBC for a list of programs in which a particular issue was touched upon over a period of time. The list ran in several pages and represented many hours of programming. It was clear that all shades of opinion had been reflected, but who was to judge whether the treatment was balanced? At one point the Chairman replied to a complaint from a member of Parliament:

I must say that when the Board has investigated the total coverage given by the CBC to particular issues, it has seemed to be that an adequate opportunity has been given to the exposure of divergent views. I admit the word "adequate" is difficult to define. Perhaps it would be better to say we have found no evidence that the CBC is promoting a particular issue.

The fairness principle was extremely difficult to administer, and after considerable debate in the Parliamentary Committee, the new Act enshrined the right of broadcasters to freedom of expression—to editorialize and to take positions on controversial matters.

The Board did have a regulation prohibiting the obscene or indecent. The Board was reluctant to exercise the role of censor; and there was only one prosecution under the regulation. The private broadcaster pleaded guilty and dismissed the employee involved. It is true that complaints of indecency or obscenity were more often directed at the CBC and the Corporation agreed it was subject to the regulation of the Board. The Board never took action against the CBC although some members would have chosen to do so.

It was significant that the successive governments appeared to hold the Corporation directly accountable. In the early case of "Preview Commentary," the minister made his move without any reference to the Board; and later the government did not implicate the BBG in the affair of "This Hour Has Seven Days." In both cases the government found itself involved in a management-employee dispute and dealt directly with the employees of the CBC.

It is doubtful that the outcome would have been much different if the Board had sought to impose its judgement. What seemed evident was that frequent or substantial departures from generally accepted views in public broadcasting can hardly fail to involve Parliament. It would be expected that offended members of the public would take their complaints to their ministers or to members of the Cabinet; and that members would raise the issue in the House. The worse that could happen would be for the government to intervene continuously in decisions for which the appointed Directors should be held accountable. If they were prepared to accept the complaints as legitimate, what could they do about it? Neither the Board nor the government could hire or fire producers. Only the government could change the Directors.

The Liberal Government eventually found itself in the position that it was not prepared to defend the CBC; it appeared to find the complaints legitimate. The sense of frustration in Parliament culminated in Miss LaMarsh's outburst about "rotten management" and the subsequent support she received in the House. In commenting on this in her book, Miss LaMarsh said: "Why did I refer to 'rotten management'? Did I have the right to do so, since I was the Minister who reported to Parliament for the CBC? I didn't manage it, nor could I affect the day to day management decisions no more than the Cabinet as a whole could. We could only hire and fire."[12] This was precisely so; and the Chairman of the Board was led to say the same thing before the Standing Committee on Broadcasting in 1967. The government appointed all the Directors of the Corporation and its chief executive officer. It seemed elementary that, if the government lost confidence in the performance of one of its agencies, its proper recourse was to change the people it had appointed to be accountable. It is not a sufficient answer to say that this would be difficult for a government to do.

The Committee on Broadcasting, 1965 obviously believed that the BBG should have exercised more control over private broadcasting. Three of the most contentious issues about private broadcasting were: advertising content, Canadian content and local program content. The flow of information to the Board on these matters was less well organized than it might have been. A computerized management information service would have improved the situation. But if the BBG were at fault in not exercising more control in these areas, the problem was not so much lack of information as the problem of the exercise of judgement. No one disputes that, if private broadcasting is to be permitted, private broadcasters must be allowed to receive revenue from advertising. If the public as audience finds the advertising irritating, there is a problem of reconciling the needs of broadcasting stations with the preferences of the audience. Perhaps more information would result in more definite answers. Everyone knew that the amount and nature of Canadian content were the subject of contention. The public seemed to support a policy of Canadian broadcasting but the audience frequently preferred to view U.S. programs. Information clarified the factors, but the conflicting elements still had to be reconciled. The question of the responsibility of the local station for local programming was constantly before the Board, and, in retrospect, it would seem that the Board managed to devise a satisfactory approach to this problem. But the essence of the problem was the adaptation of programming to the circumstances of the particular community. To regulate appropriately for each community, the regulatory authority would have to know as much about the community as the local broadcaster did. This would be difficult. Progress has been made in informing the new regulatory authority (the CRTC) but it would seem that after all the new information has been weighed and conclusions are drawn, many people will still contend that some or all conclusions made by the CRTC have been wrong.

The Board was criticized for not exercising sufficient surveillance over stations, that is, for not getting enough information to detect all infractions of regulations. If the goal was to extract the pound of flesh from every licensee who, even inadvertently, broke a regulation, then to meet this goal it would be necessary to monitor every station all the time. With prevailing techniques the effort and expense would have been enormous. If the more limited goal of discouraging deliberate infractions is acceptable, less costly methods would be sufficient. In reply to a question from a member of the Parliamentary Committee, the Chairman compared the problem to one of deciding how many cruiser cars to put on the highway in order to catch offenders of the speed limit. There was no demonstrably right answer. Perhaps the Board should have done more monitoring; the subject was discussed often.

The Chairman did not want to offer either apologies for nor defence of the financial administration or the tight budget under which the BBG operated between 1958 and 1966. His Scottish ancestry and Presbyterian upbringing, vivid recollections of the 1930s, and experiences as a University President during the 1950s all predisposed him to what might be described as a proper sense of responsibility for the expenditure of public money. They may have conditioned him to levels of expenditure no longer appropriate to the 1960s. It was gratifying that the Board drew no comments from the Auditor General; and up to 1966 had no difficulty with the Treasury Board. He could recall only one criticism of Board expenditure. It came from an MP and had reference to the size of an envelope in which an announcement, smaller than usual, had been mailed. The Board was able to reply that it was acting on advice that it was more economical to standardize the size of the envelope. The Chairman was satisfied that there was no waste of public money by the BBG.

Dave Sim shared many of the Chairman's prejudices. He used to say that they were both being dragged into the twentieth century. Both had supported estimates of $2 million for the 1968–1969 budget. As government policy emerged, the Board was advised to make preparations for additional responsibilities, for example, the function of licensing and regulating cable systems. The reorganization plans, including the development of a computerized management information service, were largely the product of Pierre Juneau's ingenuity. He had brought new ideas to the Board and had decided opinions about its needs. The one thing he was unable to achieve was the implementation of the recommendation of the Committee on Broadcasting that appointments to the staff of the Board should be made without reference to the Public Service Commission.[13] The appalling difficulties the Board met with in efforts to secure additional staff in 1967, although no greater than we had previously encountered, did nothing to change his convictions.

The authorized funding for the Board in 1966–67 was $814,000, with substantial increases in salaries, professional services and data processing. The amount provided in the 1967–68 estimates was $1,265,800; and a submission made in mid-1967 projected expenditures of $2,036,300 for 1968–69. The program review on which the submission for 1968–69 was based, stressed that broadcasting was an expanding sector of the economy. The normal expectation was an increase of 40 or 50 stations a year. Licence fees paid by broadcasting stations had increased from $1 million in 1962 to $2.1 million in 1966–67; and further increases at the rate of $300,000 a year could be expected. The review outlined the additional functions to be expected under the 1968 Act. These included broadcasting licensing functions and licensing and regulation of cable systems, both previously performed by the Department of Transport. Arrangements were made for the transfer of more than 30 employees from the Department. Additional functions also included plans for the development of educational television.

The major increases in expenditure for 1968–69 were in Administration, Program, Licensing and Research. The increase in Administration reflected the increase in the number of full-time members, and the appointment of a Director of Administration and Personnel Service with supporting staff. The Program branch was to be reorganized into three divisions each responsible for one facet of programming, namely Public Affairs, Entertainment and Sports, and other programs including Commercial Policy. Provision was made for an extension of regional offices. The total increase in staff was about 60. Throughout the submission, emphasis was put on an increased flow of information to the new Commission, and for more extended analysis of the information secured. Mr. Fowler would have been pleased.

[15]

THE BOARD OF
BROADCAST GOVERNORS:
AN ASSESSMENT

THE BBG, UNDER THE LEADERSHIP of its Chairman, Andrew Stewart, worked diligently for ten years to implement the provisions of the 1958 Broadcasting Act. The Act introduced a new nonoperating Board to replace the Board of Governors of the CBC as the regulatory body and significantly changed the way in which broadcasting generally was to be controlled. The drafters of the Act, perhaps understandably, failed to anticipate many of the problems that would emerge. For example, the Act said that the "establishment . . . of broadcasting stations" was one of the purposes of the Board. It also said that the CBC had "power to . . . establish . . . such broadcasting stations as the Corporation considered desirable." Whose decisions should prevail? The members of the Board and its staff were not experienced broadcasters and had to meet situations for which there were no precedents. The CBC had to face adjustments including appearances, which it would have preferred to avoid, before the Board in support of licence applications. The private broadcasters, although approving of the change, generally disliked regulations. Governments tend to be schizophrenic about broadcasting which Frank Stanton, former Chairman of the Columbia Broadcasting System, once described as "captious, carping, cantankerous, and controversial." Under these circumstances

273

it is not surprising that there were tensions and that some false starts could be expected.

The long-run effect of the actions of the Board are difficult to assess, and may prove to be minor. This tentative judgement is based on the opinion that the overriding factor affecting the development of broadcasting has been technology. Marshall McLuhan's concept—the medium is the message—seems to have been more persuasive than Robert Fowler's—the only thing that really matters in broadcasting is program content; all the rest is housekeeping.

The housekeeping details seemed to have take precedence over the content. The very nature of the medium will have a profound effect on the way people view things. Technologically-driven change seemed to be ahead of the policy maker. Policy always seemed to have been reactive rather than proactive. As Gordon Fearn has phrased it:

The regulators were grappling with radio when television came along; they were focusing on television when cable systems were introduced; they returned to radio for a time when FM and stereo broadcasting were introduced; they were unsure how to respond when satellite dishes became available; and so on. As for the politicians . . . , a mixed system of competing interests seem to have led to confused priorities. At the heart of the political dilemma is the difficulty always inherent in trying to correct past choices once interests based on these choices have become entrenched.[1]

Regardless, one impact of technological development has been to offer viewers a vastly increased range of choice; and viewers have made their own choices. The Board supported public broadcasting as an instrument for advancing the national purposes; but with increased choice there came greater fragmentation of the market, and the share of the audience captured by the CBC declined. The other elements of the broadcasting system were, like the general public, not necessarily devoted to the same interpretations of the national interest as those which motivated the BBG or CBC.

If Innis's understanding of the impact on society of newspapers and magazines is correct (he really had little chance to study television), "the effects of this on Canadian culture have been disastrous. Indeed they threaten Canadian national life."[2] "Technology has shortened the impact of time in our lives, discounting the past and the future."[3] Given their higher degree of consumer acceptance, the consequences of satellite distribution, video tape recording and other electronic developments cannot help but be immense. Governments have only two options in dealing with technology, to try to limit it choice-expanding potential or to accept the inevitable and try to cushion the impact of the wider choice open to consumers. No democratic government policy or agency regulation can likely have much impact on the consequences of the wider choice offered by new electronic technology.

CHANGES, 1958–1968

The broadcasting world in Canada in 1968 was a far different world from that of 1958, in part thanks to BBG. The second television network had been introduced, nurtured through its birth pangs and sent into the world as a healthy child. Primary service had been extended to many new areas. Colour had been introduced. Progress was made in the introduction of educational television and in the opening up of the UHF band. Cable, the greatest enhancer of choice, was brought within the scope of the 1968 Act. In the quest for a system essentially Canadian in content and character, the local content regulations, per-haps the Board's greatest single contribution to broadcasting, had been introduced and modified from time to time.

PUBLIC BROADCASTING IN CANADA

Between 1958 and 1968, however, governments and Parliaments failed to establish any general plan for public broadcasting. The Broadcasting Act, 1958, required that the CBC submit a five-year budget and this provision remained in the Act until the Act was replaced. The Board understood that, after the passage of the Act, the

CBC met the requirements and submitted a five-year budget; the Board was not informed, either by the CBC or the government, of the content of these proposals. The Conservative Government did not take a position on the continuing needs of the CBC; nor did the Liberal Government between 1963 and 1968. Program budgeting was becoming increasingly widely accepted by governments and other organizations as an essential tool of management. It required the definition of objectives, the establishment of priorities, and a commitment to means. Successive governments failed to benefit from the five-year budgets of the CBC because they were unsure of the commitments they wanted to make toward the CBC.

Each government was frustrated by having to deal annually with increasing demands from the Corporation but was unwilling to accept any proposals for financing the CBC which would have obviated this necessity. The Fowler Commission proposed that the public funds to be made available to the CBC should be tied to some indicator such as population. In his fixed points of reference to the "Troika" in 1963, the Minister, Mr. Pickersgill, supported the principle of "forward financing," and the "Troika" endorsed it. The Committee on Broadcasting, 1965 reiterated the position of the Fowler Commission and recommended specifically "that the financial requirements of the CBC, both capital and operating, should be provided by a statutory grant of $25 for each television household in Canada as reported by the Dominion Bureau of Statistics."[4] The formula was to be reviewed at the end of five years. The Broadcasting Act, 1968, went into effect without any commitment on the financing of the CBC.[5]

Successive governments failed to give any useful guidance on the commercial policy of the Corporation; and the new legislation became effective without any clear definition of the commercial policy the CBC would be expected to follow. The Fowler Commission suggested that the CBC should be more aggressively commercial,[6] and this position was endorsed by the Parliamentary Committee, 1959; but it was never clear what was meant by this, other than that the CBC might be expected to reduce its demands on the public treasury by raising more commercial revenue.

There were two ways to approach public broadcasting service. The first approach assumed that it was a commercial operation. The Corporation would be then given support from the public treasury because it would "lose money" as a commercial enterprise. The CBC resisted this view and the Chairman of the BBG found himself on the CBC's side. The view of the CBC as a commercial enterprise was understandable among businessmen in Parliament and among private broadcasters. It might be applicable to other crown corporations, although it would then be difficult to know why they would not be turned over to private enterprise. It was not a view appropriate to the public broadcasting service or to the responsible corporation.

The second approach recognized that Parliament would impose certain national purposes on the CBC, purposes it recognized could be realized only by a crown corporation. Parliament would know what it was the Corporation was expected to do to advance these purposes. It should be aware of the costs involved, and should provide that these costs be met. If Parliament wished the CBC to seek commercial revenue in the market place, the CBC should be allowed to do so, but only in a manner and to an extent consistent with its purposes. If there was a conflict, the conflict should always be resolved on the side of the achievement of the purposes which Parliament prescribed and supported. Procedurally this meant approving a budget for the CBC which would sustain and advance the acceptable service, reducing the public support by the amount which would be obtained by sales, under a commercial policy consistent with the maintenance of the approved service. Parliament was not sufficiently clear as to the purposes of the CBC, and seemed oblivious to the relations between its purported purposes and its commercial policy.

One aspect of the purposes of the CBC on which Parliament did not express itself sufficiently clearly was the nature of the national network service. The CBC contributed to the confusion by insisting that its mandate was adequately expressed in such general terms as to give no significant direction to it, nor any assurances to anyone else as to how it would perform. Production of Canadian programs for network distribution was the major element in the Corporation's operating budget. It is clearly impossible to project the CBC's expenditures or the public support required without some well-defined concept of the extent to which the CBC would engage in Canadian productions. The Parliamentary Committee considering Bill C-163 came out strongly in favour of Canadian programming by the CBC and referred to more Canadian programming in prime time. But this policy meant little unless and until it was incorporated in a network schedule, and even then meant nothing until the necessary financial support was assured.

ROLE AND PROCEDURES OF THE BOARD

Like the agencies discussed in Doern's book,[7] the BBG can be deemed to have been more managerial in nature than purely regulatory. Equally, in the Canadian parliamentary context, it could not be completely independent of government—legislative or executive branch. In any case, it would appear to have been too independent as it was—a body viewed as essentially administrative by its Chairman, left by government to drift in a sea of policy ambiguities without adequate resources or powers to give full meaning to its planning, policing and promoting functions. The sea was full of unfriendly creatures—other bodies quite willing to inject into the void policy interpretations amenable to themselves rather than to the visions of the Board.[8] In such circumstances, where the Board's actions were subject to comment and criticism from a variety of quarters—the CBC, the CAB, the DOT, the CBL—it is difficult to suggest that it had been captured by any one of them.

Three Doern points deserve note. Firstly, the openness and legitimacy of the Board's processes, if not ends in themselves, were well recognized and respected. The public hearings gave an opportunity for all to be heard given the constraints of Canadian geography and the difficulties of finding adequate meeting places in the Ottawa of the 1960s. The Board put to public hearings many issues not required by the Act if it believed the public interest so required. For some, the degree of openness was tedious and time-consuming, but such were the costs of an open system.

Secondly, as the Board's processes and goals were complex, the Board should be judged on the basis of multiple performance criteria, not just one. To judge the Board's activities solely on the grounds of

Canadian content, for instance, would be unfair. One must also consider its many other concerns such as those for the expansion of primary and secondary services. Funds for the public sector were limited by government decision and in the private sector by the market place. The Board had to seek a *modus operandi* between funds for program production and system development. Generally, Canadians seemed to have shown a penchant for bigger and better hardware at the expense of program content.

Finally, as Doern suggests, where the processes are complex, failure to achieve goals may not be attributable to any one agency. Such is the case in this instance. In relatively few issues was the Board a completely free agent. In terms of its funding, it depended upon government. In terms of its staff, it had to depend upon the Civil Service Commission. With regards to most technical matters, it was dependent upon the Department of Transport. For much vital information, it depended upon the Dominion Bureau of Statistics or the regulated industry. For clear policy directives, it looked, often in vain, to government and Parliament. For compliance with its regulations, it had to depend in large part on the good will of those it was regulating (or worse still on another public agency which at times questioned its very authority). Looked at in this light, the Board was in an unenviable position, mandated by Parliament to do certain things, yet dependent on a wide range of actors which might not have shared the Board's interpretations of indistinct policies. At best, the Board's position was one in which government ambivalence made the life of the Board much more difficult.

BOARD-GOVERNMENT RELATIONS

The view one adopts of the appropriate relation between Parliament, or the government, and the regulatory agency, is significant. Parliament may frame legislation so as to leave wide latitude to the agency in determining how the broadcasting system is to be structured and operated. Or, it may define the purposes with precision, leaving the agency to administer within the more clearly defined context. The

Chairman's preference was for legislation carefully considered and enacted so that, under the administration of the agency, the developments would be consistent with the wishes of Parliament. The planning and promoting functions would then have been more readily performed. Moreover, as it was impossible for Parliament to foresee all circumstances that might arise, there should have been no objection to ministerial directives to the agency. It is unhealthy to have appointed bodies making important public policy decisions. In terms of policy, the Broadcasting Act, 1958 was inadequately considered and unfortunately drafted. The absence of any policy direction on how the structure of the broadcasting system was to develop was a constant frustration to the Board. There were undoubtedly areas of decision-making which should have been left to the administrative agency, but there were areas in which only government could act.

The members of the agency should, however, be selected on the principle of searching for, and appointing, the best qualified person available to undertake a task. To appoint the members of the "impartial and independent body" principally on the basis of partisan political affiliation is to undermine confidence in it. While the pressures to appoint friends of the governing party are undoubtedly strong, the leadership skills and the knowledge of the industry possessed by prospective appointees should also be given considerable weight in the appointment process. The agency head, the industry and the academic community should also be consulted. As hard-working and dedicated as most of the member of the Board were, its image and credibility suffered as a consequence of accusations of partisan interference.

Two of Doern's suggestions[9] bearing upon the relationship between agency and Cabinet are highlighted by the BBG's experiences. One suggested change would involve "an annual memorandum of agreement between the Cabinet and the agency outlining the Cabinet's expectation for agency performance as well as any specific policy instructions." The other would involve a published policy instrument outlining the objectives, reasons for, and time of application of the policy which the Cabinet wished to impose upon the agency. Both devices would allow a much clearer attachment of responsibility and ensure that the task of the agency would be much more clearly administrative rather than policy-making or policy second-guessing. It is not always possible to change legislation quickly or on a regular basis. The Conservative Government assumed power in 1957 with certain broadcasting policy imperatives in mind. The second television network and the Canadian content regulation were manifestations of these. The BBG was envisaged as an agent of change. Yet the implementation of these changes produced ramifications which the Board could not, and the government in the short run was apparently unprepared to, mitigate. The Board in effect became the victim of government inertia and of a concept of agency independence which precluded legitimate communication between government and Board on matters of policy. It was right to argue that decision-making on some subjects such as licensing be put at arms length from partisan pressures.[10] It was not right to force an appointed body to make or to be held responsible for decisions such as those related to the funding of the CBC which can only be regarded as political. Implementation of the two Doern suggestions would have helped to clarify the policy-making process and the assigning of political responsibility.

Matters of public policy are, in theory, the responsibility of the elected representative of the people, they, in the long run, being responsible to the people. Perhaps Dr. Stewart was correct to question the effectiveness of broadcasting in achieving political and cultural ends unless there was clearly present "the disposition of the public to support the [political and cultural] purposes." The experience of the BBG, and of the CRTC since 1968, even with its vastly enhanced powers and resources, may provide evidence of the possibility that the Aird Royal Commission of 1929 and all such public bodies since have based their recommendations on a false premise. Aird claimed to have found "unanimity in one fundamental question—Canadian radio listeners want Canadian broadcasting."[11] The Board struggled with its mandates, but, for a variety of reasons, experience suggests that the Canadian public had developed an appetite for non-Canadian programs. Dr. Stewart suggested that viewers were schizophrenic, adopting different postures in public and in private. Richard Schultz has convincingly argued that any attempt at regulation is an exercise in futility if the regulated can escape the impact of the regulation.[12] Thanks to geography and more recently technology, the vast majority of Canadian viewers have been able to do just that. Could any amount of management or regulation short of the jamming of the American signal change that?

BROADCASTING AND PUBLIC OPINION

In their apparent ambivalence toward the CBC, governments were perhaps merely reflecting the ambivalence of public opinion. In spite of the special interest groups which show up at royal commission hearings, parliamentary committee hearings and regulatory agency licence renewal hearings, the general public has historically demonstrated its preference for non-Canadian programming. Some will argue that the viewing of predominately foreign programming is brought about by the limited amount of Canadian programming available. That may be in part true, but we must also ask why Canada is amongst the most cabled countries in the world. If there had been a loud and clear public demand for more Canadian programming would not Parliament and/or the market place have responded with more generous funding to underwrite such programming? Perhaps successive governments' delay and indecisiveness on broadcasting matters in an all too accurate reflection of the ambivalence of the general public, not just those who appear before public inquiries.

Communication between the regulatory agency, the government and Parliament must be as open and direct as is humanly possible if the public will is to be received and understood by any and all. The key actors in such communication should be the national political parties of Canada. The parties are best represented—and sometimes in a less partisan fashion—in the committees of Parliament. The particular committee which reviewed the White Paper on Broadcasting and Bill C-163 came remarkably close to a consensus on the essentials of broadcasting policy. That was a good omen.

Given the strengthening of the parliamentary committee system generally and the Standing Committee on Broadcasting, the licensing and regulatory authority, in addition to making its annual report to Parliament, should appear annually before the Committee to account for its performance. The Board should not merely submit to investigation by the Committee, it should welcome the opportunity to account for its stewardship, to present its case, to contribute to the presence in Parliament of a group of fully informed members, and to assure itself that it is carrying out the wishes of Parliament. The Committee, being given the responsibility to examine the operation of broadcasting under the legislation and to report to Parliament, might even be given some responsibility for appointments to the Board.

The conditions outlined could remove the suspicion that the Board is an instrument of the party in power, would tend to make the procedure of the Board subject to the fullest possible public scrutiny, and would establish the accountability of the Board to Parliament through a Standing Committee. Subject to these conditions, the better Board might be a full-time Board capable of dealing expeditiously and efficiently with the matters under its jurisdiction.

It would also seem preferable to avoid direct government involvement in program decisions. Parliament may choose to indicate in the legislation areas of program content which should be subject to control; and the agency must then make and administer regulations. On more than one occasion between 1958 and 1968, the government became directly involved with program content, with unfortunate results. The regulations of the agency should be proscriptive and should be kept to a minimum. It would be best if decisions on program content could be left to the creative people, but this may not be entirely possible. In practice, the licensee is, and must be seen to be responsible. The preference for unregulated program decisions is based on the assumption of there being a great variety of unrelated voices. In the Chairman's judgement, the Board was not heavy-handed in the application of its regulations and was generally sensitive to the problems of monopolistic tendencies.

CANADIAN CONTENT AND SYSTEM RESOURCES

Although the Board has been criticised by some for not applying the Canadian content regulation sufficiently rigorously, it did unswervingly support the principle. Broadcasting was viewed as a means of communication. The object of the Canadian content regulations was not directly to employ performers or to influence the cultural development of Canadians, it was to ensure the opportunity for Canadians to communicate with one another. It seemed to the Chairman that this was important to the survival of Canada as an effective political unit. The CBC had been formed not because of any general preference for public ownership, but to provide a direct means of strengthening the body politic. It was the Board's view that the private television sector should make a contribution, although a more limited one, to the same purpose. This was the reason for its support for the early creation of a private network. It was expected that the larger stations in the metropolitan centres of the central provinces would contribute to the cost of providing programs to the smaller outlying places. For the same reason, the Board was opposed to the creation of a network covering only stations in the central provinces.

The Board's view of broadcasting also implied origination of programs from a variety of locations. It was concerned that so much of the English-language programming on the CBC originated in Toronto and hoped that a similar situation might be avoided on the private network. It was hoped that control of the private network would not fall into the hands of the Toronto station. For this reason, although preferring effective ownership by a nonbroadcasting organization, the Board did not oppose the mutual ownership of the network.

THE 1968 BROADCASTING ACT

The Broadcasting Act, 1968, was passed by the House of Commons on 7 February 1968, almost four years after the "Troika" reports were submitted. What impact did the nearly five-year gestation period and the ten-year experience of the BBG period have on the new legislation? What, especially, did it say about the role of the new regulatory agency and its relationship with the CBC?

The new Act contained a statement of objectives for the broadcasting system which, amongst other things, declared that broadcasting undertakings in Canada constitute a single system "comprising public and private elements," and that the policy objectives could best be achieved "by providing for the regulation and supervision of the Canadian broadcasting system by a single independent authority."[13] The section entitled "Broadcasting Policy for Canada" stated: "Where any conflict arises between the objectives of the national broadcasting service and the interests of the private element of the Canadian broadcasting system, it shall be resolved in the public interest but paramount consideration shall be given to the objectives of the national broadcasting service."[14]

The Canadian Radio-Television Commission was made the licensing authority and cable systems were brought under its jurisdiction. The Act, provided for the issue of directives by the Government on the issue of licences. The statement of policy said that: "All Canadians are entitled to broadcasting service in English and French as public funds become available."[15] Direction on the issue of licences could be made respecting "the maximum number of channels or frequencies for the use of which broadcasting licences within a geographical area designated in the direction; the reservation of channels or frequencies for the use of the Corporation or any special purpose designated in the direction; and the classes of applicants to whom broadcasting licences may be issued."[16] These provisions effectively placed the control of the structure of the system in the hands of Parliament. Unlike the Act of 1958, the new legislation did not require the CBC to submit five-year capital programs.

The 1968 Act strengthened the position of the Commission in its control over station and network operations. It was given power to make regulations on allocation of the broadcasting time for the purpose of giving effect to the general statement of policy on programming including conditions for the operation of broadcasting stations as part of a network and the conditions for the broadcasting of network programs (the 1962 Grey Cup lives on).[17] The CBC retained the authority to make operating agreements with licensees for the broadcasting of programs.

There was little new in the new Act referring to the financing of the CBC, or the Corporation's commercial policy; although a new section was introduced requiring the Corporation to establish a Proprietor's Equity Account to which would be credited monies paid to the Corporation for capital purposes out of parliamentary appropriations.[18] Neither was there anything in the Act to imply that the CRTC had any responsibility for the budgeting of the CBC or the efficiency of its operations.

The broad policy for programming was stated as follows:

The programming provided by the Canadian broadcasting system should be varied and comprehensive and should provide reasonable, balanced opportunity for the expression of differing views on matters of public concern, and the programming provided by each broadcaster should be of a high standard, using predominantly Canadian creative and other resources.[19]

The CBC was mandated to provide a national broadcasting service to be predominantly Canadian in content and character; the national broadcasting service should (i) be a balanced service of information, enlightenment and entertainment for people of different ages, interests and tastes covering the whole range of programming in fair proportion; (ii) be extended to all parts of Canada, as public funds become available; (iii) be in English and French, serving the special needs of geographic regions, and actively contributing to the flow and exchange of cultural and regional information and entertainment, and (iv) contribute to the development of national unity and provide for continuing expression of Canadian identity.[20] The wording was not dissimilar to that of the CBC's own statement of its mandate.

With respect to the content of particular programs, the new Act retained specific provisions governing political broadcasting and continued the authority of the regulatory body to make regulations covering the proportion of time that may be devoted to the broadcasting of advertisements or announcements of a partisan political character and the assignment of such time on an equitable basis to political parties and candidates. As had been the case with its predecessor, the CRTC was given authority to regulate "standards of programs" and, under the 1968 Act, the Corporation was established for the purpose of providing the national service contemplated by section 2 "subject to any applicable regulations of the Commission." The CRTC was made responsible for the policing and enforcement of the sections of the Act dealing with political broadcasting, as well as of its own regulations. Licensees violating the sections on political broadcasting were made liable on summary conviction to a fine not exceeding five thousand dollars, and the fine for violating the provisions of any regulation was set at a maximum of twenty-five thousand dollars for a first offence and fifty thousand dollars for each subsequent offence.

Perhaps the major change in the Act was to give the CRTC authority to impose conditions with respect to programming on licensees including the CBC. Licences were to be granted for terms not exceeding five years and subject to such conditions related to the circumstances of the licensee as the newly-created Executive Committee of the CRTC deemed appropriate for the implementation of the broadcasting policy enunciated in section 2 of the Act. In the case of broadcasting licences issued to the Corporation, conditions were to be as the Executive Committee deemed consistent with the provision, through the Corporation, of the national broadcasting service contemplated by section 2 of the Act.[21] The Executive Committee and the Corporation were required, at the request of the Corporation, to consult with regards to any conditions that the Executive Committee proposed to attach to any broadcasting licence issued to the Corporation.[22] If the Executive Committee attached any condition to a broadcasting licence that the Corporation thought would impede its provision of the national broadcasting service, the Corporation might refer the condition to the Minister for consideration. The Minister, after consultation with the Commission and the Corporation, might give to the Executive Committee a written binding directive with respect to the condition.[23] A directive given by the Minister must be published in the *Canada Gazette* and laid before Parliament within fifteen days after the making thereof.[24] The Act further provided that

When the Commission, after affording to the Corporation an opportunity to be heard in connection therewith, is satisfied that the Corporation has violated or failed to comply with any condition of a licence issued to it, the Commission shall forward to the Minister a report setting forth the circumstances of the alleged violation or failure, the findings of the Commission and any observations or recommendations of the Commission in connection therewith, and a copy of the report shall be laid by the Minister before Parliament within fifteen days after receipt thereof by him.[25]

The powers given to the Commission to place conditions on the licences of both CBC and private stations, and to regulate the allocation of broadcasting time and the broadcasting times to be reserved for network programs, *in principle* enabled the Commission to control the "mix" of programs in both the public service and the private service. In doing so, the Commission would have to grapple with the problems of the effects on the audience of the stations, public and private, and with the financial consequences. In interpreting the "circumstances of the licensee," the Commission would not wish to impose conditions which would make it impossible for the private station to operate. The main contention with the Corporation might well be whether the CBC could meet the program conditions with the resources available to it. The matter of CBC resources was in no way resolved by the new Act.

CONCLUSIONS

The new Act clearly put the CRTC in a stronger position in matters relating to government, to the CBC and to the private sector. Some things had been learned from the ten-year period and from the trials and tribulations of the shedding of the single station policy, the introduction of the two board system, the second television network, the Canadian content regulations and a variety of types of new technology.

In trying to assess the work of the Board, it seems appropriate to note the words of the Law Reform Commission of Canada:

Ambiguous statutory mandates mean that many regulatory agencies are a source of both primary and secondary policy-making.

Legal reformers acknowledge that some vagueness is inevitable, but they suggest that obscure mandates lead to public confusion about the goals and priorities of agencies, to problems of regulatory enforcement when agencies are challenged by interest groups to justify their policies and decisions, and to difficulties in evaluating how effectively agencies are performing in terms of the policy framework set by the legislature.[26]

The BBG was in many respects a pioneer travelling in murky waters. Whatever its strengths and weaknesses, it did preside over a virtual revolution in Canadian broadcasting, testing the waters as it went, some times innovating, at other times relying on the tried and true, in either case providing a beacon for the future. Looking at the unfolding of Canadian broadcasting since 1968, with a knowledge of the BBG's experience in mind, one can only conclude that "the more things change. . . . plus ça change. . . ." It is a matter of regret that so little has been achieved in harnessing private as well as public resources in pursuit of national purposes within the Canadian broadcasting system.

The measure of the BBG can perhaps best be taken by an application of the conflicting theories surrounding the proper roles of regulatory agencies outlined by Thomas and Zajcew. As they suggest, without a clear theory of regulatory agencies, conflicting assessments of the appropriate role will arise, one stressing the policy-making function, the other the adjudicative function.

First [regulatory agencies] are said to behave in a legitimate and responsible fashion when they adhere to the policy intentions of elected representative in cabinets and legislatures. Second, legitimacy for regulatory decision-making can have a procedural basis. It arises from the process of independent, non-partisan decision-making, open hearings, fairness to all sides, a reliance upon professional analyses, and the application of clear criteria on a constant basis.[27]

Certainly, Dr. Stewart liked to think of the Board as fulfilling the first role. In the absence, however, of the clear policy intentions of elected representative in cabinets or legislatures, he and the Board were forced more into the second role, stressing openness, consistency, fairness and a nonpartisan stance in its decision-making. Unfortunately, in the minds of some, the intended legitimacy was denied because of perceived partisan bias. As Dr. Stewart noted, the case can never be proved.

One may try to take broadcasting out of politics, but it is difficult to take politics out of broadcasting. Where the stakes, psychological or economic, are high, so too will be the pressures brought to bear by the various interests involved. If the public interest is to be protected the need for planning, promoting and policing will be ever present. Regardless of the difficulties encountered, those associated with the Board of Broadcast Governors did their best to fulfil the role inherent in the Brown-John definition of a regulatory agency,[28] to sustain the public interest as they saw it and, in no small measure, contribute directly or indirectly to the evolution of Canadian television and the policy underpinning it.

EPILOGUE

The Beauties and the Board (from left to right): Carlyle Allison, Vice-Chairman, Julliette, entertainer, Irene J. Gilbride, BBG, Andrew Stewart, Chairman, Joan Fairfax, entertainer, Edward Dunlop, BBG, Joyce Hahn, entertainer, and Waldo Helden, CFRB, Toronto. *Photograph by Gilbert A. Milne & Co. Limited, EM 3–1166–7, Cunningham, 37605–9. Used with permission of the City of Toronto Archives.*

THE CHAIRMAN'S SANITY BLANKET:
REGULATORY HUMOUR

GIVEN ALL THE CIRCUMSTANCES under which the Board had to operate, a sense of humour was helpful. In times of frustration, I would frequently amuse myself with limericks. This one had to do with the protestations of the representatives of a Toronto radio station against the competition:

> The efforts of Sedgwick and Cran
> would keep C.F.R.B. in the van
>   if it weren't for rotters
>   like CHUM'S Alan Waters.
> "Mr. Chairman, please roll on the Ban."

On two occasions I prepared descriptions of fictional meetings in the form of one scene plays. The later one described a meeting of the "Troika," the principal characters being Ouimet, Jamieson and myself. This piece was discovered by Dick Lewis, publisher of the trade magazine *The Canadian Broadcaster* and was published in the issue of 3 October 1963. The earlier effort was a description of a mythical, *in-camera* meeting of the BBG. It went as follows:

MEETING OF THE BOARD OF BROADCAST GOVERNORS:
A Short Play for Television.

The time is 8:30 p.m. Fourteen members of the Board are sitting around a table in a dingy room in a third class hotel. Payola is not in evidence.

There are two pictures on the wall. "The Fathers of Confederation" and "Napoleon's Retreat from Moscow." The table is bare except for some glasses and a jug. It contains iced water.

The Chairman, dressed in rough tweed jacket and kilt of the Hunting Stewart tartan, is playing with his sporran. The Vice-Chairman, pipe firmly in his teeth, has his gaze fixed on the pictures on the wall opposite him. The third full-time member is reading the racing page from his favourite newspaper.

Other members are variously engaged; but all display an air of expectancy. Mr. Sabourin enters. He finds himself a chair between the ladies and is seated.

CHAIRMAN: *(in his barely audible tenor)* "Will you please come to order."
(Mr. Burge continues his animated conversation with Dr. Mackay.)
CHAIRMAN: *(apparently raising his voice)* "Will you come to order, please."
DR. FORSEY: "I think the Chairman is trying to say something. But he persists in mumbling and I can't make out what he's saying. Would you mind speaking louder?"
(Chairman shows signs of strain. He bangs on the table with a glass. It breaks.)
DR. DAVIES: "Naughty! Naughty!"
(A measure of order is finally achieved.)
CHAIRMAN: "We have to consider the 25th, or is it 24th, application for second television licences."
(Mr. Mills, Secretary to the Board, hurriedly produces some pieces of paper.)
MR. BROWN: "We haven't passed the minutes of the last meeting."

MR. DUNLOP: "Two weeks ago I sent a couple of corrections to the Secretary. I was recorded as referring to the Toronto station as the "Flagship." I'm sure I never used that word."

DR. FORSEY: "I noticed that a word on the 2nd line of the 3rd paragraph on page 4 was misspelled. It should be r-o-u-t-e, not r-o-o-t."

MR. ALLISON: "I move the adoption of the minutes."

MR. BURGE: "Let's make it unanimous."

CHAIRMAN: "Oh dear. Where were we? Oh yes. The television applications."

DR. DAVIES: "Mr. Chairman, may I say a word. I was particularly impressed by the interest and concern shown by the President of the Outer Space Company in programming for our senior citizens."

MRS. GILBRIDE: "He's working far too hard. It'll be a great relief to his wife if he doesn't get it."

DR. CONNELL: "I got the impression there was a cavity in his contour."

MR. HAIG: "He had only one Brownie Camera."

MR. WILSON: "I was surprised that the height of his antenna was minus 500."

SEVERAL MEMBERS: *(not including Mr. Brown)* "How come?" "or. . . ."

MR. WILSON: *(Leaning into the table)* "EHAAT stands for. . . ."

MR. ALLISON: "Mr. Chairman, we ought to consider some of the other applicants. I liked the cut of the principal in the Barber application."

DR. DAVIES: "Hair, hair."

(At this point Mr. Duchemin leaves to get cigars.)

CHAIRMAN: "Was there a Barber application? Which one was it?"

MR. MILLS: "Number 18."

CHAIRMAN: "Oh dear, I seem to have lost the brief."

(Mr. Mills staggers over with Volume 1.)

MR. MILLS: "I'll have to get a porter to bring Volumes 2–10, including the last minute revisions of the addendum to the supplementary brief."

(He exits.)

MR. MARSHALL: "I knew Hamish McAlpine, the Programme Director for Tomahawk, when he was a lad at Grand Falls." *He adds (sadly),* "But he's changed since he went to Canada."

DR. MACKAY: "The Tomahawk application was heard a year ago. I remember. I was there."

CHAIRMAN: *(aside)*: "It's all so confusing."

MR. PEARSON: "May I remind you of Section 12 of the Act."

SEVERAL MEMBERS: "Oh forget it."

(Mr. Pearson takes this as a joke, he laughs.)

MR. SABOURIN: *(Whose teeth are chattering, is heard to remark.)* "The water was cold."

MR. BROWN: "Mr. Chairman, I object."

(The Chairman didn't hear. There is something on his mind. He wears a sad smile. He is heard to mutter "Quaecumque Vera." It is the motto of the University of Alberta.)

THE TWO LADY MEMBERS SIMULTANEOUSLY: "They are all so nice. Why aren't there more channels?"

(The Technical Advisor is evidently equal to the occasion, but . . .)

DR. DAVIES: "It is a difficult decision calling for clear heads. I suggest we sleep on it."

CHAIRMAN: *(plaintively)* "But there are a number of urgent matters on which. . . ."

(He realizes he is alone with the Vice-Chairman. Mr. Duhamel reluctantly removes his eyes from the "Fathers of Confederation." They exit together.)

CURTAIN

THE PUBLIC HEARINGS: VOX POPULI

The licensing of second stations was an event of immense importance. Roy Thomson, in suggesting that a television licence was a licence to print money, was not alone in anticipating substantial profits from television licences. There was immense interest in the hearings on the part of the public and among those with special interests. And the element of competition created a dramatic atmosphere. The public hearings were, however, not without lighter moments.

Probably the wittiest presentation was made by Leonard Brockington, sometime Chairman of the Board of the CBC and Chancellor of Queen's University. It was Brockington who, when asked why he had given up writing Mackenzie King's speeches, said he was tired of acting as a midwife to an intellectual virgin. At the time of the BBG hearings, he was assisting in a Toronto application in which the J. Arthur Rank organization was involved.

Mr. Chairman, ladies and gentlemen of the Board. I am sure you will be very glad when once again silence becomes our mother tongue. And I am very diffident and somewhat reluctant to add to your burden. Now I am going to be rather informal, but I think you probably know as well as I do that an impromptu speech is not worth the paper it is written on. I am aware too that you all know the truth of the Italian proverb that words are the daughters of earth and things are the sons of heaven. I am sure you know too that while sentiment cannot dominate fact, that great is its power nevertheless, and that in enterprises like these the most momentous facts can be insignificant with sentiment.

Now it is fine that no matter what opinions we ever held or hold, or whatever our personal preference is, that commercial television is here to stay as part of the picture of North American life. Investors and artists also need the security of a reasonable profit for their sakes and ours. Because if we went around without any profit motive, we would find ourselves in the position of the poet in "Patience" who said to the other poet, "you know what it is to long for the infinite and to be brought to face daily the multiplication tables."

I used to say long ago that the two greatest audiences in the world were, and perhaps the two best, were those who do not go to the moving pictures and those who do not listen to the radio and I recall the limerick that said:

The young folk who frequent picture palaces
have no use for psychoanalysis.
        and although Dr. Freud
        would be distinctly annoyed,
they cling to their long standing fallacies.

Mr. Brockington concluded by recalling when Mr. Bernard Shaw was once again asked what he thought of television, replied: "I am afraid to look."

Bernard Braden was a Canadian who had gone to the United Kingdom. He was appearing on behalf of BC Television. Braden said: "A man in Nottingham once said to me: 'You are the only Canadian I have ever met who was not in uniform or on skates.' Several years ago a distinguished English writer said to me: 'I understand there is a Canadian company of actors coming to the Edinburgh Festival this year. I am looking forward to seeing some Canadian plays. What are they doing?' I had to tell him that the plays were Hamlet and Henry V by William Shakespeare. There was a pause and he said to me: 'Are they aware that we do this kind of thing ourselves adequately, from time to time?'"

Dr. Forsey (later Senator Forsey) and Dr. Emlyn Davies, the Baptist minister from Toronto, could be relied upon to brighten things up. On one occasion during the questioning of Finaly MacDonald (now Senator MacDonald) in Halifax, both Forsey and Davies got involved. Davies asked MacDonald; "I would like to ask how anyone is vitally wholesome." MacDonald relied "vitally wholesome is the same as vulgarly healthy." At which point Forsey interjected: "I thought it was like the man in Montreal who said he was unscrupulously honest."

My own intervention which pleased me most was in Toronto. J.S.D. Tory, representing Summit Television, was assisted by a young man Campbell:

CHAIRMAN: *(with tongue in cheek)*: "I notice between 11:00 and 12:00, Mr. Campbell, five times a week you have an hour-long programme 'Tonight in Toronto.' Do you think you will have any difficulty in finding material to fill this programme?"

CAMPBELL: "I am not quite clear why this is so amusing. I could take the question quite seriously. No, we do not anticipate any difficulty."
CHAIRMAN: "Thank you. Mrs. Gilbride and I will do some research on this for you."
TORY: "I have just explained it to him."

Dr. Forsey again provided some relief when, on an August afternoon—hot and steamy as only Ottawa can produce them, he took an applicant to task. As the public hearing was continuing after lunch on the Friday (they usually ended by Thursday afternoon!), I had asked all those yet to appear not to read their briefs but to summarize them as succinctly as possible. The first applicant after lunch started reading his brief. I finally broke in and reminded him of my plea. He weakly held up his left arm, pleading the absence of his watch for his oversight. With this, Dr. Forsey, in a stage whisper that all could hear, opined: "Thank God there is a calendar on the wall!"

REFLECTIONS ON BBG GENERAL REGULATIONS

The Canadian content regulations were not the only regulations of the Board. The Radio (AM) Broadcasting Regulations which applied to both radio and television as were in effect at January 1964 included, *inter alia* regulations governing advertising, including liquor advertising; prohibiting abusive comment on race or religion; prohibiting "any obscene, indecent, or profane language"; prohibiting any program involving "a lottery, gift programme, or similar scheme in which the contestant paid in order to be eligible for a prize."

In February 1963 an article of mine entitled "The Necessity For Government Supervision of Advertising on Radio and Television in Canada" was written for publication in *The Commerceman*, Queen's

University. In the article I wrote: "There is much to be said against general regulations imposed by a licensing authority. No intelligent person close to the regulatory process can fail to appreciate this. General regulations remove the responsibility from those directly involved and diminish their sense of responsibility; they thwart creativeness; and they impose a degree of rigidity which makes it impossible to meet the needs of particular situations. In relation to particular situations, a general regulation may seem to make no sense at all."

On advertising in the media, the article in *The Commerceman* said it seemed abundantly clear that a very large proportion of the audience would greatly prefer not to have commercials inserted into the broadcasting service. The antipathy rose from the nature of the medium. It was uniquely difficult to escape from commercial messages on radio and television and resentment was expressed by registering complaints. The Board responded to complaints by regulating the time and distribution of advertising messages.

I once replied to a lady in Vancouver "The Board has no regulation referring to 'abusive comment' on mothers-in-law. I am forwarding your letter to CKNW."

From time to time the Board had complaints about wrestling, on the grounds that it was either "legal murder" or "phoney." In one reply I pointed out that "Professional wrestlers usually live to a ripe old age and turn out to be very successful businessmen." And, "having watched a hockey game last night, [the charge] would seem to apply equally to Canada's national game." Later I was able to point out that the Board had passed a regulation prohibiting the broadcasting of "contests the results of which are known in advance." As a result of this regulation, wrestling was advertised as an "exhibition."

The Board prohibited the advertising of spirituous liquors and had regulations governing advertising of beer and wine. The temperance forces, led by Dr. Mutchmore, opposed the regulations. It was within the jurisdiction of the provinces to regulate the advertising of beer and wine. This occasionally exposed differences of opinion between the Board and the Liquor Control Board of Ontario. At one point the LCBO prohibited the representation of any curved object that looked like a bottle. I expressed myself in limerick form:

Said Le Brasseur "we ought to be able
to show a curvac-e-ous label."
The answer was no
from the LCBO
a flat one is mutchmore suit-able.

The outstanding case on "abusive comment" involved radio station CJOR, Vancouver, and the "hot-line" program of Pat Burns. I was always fascinated by the MC's on open line programs who would offer their views, for hours on end, on any subject under the sun. Joe Pyne was the first of the kind we encountered and when in Montreal I invited Pyne to lunch so I might be exposed to the phenomenon. I concluded it was glandular and there was not much could be done about it. Pat Burns was a master of the sweeping generalization. Doctors were quacks; lawyers were shysters; police were bullies; and advertisers, with the notable exception of those selected to sponsor his programs, were liars. Burns became a sensation. The station's ratings rocketed, and with them the profits. The audience included those who were mesmerized by him and others looking for grounds for complaints. The local member of the Board, Joe Brown, faced a barrage of letters.

Brown seemed to favour prosecution. Initially I replied that we needed a case which would be both successful in the courts and overwhelmingly approved by the public. I did not believe we had such a case. Later Burns became engaged in controversy over Canadian Indians whom he had characterized as dirty, unreliable, and slothful. I wrote Brown: "I have felt that the reference to Indians might give us a case on which we could get a conviction." In December 1964 we sought to engage an independent counsel in Vancouver to study Burns's statements about Indians. The lawyer we approached eventually agreed and his advice was that the Board could probably get a conviction. The Board, however, had other plans for CJOR. It recommended against the renewal of the licence to the owner.

While the Burns case was the most difficult and protracted one with which the Board had to deal, controversy was also caused by such notables as Gordon Sinclair and Pierre Berton who, intentionally or not, became thorns in the side of the regulatory agency. Mr. Berton's actions provided an opportunity for the Board to rescind a regulation inherited from the CBC regulatory era which required that all scripts dealing with the subject of birth control be submitted to the Board for prebroadcast vetting.

Most of the complaints related to "good taste" involved productions of the CBC. I do, however, remember that the very first complaint that the Board received was lodged against a private radio station. The complainant was offended by a story told by a disc jockey. A lady entered a dentist's office and said "Doctor, I am so nervous I would as soon be pregnant." The dentist replied, "Madam, make up your mind, I may have to adjust the chair."

In December 1966 I prepared for the part-time members of the Board a lengthy memorandum on the responsibility for programs broadcast by the CBC. I noted that under questioning before a Parliamentary Committee, the full-time members had found themselves required, without direction from the full Board, to declare their position. The statement by the full-time members concluded "On balance, we think it would be preferable if the CBC Directors were held clearly responsible for the 'quality' or 'public acceptability' of their programmes." The memorandum noted that the public service is not subject in the same way as are private broadcasters to conditions in the market including the preferences of users; and said that the fundamental issue appeared to be whether or not those responsible for the public sector should be more "experimental," and "more liable to make mistakes." The full-time members were inclined to agree that the public service should be more experimental than the private service.

In replying to complaints about CBC programs, I frequently defended the Corporation. I also found it exasperating, hence:

> The producers of CBC's Quest
> have a theory to hold interest,
> in a pig's eye
> with vox populi
> they really want rape and incest.

However, in reply to one MP I wrote "The Board does have a regulation prohibiting obscene, indecent and profane language. While the content of some of the Quest programmes may be suspect under the regulation, this is not the essential point of your concern. Actually, I do not envy the Corporation its responsibility to select programmes. I find myself generally in sympathy with the experimental approach of the Quest series and many of the programmes seem to me to have considerable value."

Joe Brown, who was without doubt the most conscientious of all the part-time members of the Board, found some of the CBC programs grossly offensive. In December 1966 he wrote to me saying "your personal note of Friday last (9th) arrived today. I am unhappy that you, and the permanent members, "do not feel that either the full-time members, the executive, or an ad hoc committee of the Board, should decide to prosecute the CBC over what I claim was a violation of the Board's television regulation 5(c) with regard to obscenity as portrayed on the CBC programme Sunday on November 27."

On 14 January 1967 Mr. Brown wrote a lengthy memorandum addressed to the members of the Board giving his reasons in support of a reference to the courts. The Board took action; and on 13 March I wrote Mr. Ouimet advising him that the Board had retained a counsel and that a portion of the Sunday program of 26 November 1966 was found to be "indecent" within the meaning of "indecent" in Section 5 of the regulations. In his letter of acknowledgement, Mr. Ouimet said: "you also indicate that by action of the Board of Broadcast Governors you have been instructed to advise the Corporation that, in the event of any similar occurrence, the Board would be obliged to proceed against the Corporation in the manner provided under the Broadcasting Act." Mr. Ouimet asked for a copy of the opinion so that they could consider the reasoning behind it.

When I became familiar with the Act, I noted that the Board was not required to give reasons for its decisions. I raised the point with the Minister. Mr. Nowlan said "Never give reasons, they only cause trouble." The reason most often given by the Board was that the decision was "in the public interest."

My limerick intended as a comment on the "Troika" perhaps sums up the whole BBG experience:

> The Troika is surely a queer,
> three horses, no lead and no rear.
>   A stud CAB,
>   and a mare CBC,
> But the BBG's gelded I fear.

APPENDICES

APPENDIX I

App. I.1 *Prime Ministers of Canada and Ministers Responsible for Broadcasting Matters, 1958–1968*

PRIME MINISTER

John G. Diefenbaker   21 June 1957 - 22 April 1963

RESPONSIBLE MINISTERS

RADIO ACT[1]

G. Hees   21 June 1957 - 10 October 1960
L. Balcer   11 October 1960 - 22 April 1963

BROADCASTING ACT[2]

G.C. Nowlan   21 June 1957 - 8 April 1962
E.G. Halpenny   9 April 1962 - 22 April 1963

PRIME MINISTER

Lester B. Pearson   22 April 1963 - 20 April 1968

RESPONSIBLE MINISTERS

RADIO ACT

G.J. McIlraith   22 April 1963 - 2 February 1964
J.W. Pickersgill   3 February 1964 - 18 September 1967
P.T. Hellyer   19 September 1967 - 20 April 1968

BROADCASTING ACT

J.W. Pickersgill   22 April 1963 - 2 February 1964
M. Lamontange   3 February 1964 - 17 December 1965
J. LaMarsh   18 December 1965 - 9 April 1968
J.J. Connelly   10 April 1968 - 20 April 1968

1 Minister of Transport
2 All occupied the office of Secretary of State except Mr . Nowlan
who was Minister of National Revenue.

APPENDIX II

App. II.1   *Board of Broadcast Governors Appointments 1958–1968*

BY APPOINTING PARTY AND OCCUPATION AT TIME OF FIRST APPOINTMENT

	CONSERVATIVE			LIBERAL		
Occupation	Full-time	Part-time	Total	Full-time	Part-time	Total
Business	–	3	3	–	7	7
Legal	–	3	3	–	2	2
Journalism	2	1	3	–	–	–
Education	1	2	3	1	3	4
Other Professional	–	2	2	–	2	2
Social Service	–	3	3	–	1	1
Civil Service	–	1	1	2	–	2
Agriculture	–	1	1	–	1	1
Labour	–	1	1	–	–	–
Entertainment	1	–	1	–	–	–
	4	17	21	3	16	19

BY GENDER

	CONSERVATIVE			LIBERAL		
	Full-time	Part-time	Total	Full-time	Part-time	Total
Male	4	15	19	3	14	17
Female	–	2	2	–	2	2
	4	17	21	3	16	19

BY LANGUAGE GROUP AND PROVINCE

	CONSERVATIVE	LIBERAL	TOTAL
British Columbia	1	1	2
Alberta	1(1)[1]	1(1)[1]	2(2)[1]
Saskatchewan	1	–	1
Manitoba	1(1)[1]	1	2(1)[1]
Ontario	5	4(2)[1]	9(2)[1]
Quebec	6(2)[1](5)[2]	5(5)[2]	11(2)[1](10)[2]
New Brunswick	1	2	3
Nova Scotia	1	2	3
Prince Edward Island	2	2	4
Newfoundland	2	1	3
Total	21	19	40

1 Full-time appointments
2 Francophone appointments
Source: BBG Biographical Information on the Members of the Board

App. II.2 *Part-time Members of the Board*

ORIGINAL APPOINTMENTS

JOSEPH BROWN; Vancouver; businessman. Reappointed 6 December 1963; and a member of the Board at March 1968. Apart from the Chairman, the only member of the Board to serve throughout the life of the BBG.

MABEL CONNELL; Prince Albert; dentist. Died 19 August 1963.

EMLYN DAVIES; Toronto; Baptist minister. Term expired 9 November 1963.

ROY DUCHEMIN; Sydney; publisher. Term expired 9 November 1963.

EDWARD DUNLOP; Toronto; executive. Resigned 12 September 1963 for business reasons.

EUGENE FORSEY; Ottawa; Trade Union—Research. Resigned 29 August 1962 in disagreement with his colleagues on applications for licences in Quebec City.

ROBERT FURLONG; St. John's; judge. Resigned 14 May 1959 to become Chief Justice, Newfoundland.

IRENE J. (MRS. R.G.) GILBRIDE; Montreal; volunteer social worker. Resigned 29 April 1961 on grounds of age.

GUY HUDON; Quebec City; Dean, Faculty of Law, Laval University. Resigned 29 August 1962 in disagreement with his colleagues on applications for licences in Quebec City.

COLIN MACKAY; Fredericton; President, University of New Brunswick. Term expired, 9 November 1963

IVAN SABOURIN; St. Jean-Iberville; lawyer. Term expired, 9 November 1963.

J. DAVID STEWART; Charlottetown; businessman. Resigned 7 December 1959 to seek election, successfully, in the provincial legislature.

FURTHER CONSERVATIVE APPOINTMENTS TO APRIL 1963

LOUIS BURGE; St. Peter's Bay, P.E.I.; farmer and merchant. Appointed 7 December 1959 to replace Col. David Stewart. Term expired 6 December 1964.

LESLIE MARSHALL; St. John's; businessman. Appointed 7 December 1959 to replace Chief Justice Furlong. Term expired 6 December 1964.

JOHN LEWIS; Montreal; insurance. Appointed 28 April 1961 to replace Mrs. Gilbride. Resigned 30 July 1965 for business reasons.

CHARLES CHAMBERS; Toronto; trade unionist. Appointed 29 November 1962 to replace Dr. Forsey. Resigned 3 August 1963 for business reasons.

CLAUDE GAGNON; Quebec City; lawyer. Appointed 18 October 1962 to replace Dean Hudon. Reappointed 18 October 1967. Member of the Board at March 1968.

LIBERAL APPOINTMENTS AFTER APRIL 1963

JOHN COYNE; Ottawa; lawyer. Appointed 3 August 1963. Resigned effective 31 December 1967.

JOSEPH GRITTANI; Toronto; insurance. Appointed 12 September 1963. Member of the Board at March 1968.

FRED HOLMES; Windsor; retired businessman. Appointed 6 December 1963. Member of the Board at March 1968.

JEAN PAUL LEFEBVRE; Montreal; educator. Appointed 6 December 1963. Resigned 5 May 1966, to seek election, unsuccessfully, to the provincial legislature.

LORRAINE SWEATMAN; Winnipeg; housewife. Appointed 6 December 1963. Member of the Board at March 1968.

THOMAS WATSON; Fredericton; Presbyterian minister. Appointed 6 December 1963. Resigned 17 November 1967 to return to Scotland.

WILLIAM WOODFINE; Antigonish; Professor of Economics, St. Francis Xavier University. Appointed 6 December 1963. Resigned 3 May 1967 for sabbatical year.

KEIR CLARK; Mount Stewart, P.E.I.; businessman. Appointed 13 April 1965. Resigned 2 June 1966 to seek election, successfully, in the provincial legislature.

EDOUARDINA DUPONT; Trois Rivieres; businesswoman. Appointed 21 October 1966. Member of the Board at March 1968.

MAJOR REID; Souris, P.E.I.; farmer and merchant. Appointed 21 October 1966. Member of the Board at March 1968.

GUY ROCHER; Montreal, Professor of Sociology, University of Montreal. Appointed 21 October 1966. Member of the Board at March 1968.

GORDON THOMAS; St. Anthony, Newfoundland; physician. Appointed 21 October 1966. Dr. Thomas was the only part-time member of the BBG appointed to the CRTC.

GEORGE URQUHART; St. John; businessman. Appointed 2 February 1967. Member of the Board at March 1968.

IAN STOTT; Sydney; businessman. Appointed 15 June 1967. Member of the Board at March 1968.

APPENDIX III

App. III.1   *Senior Staff Appointments Board of Broadcast Governors 1958–68*

OFFICE

DATE OF APPOINTMENT[1]

SECRETARY

M.M. McLean	Seconded
F. Whitehead	Seconded
W.D. Mills	22 June 1959
F.K. Foster	8 March 1965

ASSISTANT SECRETARY

G.A. Plante	11 March 1960
J. LaPerriere (later Chief, Administrative Services)	8 September 1964

COUNSEL

A.B.R. Lawrence	12 December 1958 (on retainer)
W.C. Pearson	28 September 1959
M.M. Goldenberg	12 October 1966

ASSISTANT COUNSEL

F.R. Côté	26 November 1965
J.M. Demers	1967–68

RESEARCH DIRECTOR - PROGRAMME

J.R. McLean	4 April 1960

ASSISTANT DIRECTOR - PROGRAMME

Aime Grandmaison	13 August 1961
L. St. Amand	1966–

RESEARCH DIRECTOR - ECONOMICS

J. Dawson	2 May 1960 (to 13 February 1964)

ASSISTANT DIRECTOR - ECONOMICS

H. Batchelor (later Acting Director-Economics and Senior Financial Analyst)	1 September 1961

TECHNICAL ADVISOR

W.R. Wilson	10 November 1959

ADMINISTRATIVE OFFICER

P.E. Meunier	20 April 1959 (to 1962)

1 Appointment to 31 March 1968 unless appointment of successor indicated.

APPENDIX IV

App. IV.1   *Board of Broadcast Governors Personnel and Financial Statistics 1958–1968*

	PERSONNEL[1]	VOTE	FINANCES EXPENDITURES	BALANCE
1958–59	7	72,000	46,833	25,167
1959–60	22	223,889	188,846	35,043
1960–61	28	298,420	281,468	16,952
1961–62	31	331,170	311,515	19,655
1962–63	34	357,935	353,913	4,022
1963–64	34	362,731	341,523	21,208
1964–65	35	390,300	367,645	22,655
1965–66	37	493,000	382,326	110,674
1966–67	64	814,100	601,813	212,287
1967–68	120	1,265,800		

1 Personnel figures do not include full-time members of the Board
Sources: All information but the 1967–68 financial figures were derived from the BBG Annual Reports, 1958–59 to 1967–68.

APPENDIX V

App. V.1   *Broadcasting Stations Licensed in Canada at 31 March 1960*

	CBC RADIO			CBC TELEVISION			TOTAL		
	Stations	LPRT	Total	Stations	SS	Total	Stations	LPRT /SS	Total
British Columbia	2	35	37	1	–	1	3	35	38
Alberta	2	5	7	–	–	–	2	5	7
Saskatchewan	1	–	1	–	–	–	1	–	1
Manitoba	2	–	2	2	–	2	4	–	4
Ontario	4	21	25	3	1	4	7	22	29
Quebec	4	2	6	2	–	2	6	2	8
New Brunswick	2	4	6	1	–	1	3	4	7
Nova Scotia	2	6	8	1	3	4	3	9	12
Prince Edward Island	–	–	–	–	–	–	–	–	–
Newfoundland	–	–	–	3	–	3	3	–	3
Territories	5	1	6	–	–	–	5	1	6
Totals	24	74	98	13	4	17	37	78	115

Source: BBG, *Annual Report*, 1959–60, Appendix B

App. V.2   *Broadcasting Stations Licensed in Canada at 31 March 1968*

	CBC RADIO			CBC TELEVISION			TOTAL		
	Stations	LPRT	Total	Stations	SS	Total	Stations	LPRT /SS	Total
British Columbia	2	67	69	3	11	14	5	78	83
Alberta	2	6	8	2	7	9	4	13	17
Saskatchewan	1	1	2	–	–	–	1	1	2
Manitoba	2	3	5	2	5	7	4	8	12
Ontario	5	49	54	3	12	15	8	61	69
Quebec	5	22	27	3	5	8	8	27	35
New Brunswick	4	10	14	1	–	1	5	10	15
Nova Scotia	2	12	14	2	4	6	4	16	20
Prince Edward Island	–	–	–	–	–	–	–	–	–
Newfoundland	5	13	18	7	4	11	12	17	29
Territories	4	18	22	1	–	1	5	18	23
Totals	32	201	233	24	48	72	56	249	305

Source: BBG, *Annual Report*, 1967–68, Appendix B
LPRT = Low Power Relay Transmitter
SS = Satellite Station

PRIVATE RADIO			PRIVATE TELEVISION			TOTAL			GRAND TOTAL		
Stations	LPRT	Total	Stations	SS	Total	Stations	LPRT/SS	Total	Stations	LPRT/SS	Total
23	–	23	4	3	7	27	3	30	30	38	68
17	–	17	5	–	5	22	–	22	24	5	29
14	–	14	6	–	6	20	–	20	21	–	21
9	–	9	1	–	1	10	–	10	14	–	14
67	–	67	14	3	17	81	3	84	88	25	113
43	1	44	9	2	11	52	3	55	58	5	63
9	–	9	2	–	2	11	–	11	14	4	18
11	–	11	1	2	3	12	2	14	15	11	26
2	–	2	1	–	1	3	–	3	3	–	3
7	–	7	2	1	3	9	1	10	12	1	13
–	–	–	–	–	–	–	–	–	5	1	6
202	1	203	45	11	56	247	12	259	284	90	374

PRIVATE RADIO			PRIVATE TELEVISION			TOTAL			GRAND TOTAL		
Stations	LPRT	Total	Stations	SS	Total	Stations	LPRT/SS	Total	Stations	LPRT/SS	Total
38	–	38	12	73	85	50	73	123	55	151	206
20	–	20	7	18	25	27	18	45	31	31	62
18	–	18	11	16	27	29	16	45	30	17	47
12	–	12	3	3	6	15	3	18	19	11	30
83	2	85	16	10	26	99	12	111	107	73	180
57	2	59	13	36	49	70	38	108	78	65	143
9	–	9	4	4	8	13	4	17	18	14	32
14	–	14	3	6	9	17	6	23	21	22	43
2	–	2	1	–	1	3	–	3	3	–	3
10	–	10	3	5	8	13	5	18	25	22	47
–	–	–	–	–	–	–	–	–	5	18	23
263	4	267	73	171	244	336	175	511	392	424	816

App. V.3   *Net Increase in Broadcasting Stations in Canada*
March 1960 - March 1968

	CBC RADIO			CBC TELEVISION			TOTAL		
	STATIONS	LPRT	TOTAL	STATIONS	SS	TOTAL	STATIONS	LPRT	TOTAL /SS
1968	32	201	233	24	48	72	56	249	305
1960	24	74	98	13	4	17	37	78	115
Increase in Stations	8	127	135	11	44	55	19	171	190
Percentage Increase	33	171	137	84	1100	323	51	219	165

LPRT = Low Power Relay Transmitter
SS = Satellite Station

PRIVATE RADIO			PRIVATE TELEVISION			TOTAL			GRAND TOTAL		
Stations	LPRT	Total	Stations	SS	Total	Stations	LPRT/SS	Total	Stations	LPRT/SS	Total
263	4	267	73	171	244	336	175	511	392	424	816
202	1	203	45	11	56	247	12	259	284	90	374
61	3	64	28	160	188	89	163	252	108	334	442
30	300	31	62	1454	335	36	1358	97	38	371	118

APPENDIX VI

App. VI.1   *Private Radio and Television Income Statistics 1961–68*

YEAR	NUMBER OF STATIONS RADIO/TELEVISION	NET INCOME	NET INCOME TO TOTAL ASSETS	NET INCOME TO SHAREHOLDERS' EQUITY
1961	194/55	(2,675)	–	–
1962	198/58	1,754	1.6	4.5
1963	239/63	5,462	4.8	12.8
1964	265/66	10,002	8.2	20.3
1965	281/65	13,942	10.7	23.8
1966	291/65	15,051	9.8	20.9
1967	305/66	15,569	9.4	19.23
1968	319/68	17,107	11.5	22.7

Source: Canada, Dominion Bureau of Statistics, *Radio and Television Broadcasting*, 1961–68, Catalogue #56–204.

NOTES

PREFACE

1. See Frank W. Peers, *The Politics of Canadian Broadcasting 1920–1951* (Toronto: University of Toronto Press, 1969); Idem, *The Public Eye: Television and the Politics of Canadian Broadcasting, 1952–1968* (Toronto: University of Toronto Press, 1979); E. Austin Weir, *The Struggle for National Broadcasting in Canada* (Toronto: McClelland and Stewart, 1965); and Marc Raboy, *Missed Opportunities: The Story of Canada's Broadcasting Policy* (Montreal and Kingston: McGill-Queen's Press, 1990).

2. G. Bruce Doern, ed., *The Regulatory Process in Canada* (Toronto: Macmillan, 1978). Although later analyses of the regulatory process abound, it was decided to adopt the Doern model because it is based on concepts more applicable to the BBG period than the contemporary ones. In choosing this framework we are less likely to fall into the sin of presentism, that is the judging of past performance by present standards. Amongst other works which might be usefully studied are: Stephen Brooks, *Public Policy in Canada: An Introduction*, 2d ed. (Toronto: McClelland and Stewart, 1993); C. Lloyd Brown-John, *Canadian Regulatory Agencies* (Toronto: Butterworths, 1981); G. Bruce Doern and Richard W. Phidd, *Canadian Public Policy: Ideas, Structure, Process*, 2d ed. (Scarborough: Nelson Canada, 1992); Kenneth Kernaghan and David Siegel, *Public Administration in Canada*, 2d ed. (Scarborough: Nelson Canada, 1991); Richard Schultz and Alan Alexandroff, *Economic Regulation and the Federal System* (Toronto: University of Toronto Press, 1985); and Paul Thomas and Orest W. Zajcew, "Structural Heretics:

Crown Corporations and Regulatory Agencies," in Michael Atkinson, ed., *Governing Canada: Institutions and Public Policy* (Toronto: Harcourt Brace Jovanovich Canada Inc., 1993)

3. Schultz and Alexandroff, *Economic Regulation*, pp. 2–3.

4. Brown-John, p. 35.

5. Schultz and Alexandroff, pp. 5–8.

1 THE EVOLUTION OF CANADIAN TELEVISION POLICY

1. Canada, Parliament, House of Commons, Special Committee on Radio Broadcasting, 1938, *Final Report*, p. 194. Numerous references to the issue appear throughout the Minutes and Proceedings of Evidence, e.g., pp. 5, 54, 57, 66, 145–46, 156.

2. Royal Commission on Radio Broadcasting, *Report* (Ottawa: King's Printer, 1929), p. 6.

3. With the introduction of television, the name of the Association was changed to "The Canadian Association of Radio and Television Broadcasters." In 1958, however, the simpler name "Canadian Association of Broadcasters" was reinstituted. It will be used throughout this study.

4. Canada, Royal Commission on Broadcasting, *Report* (Ottawa: Queen's Printer, 1957), p. 136.

2 THE BOARD OF BROADCAST GOVERNORS: CONSTITUTION AND FUNCTIONS

1. See Appendix I for a listing of Prime Ministers and ministers responsible for broadcasting, 1958–1968.

2. Dr. Stewart noted in his memoir: "I was appointed as Chairman of the BBG when the Diefenbaker Government was in office and served under Mr. Pearson's administration. I had never identified myself with any political party. Mr. Ray Milner, of Edmonton, persuaded me to attend the Conservative convention at Port Hope at which Mr. Bracken was elected leader of the party. I went as an adviser on agricultural problems. This connection may have led to the invitation to chair the Royal Commission on Price Spreads for Food Products, and later to chair the BBG. I believe I met Mr. Diefenbaker on three occasions, only once after my appointment to the Board. It was at a garden party. I was not an admirer of Mr. Diefenbaker. I found him pompous. I

had been appointed by the Liberal Government of Mr. St. Laurent as a member of the Royal Commission on Canada's Economic Prospects (Gordon Commission) and had met Mr. Pearson first at Walter Gordon's house. Later, Mr. Pearson visited the University of Alberta. After moving to Ottawa, I found Mr. Pearson a strong supporter of International House, of which I was for a time President. I saw him on broadcasting matters on a number of occasions. I liked Mr. Pearson. I found him unpretentious. I am not sure that either of the Prime Ministers had much of a grasp of what broadcasting was all about.

"I was associated with five ministers responsible for broadcasting: Nowlan and Halpenny (Conservatives) and Pickersgill, Lamontagne and LaMarsh (Liberals). The relationship with the minister is a sensitive one. The Chairman must be prepared to protect the independence of the agency. At the same time, the minister must be in a position to report to Parliament and frequently to defend the agency. When the Board's estimates were before the House, the Chairman had to sit on the floor in front of the minister. I had no difficulty with any of the ministers. Pickersgill was knowledgeable about broadcasting and Miss LaMarsh made herself well-informed."

3. The Prime Minister suggested that the announcement of the decision not to reappoint Mr. Allison had been delayed in the event that the Conservative Party should have won the election of 8 November 1965 and wanted to reappoint him. Regardless, he agreed that the decision of Cabinet should have been communicated to both Messrs. Stewart and Allison when it was taken and apologized for the failure to do so. (Letter, Rt. Hon. L.B. Pearson to Andrew Stewart, 24 November 1965. Pearson papers, MG26 N4, Vol. 12, file #352/B863.1)

4. Dr. Stewart's initial appointment was for seven years, but after the return to power of the Liberal Party in April 1963, the Chairman wrote to assure the new Prime Minister, Mr. Pearson, that his resignation would be offered at any time the Prime Minister might request it. Again, on 4 May 1964, the Chairman wrote the Prime Minister, referring to the possibility that new legislation might be enacted before the end of his term as Chairman in November 1965 and saying he would not be available for the administration of broadcasting after amendment to the legislation, should this amendment occur before that date. It soon became apparent that the new legislation could not be enacted by November 1965. Following up conversations with the Hon. J.W. Pickersgill, then Secretary of State, the Chairman wrote to him saying that, if the Prime Minister and his colleagues wished it, he would be prepared to continue until 30 June 1966, or until the new legislation was enacted, if that occurred earlier. On 14 July 1965, the Prime Minister announced that

Dr. Stewart had agreed to remain as Chairman of the BBG until the new legislation came into effect, and the necessary order-in-council was passed reappointing him to that position for another seven years. On 11 July 1966, following publication of the White Paper on Broadcasting, the Chairman once more wrote the Prime Minister saying that he was intrigued with the possibilities of the proposals in the White Paper. He would be happy to continue as Chairman if the Prime Minister so wished. He assured the Prime Minister, however, that should be wish to appoint someone else to the position, he would be entirely satisfied with his decision.

On Monday, 23 February 1968, the Chairman received a call from the Secretary of State, the Hon. Judy LaMarsh. Miss LaMarsh explained that the Government wished to appoint Pierre Juneau, Vice-chairman of the BBG, as chairman of the body soon to supersede the BBG as the regulatory agency, the Canadian Radio-Television Commission (CRTC). Miss LaMarsh reiterated a view she had previously expressed that the BBG under Dr. Stewart's chairmanship had not been "tough enough" with the broadcasters and referred to the advantage of appointing a French-speaking Canadian as chairman of the CRTC.

Dr. Stewart's inability to communicate in French was a serious limitation. He found it very embarrassing to deal with unilingual French Canadians when they came to his office on business. He made some limited and unsuccessful efforts to correct the problem. On one occasion, on his way to Toronto, he took along a French novel to try to read on the train. Some days later a newspaper reported that he had been seen on the train reading a book in French, "he had reached page 11."

From its first printing, the new bill—Bill C-163—contained a transitional section which provided that the chairman of the BBG would become chairman of the new CRTC. All other appointments made under the Broadcasting Act, 1958, would be terminated. Although frequent amendments were made to the draft bill, the clause continuing the appointment of the chairman was retained and remained in the bill at February 1968. The object was clearly to avoid possible controversy over appointment of the chairman of the new body. All that was required was Dr. Stewart's resignation as Chairman of the BBG. He assured Miss LaMarsh that the Government's decision created no problem.

The incredible defeat of the Government on the tax bill had brought Mr. Pearson home from Jamaica. When Dr. Stewart saw him, the Prime Minister was obviously anxious to receive the Chairman's letter of resignation, which was left with him. In a letter of 11 March, the Prime Minister suggested Dr. Stewart's resignation might take effect on 18 March, and that was agreed to.

Monday, 18 March arrived, however, without an announcement having been made.

The Prime Minister's 11 March letter also contained the following:

> As you leave the post, a very difficult and important post, which you have filled with such devotion and distinction for the last ten years, may I thank you, both officially on behalf of the Government and personally, for the efficient and unselfish service to Canada that you have given; following upon so many other years of service to the country in more than one capacity. The Canadian Government and, indeed, the Canadian people are very much in your debt. (Pearson papers, MG26 N4, Vol. 12, File #352/B863.11)

5. See Appendix II for an analysis of appointments to the Board, 1958–68. Because Messrs. Brown and Gagnon were reappointed by the Liberals, the actual number of part-time appointments is calculated as 33 for the 31 people involved.

6. See Chap. 4 for a detailed discussion of the Toronto applications and Chap. 12 for the details of the Barrie application.

7. In considering the initial appointments to the BBG in 1958, Mr. Nowlan stressed in Cabinet "the importance of the representative character of the board as well as the necessity to make it politically as neutral as possible. He thought that persons selected should be persons of outstanding quality." (Cabinet documents, RG2 A5a, Vol. 1899, 21 October 1958, p. 4)

8. See Appendix III for a list of the senior staff of the BBG, 1958–68.

9. See Appendix IV for details of BBG staffing and financing, 1958–68.

10. At the University of Alberta, the Chairman had become a constant listener to the CBC radio and an advocate for the public system. At the same time, he realized that CBC radio had a relatively small audience; and he understood the assertion by Jack Kent Cooke that the sounds emanating from his station CKEY, Toronto, represented "the authentic folk music of the North American continent." As one trained in economics, the Chairman had some sympathy with the private service which tended to respond to market conditions.

11. Canada, Parliament, House of Commons, *Hansard*, 18 July 1959, p. 6300.

12. BBG, *Public Announcement*, "Announcement by Board of Broadcast Governors on Applications for Second Television Licences," 28 July 1959.

13. BBG, *Public Announcement*, 28 July 1959.

14. BBG, *Public Announcement*, "Announcement Regarding Radio (TV) Broadcasting Regulations," 18 November 1959.

15. See Appendix V for data on licensing of stations during the period.

16. Hon. J.W. Pickersgill, Statement re Broadcasting to the Canadian Association of Broadcasters, Toronto, 1 May 1963, p. 1.

17. See Peers, *The Public Eye*, pp. 393–401 for a detailed discussion of the charge.

3 CANADIAN CONTENT

1. Canada, Parliament, House of Commons, *Hansard*, 18 July 1959, p. 6300.

2. BBG, *Public Announcement*, "Announcement by the Board of Broadcast Governors on Applications for Second Television Licences," 28 July 1959, p. 1.

3. BBG, *Public Announcement*, "Announcement Regarding Radio (TV) Broadcasting Regulations," 18 November 1959, p. 5.

4. Ibid., pp. 6–7.

5. Ibid., p. 12.

6. Ibid., pp. 13–14.

7. BBG, *Annual Report, 1962–63*, p. 13.

8. BBG, *Public Announcement*, "Announcement Regarding Radio (TV) Broadcasting Regulations"' 18 November 1959, pp. 13–14.

9. BBG, *Annual Report, 1962–63*, p. 12.

10. *Canada Gazette*, SOR/62–79, 23 May 1962, p. 3.

11. BBG, Circular Letter #68, 15 June 1962.

12. BBG, Circular Letter #18, 2 August 1960.

13. BBG, Circular Letter #67, 15 June 1962, p. 2.

14. BBG, Circular Letter #33, 19 May 1961, p. 2.

15. BBG, Circular Letter #73, 6 September 1962, p. 2.

16. BBG, *Annual Report, 1962–63*, p. 13.

17. Canada, Parliament, House of Commons, *Hansard*, 18 August 1958, p. 3749.

18. Andrew Stewart, "Communication Problems Between Canada and the United States," Address to the Canadian-American Relations Seminar, Assumption College, Windsor, Ontario, 11 November 1961.

19. Andrew Stewart, Address to the Annual Meeting of the Canadian Association of Broadcasters, Toronto, 18 April 1967.

20. Ibid.

21. Andrew Stewart, "Communication Problems Between Canada and the United States," Address to the Canadian-American Relations Seminar, Assumption College, Windsor, Ontario, 11 November 1961.

22. Andrew Stewart, "Canadian Broadcasting" Address to the Hamilton Association, Hamilton, Ontario, 28 January 1961.

4 THE INITIAL SECOND STATION APPLICATIONS

1. BBG, *Press Release*, 20 July 1959.

2. BBG, *Press Release*, 11 August 1959.

3. BBG, *Announcement by Board of Broadcast Governors on Applications for Second Television Licences*, 28 July 1959.

4. BBG, *Announcement re Hearings in January, March, May and June*, 8 October 1959, p. 3.

5. BBG, *Announcement*, 30 January 1960, p. 2.

6. BBG, Public Hearing, Toronto, 16 March 1960, *Transcript of Evidence*, p. 300.

7. The Cabinet in discussing the Board's recommendation noted that it could not at that stage rule out the recommended applicant merely because one of the individuals involved owned a newspaper. If that were to be a consideration, it should have been laid out in the ground rules. As well, Toronto did have a healthily competitive newspaper situation. Further, the Cabinet noted that the Board's recommendation had been unanimous. The "supporters of several political parties" making up the Board had independently reached their own decision based on the presentations made to them. For the Cabinet to reject such a recommendation "would really constitute political interference." (Cabinet papers, RG2 Vol. 2746, Vol. 77, 28 April 1960, p. 10.)

8. See pp. 249–57.

9. BBG, Public Hearing, Toronto, 16 March 1960, *Transcript of Evidence*, p. 175.

10. Ibid., p. 193.

11. Ibid., p. 511.

12. Dr. Stewart recalled: "I became quite involved and concerned about the process of decision-making in the case of competing applications for licences. The applicants went to great trouble and expense in preparing and presenting their applications. They had to have, and be seen to have, a fair break.' It seemed so important to arrive at the 'right' decision and to do so by a defensi-

ble process. My concerns were explored in a paper on 'The Board of Broadcast Governors' presented to the Canadian Bar Association (September 1960) and in a talk on 'The Administrator as Judge' to a Senior Officers' Course on Government Administration at Arnprior. Applicants frequently would choose to come to see the Chairman in advance of the hearing of their applications. As I believed in an 'open door' policy, I rarely if ever refused to see applicants; but I wonder if it were wise. It was always necessary to avoid any commitment and to make it clear that the decision was made by the full Board and not by the Chairman alone.

"It was also my opinion that if among the members of the Board there was some factor which would lead them to reject any application, this should be known to prospective applicants. There should be an announcement of policy referring to it. In dealing with the application by Mr. Bassett of *The Toronto Telegram*, I voted against it because I felt that the owner of a newspaper in a metropolitan centre should not also own a television station. This matter had come up in the earlier Winnipeg hearings. Here the Board rejected the application by the Siftons, owners of *The Free Press*. However, the majority of the members of the Board, perhaps with knowledge of the pending Bassett application in Toronto, recorded that their decision did not create a precedent. In other words, the Board rejected the policy of refusing a licence to a local newspaper. I exercised my right to vote according to my own view.

"It was also important that the procedures followed by the Board were seen to be fair. The Board adopted procedures which enabled it to deal expeditiously with applications. It was a matter of satisfaction that applications were placed on the agenda and a decision was announced in the shortest possible time. There was never any backlog of applications. Although the procedures of the Board were not identical to those of the courts, e.g.: the Board did not provide for cross examination, I do not recall any case of a complaint by an applicant that the Board procedures prevented him from having a fair hearing.

"My most profound concern was with the imponderables which had to be weighed in coming to a decision and with the assessment of the objectives. This was a theme I elaborated on in talking to the Canadian Bar Association. The Board published a list of factors it would take into consideration in assessing an application. How do you measure the significance of the composition of the Board of Directors of a company and weigh this against the general plan of financing? How do you come to the conclusion that one promise of performance provides a higher standard than another? What does 'in the public interest' really mean?

"I came to the conclusion that there might not be a 'right' decision; but it was important that an effort be made to find one. In my talk to the Officers' Course I said, 'The process of arriving at a judgement is an exercise which requires effort. . . . No one should be put in a position of responsibility for making a significant judgement in public affairs unless he has demonstrated the discipline and consistent practice of considered judgement. . . . No administrator is as competent as he should be and no good administrator is as competent as he would like to be. . . . After he has gathered some experience. . . . he has acquired something of value to the administrative process which attaches to himself. . . . There is, therefore, the prospect in the pooling of experience. . . . of strengthening the general management of public affairs.'

"In the same talk I stressed the advantage of providing for some review mechanism. The Broadcasting Act provided that the Board recommend on the issuing of licences. All recommendations of the Board were subject to review by the Governor-in-Council. I am not sure this was the kind of review I had in mind in my talk."

13. BBG, Public Hearing, Toronto, 16 March 1960, *Transcript of Evidence*, pp. 657–58.

14. Ibid., pp. 252–53.

15. Ibid., p. 272.

16. BBG, Public Hearing, Ottawa, 25 June 1960, *Transcript of Evidence*, pp. 400–401.

17. Joseph Sedgwick, Letter to the Editor, *The Globe and Mail*, 29 March 1960. At least one member of the Board was so outraged by Mr. Sedgwick's accusations that he refused to participate "in any deliberations, either in public hearings or at *in-camera* meetings of the Board, or any case in which Mr. Sedgwick presented arguments to us "unless Mr. Sedgwick apologized to the Board and purged himself of his contempt." Mr. Sedgwick declined the opportunity when it was offered to him. The member consistently stuck to his abstention. See Spry Papers, National Archives of Canada, MG30 D-297, vol. 123, File #2.

5 THE TORONTO STATION AND THE INVOLVEMENT OF ABC

1. The net loss for the year 1961 for the private sector as a whole was $2,674,577. The aggregate operating loss of the television stations, totalling $3,271,037, was partially offset by profits in the radio segment. Canada, Dominion Bureau of Statistics, *Radio and Television, 1961* (Ottawa: Queen's

Printer, June 1963), Tables 4, 5 and 6. See Appendix VI for private sector income statistics, 1961–68.

2. BBG, *Public Announcement*, 28 August 1961.

3. Spry Papers, National Archives of Canada, MG30 D-297, Vol. 123, File #2. Letter circulated by an unidentified member of the Board to other members.

4. Andrew Stewart, letter to Hon. Leon Balcer, 27 September 1961, pp. 2–3.

5. Andrew Stewart, letter to John Bassett, 17 November 1961, p. 2.

6. Andrew Stewart, letter to Donald Coyle, 12 January 1962.

7. Andrew Stewart, letter to Spencer Caldwell, 22 January 1962. It is evident that the Chairman found the experience with the Toronto licence a traumatic one. Among a number of strong applications the Board had recommended the Bassett application either, as Mr. Sedgwick alleged, because of Mr. Bassett's allegiance to the Conservative Party, or because of the excellence of its submission and its outstanding promise of performance. If it was the latter, then the Board had been grossly mislead; and it should have known better. The situation was exacerbated by the involvement of a U.S. network in the reorganization.

6 THE CTV NETWORK

1. BBG, *Press Release*, Calgary, 17 May 1960. Under the Radio (TV) Broadcasting Regulations, a network was defined as "an organization or arrangement employing electronic connections (including connections by Hertzian waves and cables) between two or more stations for the presentation of programs, but does not include the operation of a licenced [sic] satellite station."

2. Ibid.

3. BBG, *Press Release*, "Television Networks," 30 June 1960, p. 2.

4. Ibid., p. 3.

5. Ibid.

6. Andrew Stewart, Memo to Board, 17 August 1960, pp. 6–7.

7. BBG, Public Hearing, Ottawa, 1–2 September 1960, *Transcript of Evidence*, pp. 20–48.

8. Ibid., pp. 114–42.

9. Ibid., pp. 143–45, 155–58.

10. Ibid., p. 156.

11. Ibid., p. 159.

12. Ibid., p. 160.

13. Ibid., pp. 196–200.

14. Ibid.

15. Ibid., pp. 183 ff.

16. Ibid., pp. 243–45, 245–95.

17. BBG, *Announcement*, 9 September 1960, p. 7.

18. Ibid.

19. Ibid., pp. 8–9.

20. Ibid., pp. 9–10.

21. BBG, *Public Announcement*, 14 October 1960.

22. Ibid., p. 4.

23. Ibid.

24. Ibid., p. 3.

25. Canada Gazette, Part II, SOR/60–470, 26 October 1960, pp. 1352–56.

26. BBG, *Statement on Administrative Policy Regarding Television Networks*, 19 December 1960.

27. BBG, *Annual Report, 1963–64*, p. 17.

28. BBG, *Public Announcement*, "Cross-Programming," 7 December 1961.

29. BBG, *Annual Report, 1961–62*, p. 11.

30. BBG, Public Hearing, Ottawa, 23 February 1966, *Transcript of Evidence*, pp. 167–82.

31. Ibid., pp. 182–98.

32. Ibid., pp. 199–211.

33. Ibid., pp. 211–34.

34. BBG, *Public Announcement*, 4 March 1966, pp. 1–2.

7 THE GREY CUP GAME, 1962

1. The Cabinet received recommendations that the new Broadcasting Act should include *inter alia* provisions for:

1) a new regulatory Board with power over all stations including CBC stations along the lines recommended by the Royal Commission (Fowler);

2) reporting channels for the CBC directly to Parliament rather than through the new Board;

3) the introduction of competition in the TV field; and,

4) the new regulatory Board composed of three or five full-time members, not a larger part-time membership. (Obviously this point did not come to

pass.) (Cabinet papers, RG2 B2, Vol. 2741, n.d., file #C-20–5, #92–58, p. 2.)

An earlier meeting of Cabinet had agreed that the bill "should be drafted in general terms and not attempt to spell everything out in black and white." (Cabinet papers, RG2 A5a, Vol. 1898, 12 July 1958, p. 10.)

2. BBG, *Press Release*, 9 March 1961, p. 1.

3. BBG, *Press Release*, 20 November 1961, pp. 1–2.

4. Andrew Stewart, letter to S. Caldwell, 30 May 1962.

5. Andrew Stewart, letter to J. Bassett, 11 June 1962.

6. J.A. Ouiment, letter to J. Bassett, 11 June 1962.

7. BBG, Public Hearing, Ottawa, 18 August 1962, *Transcript of Evidence,* pp. 1004–06.

8. S. Caldwell, telegram to J.A. Ouimet, 12 July 1962.

9 BBG, *Grey Cup Game Broadcast, 1962* (Memorandum from the Board to the Canadian Broadcasting Corporation and the CTV Network), 6 July 1962, p. 1.

10. BBG, Memo, Counsel, BBG to Secretary of State, 2 October 1962. Support for the Board's position was also drawn for the principle in the Privy Council case: Attorney-General for Canada versus Hallet and Curry Ltd., 1952 Appeal Cases at p. 427.

11. Andrew Stewart, telegram to J.A. Ouimet and S. Caldwell, 18 July 1962.

12. BBG, *Press Release*, 18 July 1962.

13. CBC, *Press Release*, CBC Information Services, 15 November 1962, pp. 1–2.

14. C.F.H. Carson, letter to J.A. Ouimet, 13 November 1962.

15. BBG, Public Hearing, Ottawa, 18 August 1962, *Transcript of Evidence*, 1009A - 1009B.

16. Ibid., p. 1009B. Mr. Ouimet later wrote in his memoir: "It was particularly unpleasant to have to clash openly with Dr. Stewart, the Chairman of the BBG, for whom I had much respect and affection." (J.A. Ouimet, Memoire, Notes for Archives, MG30 E481, Vol. 46, Section E, Binder #2, p. 105.)

17. Andrew Stewart, letter to J.A. Ouimet, 24 August 1962.

18. BBG, *Press Release*, 22 October 1962, pp. 1–2. The Press Release noted the various deadlines which would have to be met if the regulation was to appear in the *Canada Gazette* of 28 November, prior to the 1 December Grey Cup Game.

19. *Canada Gazette*, Part II, SOR/62–471, 12 December 1962, p. 1304.

20. Andrew Stewart, letter to J.A. Ouimet, 14 November 1962, pp. 1–2.

21. CBC, *Press Release*, CBC Information Services, 15 November 1962, pp. 4–5. CTV Network had issued a strongly worded press release on 13 November 1962 stressing its frustration and bewilderment at the CBC's "irresponsible behaviour." (Pearson Papers, MG26 N6, Vol. 25, file # 352.)

22. Andrew Stewart, letter to J.A. Ouimet, 20 November 1962, pp. 1–2.

23. For example, see *The Globe and Mail*, 20 August 1962.

24. For example, see Canada, Parliament, House of Commons, *Hansard*, 1962–63, pp. 150, 493, 736, 1170, 1506–08, 1559–61, 1701.

25. BBG, *Public Announcement*, 3 January 1963, p. 8.

26. According to evidence in the Ouimet papers, Mr. Driedger had advised the Minister that the Cabinet should intervene "before the controversy got too far out of hand." (Ouiment papers, Grey Cup, MG30, E481, Vol. 25, "Notes on a conversation with Mr. Driedger, Deputy Minister of Justice," 8 November 1962, p. 3.

8 ALTERNATIVE TELEVISION SERVICE AND THE CONSERVATIVE GOVERNMENT

1. Canada, Parliament, House of Commons, *Hansard*, 18 July 1959, p. 6300.

2. Canada, Parliament, House of Commons, Committee on Broadcasting, *Minutes of Proceedings and Evidence*, #14, 22 June 1959, p. 479.

3. BBG, Public Hearing, Calgary, 10–12 May 1960, *Transcript of Evidence*, pp. 488–97.

4. Ibid., pp. 497–510.

5. Ibid., pp. 510–16.

6. Ibid., pp. 526–30.

7. Ibid., pp. 230–42.

8. Ibid., pp. 150–230.

9. Order-in-Council, P.C. 1960–1113, 12 August 1960.

10. The CBC, on the other hand, felt that the BBG was the major cause of problems in the broadcasting system. Statements from the Corporation's "Analysis by Corporate Affairs of Statements by Chairman of the BBG about National Broadcasting" (23 November 1961) are revealing. "The BBG is developing a concept of the national broadcasting system which appears to differ quite markedly from that which has prevailed since 1936." (p. 3) "He (Dr. Stewart) does not state that it was the BBG which introduced these tensions to a very great extent through its insistence on a privately-operated sec-

ond television network." (p. 5) "Consequently, to the degree that current tension exist because of a second network, the BBG must accept responsibility." (p. 10). (Ouimet papers, MG30, E481, Vol. 1, file A-12, "Board Agenda Material, 1958–65.") The BBG, of course, was only carrying out governmental policy with regard to the creation of a second television network.

Nevertheless, in his memoir, Mr. Ouimet commented: "Edmonton, Quebec City, St. John's, We finally won all three licences, but what a waste of time!" (J.A. Ouimet, Memoire, Notes for Archives, MG30 E481, Vol. 46, Section E, Binder #2, p. 105.)

11. BBG, *Public Announcement*, "Statement of General Policy with Respect to Rebroadcasting Stations," 11 December 1961.

12. BBG, *Public Announcement*, "The Extension of Alternative Services," 20 December 1962, p. 4.

13. Ibid., p. 9.

14. For a more detailed discussion of this point, see: F.W. Peers, *The Public Eye*, pp. 118–19, 266, 306–7.

15. Andrew Stewart, letter to Mary O'Brien, Secretary, Citizens' Committee Supporting CBC-TV, 11 January 1963, pp. 2–4.

16. Andrew Stewart, letter to Hon. Ernest Halpenny, 31 January 1963. The letter contained detailed information about the capital and operating implications of the application and noted that the estimates of annual operating losses had been increased by over $250,000 without reference to the CBC Board of Directors.

The original CBC application for the St. John's licence had been filed with the Department of Transport on 31 July 1962 to be heard in October 1962. Its processing had been delayed for financial reasons. (Ouimet papers, MG30, E481, Vol. 26, file "CBC Newfoundland Television Application-1963.")

Mr. Ouimet had written (21 February 1961) to the former minister responsible for broadcasting suggesting that it was "not only practical but desirable" that the recommendations for long-term financing of the CBC be implemented. Mr. Nowlan responded "I have made it abundantly plain in conversations with you, as well as in statements in the House of Commons, that the Government at this time has no intention of adopting a long term policy of financing the C.B.C. It is the opinion of myself and my colleagues that this is entirely unrealistic, as I said yesterday in the House of Commons." He concluded by suggesting that the whole matter was not the business of the Board anyway. (Ouimet papers, MG30, E481, Vol. 32, file "Correspondence with Government, 1958–67.")

17. BBG, *Public Announcement*, 5 April 1963, pp. 1–2.

18. Hon. J.W. Pickersgill, Address and Statement to the Annual Meeting of the Canadian Association of Broadcasters, Toronto, 1 May 1963, p. 7.

19. J.R. Baldwin, letter to Andrew Stewart, 17 April 1963, p. 1.

20. Andrew Stewart, letter to Hon. J.W. Pickersgill, 26 August 1963, p. 1.

21. Andrew Stewart, letter to J.R. Baldwin, 24 September 1963, pp. 1–2.

22. Order-in-Council P.C. 1963–1440, 3 October 1963.

23. Hon. J.W. Pickersgill, letter to Andrew Stewart, 23 August 1963, p. 1.

9 ALTERNATIVE TELEVISION SERVICE AND THE LIBERAL GOVERNMENT

1. Andrew Stewart, letter to Hon. J.W. Pickersgill, 24 September 1963, Interim Report of the "Troika," p. 4.

2. Canada, Secretary of State, *White Paper on Broadcasting, 1966* was issued over the name of the then Secretary of State, Miss LaMarsh.

3. Andrew Stewart, letter to Rt. Hon. L.B. Pearson, 8 April 1963, p. 1.

4. Andrew Stewart, Address to Canadian Association of Broadcasters, 3 May 1963, pp. 12–13.

5. Andrew Stewart, letter to Hon. J.W. Pickersgill, 24 September 1963, Interim Report of the "Troika," p. 1. The "Troika" also supported the idea that the budget of the CBC should be determined by Parliament for a period of years.

6. *White Paper*, p. 10.

7. BBG, Memo to Board, August 1966.

8. BBG, *Public Announcement*, "Extension of Television Service," 5 October 1966.

9. Andrew Stewart, letter to Rt. Hon. L.B. Pearson, 6 October 1966, p. 2.

10. Canada, Parliament, House of Commons, Committee on Broadcasting, Film and Assistance to the Arts, *Minutes of Proceeding and Evidence*, 20 December 1966, pp. 1429 ff.

11. Andrew Stewart, letter to Hon. J. LaMarsh, 23 March 1967, p. 1.

12. Andrew Stewart, letter to Hon. J. LaMarsh, 12 January 1968, p. 2.

13. BBG, *Alternative Service in Small Markets*, 4 January 1968, p. 3.

14. Ibid., p. 5.

15. Andrew Stewart, letter to Mayor R.D. Burt, Cardston, Alberta, 3 March 1967, p. 1.

16. Andrew Stewart, letter to Hon. Walter Dinsdale, 8 March 1967, p. 1.

17. Andrew Stewart, letter to Mrs. Margaret Rideout, 12 January 1967, p. 1.

18. Andrew Stewart, letter to Hon. J. LaMarsh, 9 February 1967, p. 1.

19. Later, Finlay MacDonald told the Chairman that John Bassett, looking at the haggis, said "Hell, we'll have to eat this stuff, or we'll lose our licence."

20. Andrew Stewart, letter to Hon. J. LaMarsh, 14 December 1967, p. 1.

21. *White Paper*, p. 11.

22. BBG, Internal Memorandum on White Paper, 1966.

23. Andrew Stewart, memo to Prime Minister's office, January 1967, p. 3.

24. Touche, Ross, Bailey & Smart, *Privately Owned Television Stations, Review and Analysis of the Financial Operating Results for their Financial Periods Ended in the Years 1962 to 1966*, May 1967, pp. 42 ff.

25. A major example of the problem of extension of primary service to the north was provided by the Northern Manitoba situation. In 1966, the communities of Flin Flon, Thompson, Swan River, The Pas, Swan Lake and Lynn Lake sought primary service. The Board held a public hearing on the subject involving representatives of the communities affected, the Government of Manitoba, the Manitoba Telephone System, various Labour Councils and the CBC. As with the extension of second service, the absence of clear governmental policy exacerbated the situation, now made all the more complicated by the presence of two levels of government and by government proposals to involve public agencies other than the CBC in the process. (J.A. Ouimet, letter to Hon. J. LaMarsh, 31 January 1967, Pearson papers, MG26 N4, Vol. 14, file #736,622 Conf.)

10 EDUCATIONAL TELEVISION

1. Andrew Stewart, address to the Saskatchewan Television Conference, Regina, 5 April 1960, p. 23.

2. Andrew Stewart, letter to Nora Hodgins, Ontario Teachers Federation, 7 February 1961, p. 1.

3. Andrew Stewart, letter to A.A. O'Brien, Edmonton Separate School Board, 3 March 1961, p. 1.

4. BBG, *Statement of the Policies of the Board of Broadcast Governors with Respect to Educational Television*, prepared for the ETV Conference, University of British Columbia, 31 March 1962, pp. 3–4.

5. Andrew Stewart, letter to Dr. F.B. Rainsberry, Supervisor, School Broadcasts, CBC, 27 February 1963, p. 1.

6. Meeting on Educational Broadcasting, Toronto, Ontario, 4 March 1964, *Minutes*, p. 1.

7. Ibid., p. 5.

8. Andrew Stewart, letter to M. Gosselin, 6 March 1964.

9. BBG, Memo to Minister, May 1964.

10. Andrew Stewart, letter to Hon. M. Lamontagne, 21 December 1964, pp. 1–2.

11. BBG, Memorandum to the Secretary of State re Educational Television, 12 May 1966, p. 1.

12. Ibid., p. 6.

13. *White Paper*, pp. 12–13.

14. Andrew Stewart, letter to Hon. J. LaMarsh, 30 August 1966, p. 1.

15. BBG, *Guidelines on ETV*, 2 September 1966, pp. 4–5.

16. BBG, *Public Announcement*, 25 November 1966, p. 4.

17. Ibid.

18. Ibid., p. 6.

19. Canada, Parliament, House of Commons, *Hansard*, 13 March 1967, pp. 13891–92 and 13 April 1967, pp. 14858–59.

20. Alan Thomas, letter to Andrew Stewart, 19 January 1967, p. 1.

21. CBC, *CBC Position on Education Television,* contained in J.A. Ouimet, letter to Andrew Stewart, 24 February 1967.

22. This rebuke was communicated to the Prime Minister by the Secretary of State (Pearson papers, MG26 N6, Vol. 16, Memorandum from Hon. M. Lamontagne to the Rt. Hon. L.B. Pearson, 11 April 1967.)

23. Canada, Senate, Standing Committee on Transportation and Communication, *Proceedings on Bills S-33 and C-163*, 20 February 1968, pp. 55–58.

24. Pierre Juneau, "The Federal Approach to Educational Television," a speech delivered to the National Seminar on Educational Television, 13 April 1967.

25. BBG, Memorandum, *Definition of Educational Television*, 9 November 1966, p. 3.

26. Canada, Parliament, House of Commons, Commitee on Broadcasting, Film and Assistance to the Arts, *Eleventh Report to the House*, 12 March 1967, p. 2096.

27. Andrew Stewart, Memorandum, *Re: Educational Television*, May 1967, p. 2.

28. Canada, Parliament, House of Commons, Committee on Broadcasting, Film and Assistance to the Arts, *Eleventh Report to the House*, 21 March 1967, p. 2096. Permission for the further study was granted by the House on 17 June 1967 (*Hansard*, 17 June 1967, p. 4428.)

29. Canada, Parliament, House of Commons, *Hansard*, 17 October 1967, p. 3174.

30. Ibid., 17 November 1967, p. 4428.

11 TECHNOLOGY AND TELEVISION SERVICE

1. BBG, *Public Announcement*, 30 September 1960. The CBC argued against colour on the grounds of cost, limited interest from affiliates, technical uncertainties and lack of firm public demand. (Ouimet papers, MG30 E481, Vol. 25, file "Colour Television, memo to BBG 1963.")

2. Andrew Stewart, "Expansion of Broadcasting Facilities and Services," speech to the Electronic Industry Association, June 1964, pp. 17–18.

3. Canada, Parliament, House of Commons, *Hansard*, 15 June 1965, pp. 2407–08.

4. BBG, *Public Announcements*, 18 November 1965, p. 2.

5. BBG, *Press Release #25*, 28 January 1966.

6. BBG, *Annual Report, 1966–67*, p. 15 and *Annual Report 1967–68*, p. 11.

7. BBG, *Annual Report, 1959–60*, p. 34.

8. Ouimet papers, MG30, E481, Vol. 6, file "Board Agenda Material 1958–68, #5 CATV. "Policy Statement of Provision of CBC Program Material to Community Antenna and Closed Circuit Systems," p. 2; approved by the Board 12 September 1959.)

9. Andrew Stewart, letter to Hon. G. Nowlan, 17 January 1961, p. 2.

10. BBG, *Annual Report, 1961–62*, pp. 17–18; BBG, *Press Release*, 17 April 1963.

11. BBG, *Annual Report, 1963–64*, pp. 12–14.

12. BBG, *The Regulation of CATV Systems*, 18 March 1964.

13. Canada, Parliament, House of Commons, *Hansard*, 27 November 1964, p. 10665. The Minister of Transport knew that he had no authority to regulate CATVs under the Broadcasting Act and that any power to regulate under the Radio Act on any grounds other than the narrowly technical was doubtful. He was also aware that various committees of inquiry currently studying the issues would delay a final decision for at least several months. Hence, on the advice of the Department of Justice, the $1.00 line item was inserted in the Supplementary Estimates in order to "provide the necessary authority." (J.R. Baldwin, Deputy Minster of Transport, letter to R.G. Robertson, Clerk of the Privy Council and Secretary to the Cabinet, 1 October 1964, p. 2. Pearson papers, MG26 N3, Vol. 9, file #736.662 Conf.)

14. Committee on Broadcasting, 1965, p. 254.

15. BBG, *Annual Report, 1965–66*, p. 11; *Annual Report, 1966–67*, p. 14.

16. *White Paper*, pp. 13–14.

17. Andrew Stewart, letter to Hon. J.W. Pickersgill, 22 July 1964, p. 1.

18. BBG, *Notice Concerning Special Hearing on Opening Up the UHF Broadcasting Band*, 22 August 1966.

19. BBG, memo to Rt. Hon. L.B. Pearson, "Toronto Television," n.d.

20. Rt. Hon. L.B. Pearson, letter to Andrew Stewart, 12 October 1967, pp. 1–2.

21. Andrew Stewart, letter to Rt. Hon. L.B. Pearson, 12 January 1968.

22. Andrew Stewart, letter to Rt. Hon. L.B. Pearson, 16 February 1966, p. 7.

23. Andrew Stewart, letter to Hon. J. LaMarsh, 4 November 1966, p. 1.

24. BBG, *Public Announcement*, 30 November 1966.

25. Quoted in Andrew Stewart, letter to G.G.E. Steele, Under-Secretary of State, 31 March 1967.

12 CHANNEL 3 BARRIE AND THE TORONTO MARKET

1. Joseph Sedgwick, letter to the Editor, *The Globe and Mail*, 29 March 1960.

2. Mr. Snelgrove was a Liberal candidate in the 1953 General Election in the Constituency of Simcoe North. He lost to his Progressive Conservative opponent, 8,316 to 7,796 votes. Canada, *Parliamentary Guide*, 1957, p. 395.

3. The then Prime Minister, the Rt. Hon. Louis St. Laurent, attended the official opening of CJON-TV, St. John's, in which Mr. Stirling, along with Don Jamieson, was a major shareholder. The Hon. Mr. Pickersgill was Newfoundland's representative in Cabinet. Correspondence between the Leader of the Opposition, Mr. Pearson and Geoff Stirling at the time of the passage of the 1958 Broadcasting Act would indicate something more than a casual relationship between the correspondents. (Pearson papers, MG26 N2, Vol. 25, L.B. Pearson papers, 1958–63, file #352.)

4. Canada, Parliament, House of Commons, *Hansard*, 28 January 1966, p. 376.

5. Mr. Nowlan raised the issue in Cabinet. While potential political repercussions in the upcoming provincial election were noted, Cabinet upheld the principle. Eventually Cabinet constituted the Chairman and four other members of the Board as Commissioners under Part I of the Inquiries Act to conduct a public inquiry to ascertain whether CHEK-TV had contravened the undertakings it had given to the Board. In technical terms, the crux of the issue related to the power of the station's signal which was to be strong enough to reach the northern parts of Vancouver Island but not so strong as

to cause undue interference in the Vancouver scene. (Cabinet papers, RG2 A5a, Vol. 5937, 97–60 (11 August 1958) and 103–60 (6 September 1960).)

6. Andrew Stewart, letter to Hon. J.W. Pickersgill, 1 March 1966.

7. BBG, *Press Release #29,* 25 October 1966.

8. Andrew Stewart, Notes for Secretary of State, 1 March 1966, pp. 1–2.

9. BBG, *Announcement,* 24 November 1966, p. 8.

10. BBG, *Announcement,* 25 November 1966, p. 3.

11. On 12 March 1968, in a letter to the Prime Minister, Allan J. MacEachen, a Liberal Cabinet minister from Nova Scotia nominated Mr. Stott for a position on the new CBC Board. This particular nomination was not successful, but two others made by Mr. MacEachen were, Irving Pink to the CBC Board and Gordon Hughes to the CRTC. (Pearson papers, MG26 N4, Vol. 12, file # 352/B863.3, Pers. & Conf.)

12. For an example of newspaper editorials on the subject, see *The Globe and Mail,* 25 August 1967. There seemed little public response to the editorial. Mr Pickersgill's request for a BBG study of the UHF situation was made on 6 September. Some minds were perhaps focused on the (Progressive) Conservative leadership convention then in progress.

13. Andrew Stewart, letter to Rt. Hon. L.B. Pearson re Toronto Television, 26 July 1967, pp. 1–2.

14. Andrew Stewart, letter to Rt. Hon. L.B. Pearson re Toronto Television, 18 August 1967, p. 4.

15. Public reaction to the Channel 3 Affair was considerable. Letters to the Prime Minister from Toronto area MPs and Liberal Party associations were noticeable. Even one member of the BBG wrote regretting the BBG decision and asking that the Cabinet not accept the Board's recommendation. A summary of letters received by the PM to mid-July 1967 indicated that of a total of 38 analyzed, 16 expressed concern about interference with the American channels 2 and 4; seven feared damage to the image of the Liberal Party; five each decried patronage and stressed the need for American programs because of the poor quality of the Canadian product. Five others each brought forth personal reasons. (Pearson papers, MG26 N4, Vol. 13, file #736.51, Channel 3.)

16. Ironically, in 1959, the Conservative Cabinet, after a discussion in which the Minister "could see no alternative to approval" accepted the BBG's recommendation to grant a licence to Geoff Stirling to operate a radio station in Montreal. (Cabinet papers, RG2 A5a, Vol. 2745, 17 July 1959, p. 3. Order-in-Council, 1959–868, 9 July 1959.)

17. At least one Liberal MP from the Toronto region felt deep concern

about the issue. In a letter to the Prime Minister, Robert Stanbury commented: "All Liberal members already have been hurt by it and I have little doubt that this issue alone will prove fatal for most of us in Toronto it is allowed to fester much longer." (Robert Stanbury, letter to Rt. Hon. L.B. Pearson, 30 August 1967. Pearson papers, MG26 N4, Vol. 13, file #736.5, Channel 3-part 4.) Because of redistribution between 1965 and 1968, exact comparisons are impossible. Generally, it can be said that the NDP held in 1968 the three seats it won in 1965 and that the Liberals won all the other seats, including the new ones created prior to the 1968 election. It would appear that Trudeaumania had stronger electoral appeal than broadcasting issues.

18. J. LaMarsh, *Memoirs*, pp. 246–49.

13 THE BOARD AS A REGULATORY BODY: A CASE STUDY

1. G.B. Doern, *The Regulatory Process*, p. 1.

2. Ibid. More will be said on this subject in Chapter 14.

3. Doern, p. 4.

4. Doern, p. 5.

5. Ibid.

6. Malcolm Neil, President, Canadian Association of Broadcasters, *The Globe and Mail*, 11 November, 1958, p. 3.

7. Doern, p. 4

8. See Doern, p. 4 for more detailed references. Rae and McLeod rather broadly define corporatism as "private ownership plus state control." Prethus more narrowly defines it as the circumstance in which "government delegates many of its functions to private groups which in turn provide guidance regarding social and economic legislation required by the modern state."

9. See Doern, p. 4. This phrase is used to describe the role of the state under a pluralistic concept. The concept will be discussed in greater detail later, see pp. 249–57.

10. See Appendix V for details of licences issued during the period. CBC radio stations increased 33.3% and television stations 84.6%. The increase in CBC television satellite stations was not as spectacular (1100%) as the increase in private rebroadcasters (1455%) because CBC stations were generally located in those parts of the country where the population was more concentrated or the terrain more hospitable.

11. When considering drafts of the 1958 Act, the Cabinet did have before it two proposals with regard to licensing. One would have empowered the BBG

to grant licences with the approval of the Governor-in-Council. The second was the one adopted, naming a minister of the Crown as the licensing authority, action to be taken on recommendation of the BBG and with the approval of the Governor-in-Council. This route was chosen in spite of the fact that the alternative was seen as allowing "the government more readily to avoid or meet criticism or pressure from those who have not been selected to receive a licence or those who are asking to be selected." (Cabinet documents, RG2, Vol. 2741, file #C-20–5 (1958), #195–58, p. 4.)

12. C.L. Brown-John, *Canadian Regulatory Agencies* (Toronto: Butterworths, 1981), p. 133.

13. H.N. Janisch, "Policy Making in Regulation: Towards a New Definition of the Status of Independent Regulatory Agencies in Canada," *Osgoode Hall Law Journal* 17 (1979), p. 98; J.R. Baldwin, *The Regulatory Agency and the Public Corporation* (Cambridge, Mass.: Ballinger, 1975), chap. 1.

14. G.G.E. Steele, letter to Andrew Stewart, 8 February 1963.

15. Hon. George C. Nowlan, interview with W.H.N. Hull, Ottawa, July 1959.

16. Peers, *The Public Eye*, Chap. 9, "Advice to the Perplexed Liberals." Robert Fowler, a close friend of Mr. Pearson, as well as Chairman of the two boards of inquiry (1957 and 1965) wrote to Mr. Pearson during the gestation period of the 1958 Act: "I believe the establishment of two boards would go a long way to destroy this [historic] approach—or at least to make for friction and rivalry between them which would enfeeble the single system concept." There is no evidence of Mr. Pearson's questioning the assessment. (Pearson papers, MG26 N2, Vol. 25, LBP papers 1958–68, file # 352, attached letter, p. 2.)

17. It should be noted that Dr. Stewart indicated in another place that the Board failed to gain great public confidence "mainly because of the extent of the known political association of most of the appointees." Peers, *Public Eye*, p. 216.

As with more recent patronage appointments, criticism was sometimes raised in the 1950s and 1960s about Order-in-Council appointments. One wonders to what extent such controversy was media-generated. Certainly a reading of the Cabinet minutes surrounding the 1958 appointments to the BBG (discussed in six meeting over two weeks) gives evidence of a desire to appoint people of quality, even some with no known political allegiance. Factors such as age, sex, region and occupation all drew considerable comment. Presumably the majority would have been Conservative activists. One wonders if critics of the system expect governments to appoint people with no interest in or knowledge of the governing process. (Cabinet documents, RG2 A5a, Vol. 1899, 21 October-5 November 1958.)

Before considering appointments under the 1968 Act, Mr. Pearson received the following memo from the Privy Council Office: "Appendices containing introductory notes spelling out the ideal composition which we felt you might wish to aim at obtaining, are attached herewith. These deal mainly with distribution as between men and women, between French and English speaking, and between the regions of the Maritimes, Quebec, Ontario, the west and the north." (Pearson papers, MG26 N4, Vol. 10, file #358.B863.3, Personal, p. 1.)

18. Doern, p. 7.

19. Ibid., p. 13.

20. Ibid., p. 14.

21. Ibid.

22. Trebilcock, M.J., D.G. Hartle, R.S. Prichard and D.N. Dewars, *The Choice of Governing Instruments* (Ottawa: Economic Council of Canada, 1982), p. 102.

23. Ibid.

24. T. Lowi, "Four Systems of Policy, Politics and Choice," *Public Administration Review* (1972): 299–310.

25. BBG, Submission to the Committee on Broadcasting, 1965, 7 April 1965.

26. Doern, p. 9.

27. Ibid.

28. *White Paper*, p. 11.

29. Ibid., p. 14.

30. Doern, p. 20.

31. Ibid., p. 21.

32. See LaMarsh, *Memoirs*, p. 249.

33. This calculation excludes the last two years of the BBG's existence when larger budgets were granted in anticipation of the passing of the new Broadcasting Act and the creation of the CRTC, the staff of which mushroomed quickly to many times that of the Board.

34. John Willis, "The McRuer Report: Lawyers' Values and Civil Servants' Values," *University of Toronto Law Journal* XVIII (1968): p. 353. Quoted in Doern at p. 24.

35. Dr. Stewart was appointed by the Conservatives and reappointed by the Liberals. This fact has been treated as two appointments.

36. See Appendix II.

37. As an example, one of the few Order-in-Council appointments not disparaged in recent years by the *Globe and Mail* was that of its publisher to the Senate of Canada. The then Editor of the paper, when questioned about this by Professor Hull, responded that the candidate was clearly highly qualified for the appointment. It is surely surprising that neither major federal party has not been able to find more than one qualified candidate for Order-in-Council appointments in the past number of years.

Perhaps rather than institutional changes, we need attitudinal changes and greater understanding of our system of government on the part of our media.

38. Doern, p. 1.

39. See LaMarsh, *Memoirs*, p. 244. She notes that a paucity of meetings could suggest that things were running smoothly.

14 "CAPTURE THEORY" AND THE BOARD'S EFFECTIVENESS

1. The Bernstein thesis will be considered in limited detail as it has already been discussed at length by Professor Hull. See W.H.N. Hull, "Captive or Victim? The Board of Broadcast Governors and Berstein's Law, 1958–68," *Canadian Public Administration* 26, no. 4 (Winter 1983): 544–62.

2. Doern, *The Regulatory Process*, p. 28.

3. See Paul Sabatier, "Social Movements and Regulatory Agencies: Toward a More Adequate—and Less Pessimistic—Theory of 'Clientele Capture'," *Policy Science* 6 (Amsterdam: Elsevier, 1975), p. 303.

4. Ibid., pp. 304–5. Sabatier notes . . . "that any governmental agency which is charged with, or wished to, regulate business behaviour in order to minimize harm upon consumers or their parties will be involved in political controversy, e.g. disputes over the authoritative allocation of values. In such situations the expertise available to the agency is only one of several required resources. The agency must also have the legal and/or political resources to convince and/or coerce producers into changing their behaviour. It is, in fact, highly probably that these latter two variables—rather than insufficient expertise—have been the principle limiting factors in the apparent inability of many regulatory agencies to sustain an aggressive program over an extended period of time."

5. Another analytical framework might have been used—that of the conflict resolution model employed by J.R. Baldwin in his analysis of the Canadian air transport industry. He suggests that "the role of the agency is to resolve conflict between two parties in such a way that neither part is inordi-

nately alienated from the government. This automatically restricts both the decision set and the control variables available to it." The application of this concept to the broadcasting industry could prove fascinating. See J.R. Baldwin, *The Regulatory Agency and the Public Corporation* (Cambridge: Ballinger, 1975), p. 40.

6. Bernstein, *Regulation of Business*, pp. 284–85.

7. *Committee on Broadcasting, 1965*, p. 115.

8. Ibid., p. 114.

9. Ibid.

10. Ibid., p. 115.

11. Comparisons With the BBC Fiscal Year ended 31 March 1964

	BBC	CBC
Average "on air" cost	$3,090	$1,760
Staff	11,600	5,618
Average renumeration per emp.	$3,319	$6,976
Av. num. Emp per orig output hr	2.5	.59
Av. num. Emp per "on air" hour	.44	.15
Number of networks	1	2
Daily output per studio (hours)	London .52	Toronto 1.15
		Montreal 1.31

Source: Ouimet papers, MG30 E481, Vol. 32, file, "Correspondence with the Government, 1958–67.")

12. LaMarsh, *Memoirs*, p. 266. Relations between Miss Lamarsh and Mr. Ouimet were at an all-time low. On the one hand, the CBC virtually stopped communication with "its" minister. In turn, the Minister informed the Prime Minister that:

I do not know any way within the law to make the C.B.C. follow the channel of communication, which is set out for them in the legislation, except by control of the purse. Until they have learned to direct their communications through this office they will obtain no further funds by my signature. (Hon. J. LaMarsh, letter to Rt. Hon. L.B. Pearson, 14 June 1967, p. 2. Pearson papers, MG26 N6, file #16.)

Mr. Ouimet suggested to her: "You have reached the extreme limits of ministerial irresponsibility." (J.A. Ouimet, Memoire, Notes for Archives, MG30 E481, Vol. 46, Section E, Binder #10, Misc. Notes, p. 4.)

T.C. Douglas, then National Leader of the New Democratic Party, characterized the Minister as "the perpetual teen-ager" (J.A. Ouimet, Memoire, Notes for Archives, MG30 E481, Vol. 46, Section E, Binder #2, p. 164.)

13. *Committee on Broadcasting, 1965*, p. 116.

15 THE BOARD OF BROADCAST GOVERNORS: AN ASSESSMENT

1. Gordon Fearn, "The Role of Communications Policy in Modern Culture," in *Reflections on Cultural Policy: Past, Present and Future,* Evan Alderson, Robin Blaser and Harold Coward, eds. (Waterloo: Wilfrid Laurier University Press, 1993), p. 131.

2. Ibid., p. 121.

3. Ibid., p. 127.

4. Committee on Broadcasting, 1965, p. 313.

5. There were plans for a separate CBC financing bill to be introduced into the House in the same session as Bill C-163—the 1968 Broadcasting Act. That piece of legislation was not to see the light of day. (O.G. Stoner, Memo to the Prime Minister: CBC Financing Bill, 22 January 1968. Pearson papers, MG26 N4, file #736.622 Conf.)

6. Fowler Commission, pp. 174–75.

7. Doern, pp. 350–51. The four agencies Doern and his colleagues studied were: The Canadian Transportation Commission, the National Energy Board, the Atomic Agency Board and the bodies related to the air transport industry.

8. J.Q. Wilson describes four types of political environment in which regulatory agencies can function: client politics, entrepreneurial politics, interest group politics and majoritarian politics. He defines interest group politics as: a situation in which two or more interest groups compete over agency goals and there are recognizable winners and losers as a result of regulatory action. This circumstance seems to fit the BBG's circumstance. He suggests that such an environment requires the regulator to reconcile competing interests of the regulated while at the same time recognizing the presssures of competition from other quarters, national or international. J.Q. Wilson, *Bureaucracy* (New York: Bantam Books, 1989), pp. 79–83.

9. Doern, p. 355.

10. If, as it is suggested by some, members of the Board individually gave into partisan leanings in two classic cases, CFTO-TV, Toronto and CKVR-TV, Barrie, at least comfort can be taken in the fact that there were only two such cases alleged and that they tended to neutralize each other, one being taken by a Conservative-dominated Board, the other by a Liberal-dominated Board.

11. Canada, Royal Commission on Radio Broadcasting, *Report* (Ottawa: King's Printer, 1929), p. 6.

12. Richard Schultz, "Paradigm Lost: Explaining the Canadian Politics of Deregulation," in *Governance in a Mature Society: Essays in Honour of John Meisel*, C.E.S. Franks, ed. (Montreal and Kingston: McGill-Queen's University Press, forthcoming).

13. Canada, *Statutes*, 1967–68, Broadcasting Act, Chap. 25, S.2.

14. Ibid., S.2(h).

15. Ibid., S.2(1)(a).

16. Ibid., S.22(1).

17. Ibid., S.16(1).

18. Ibid., S.45(4).

19. Ibid., S.2(d).

20. Ibid., S.2(g).

21. Ibid., S.17(1).

22. Ibid., S.17(2).

23. Ibid., S.17(3).

24. Ibid., S.17(4).

25. Ibid., S.24(3).

26. P.G. Thomas and O.W. Zajcew, "Structural Heretics: Crown Corporations and Regulatory Agencies," in *Governing Canada,* ed. Michael Atkinson (Toronto: Harcourt Brace Jovanovich, 1993), p. 135.

27. Ibid., p. 134.

28. See p. xi.

SELECTED BIBLIOGRAPHY

GOVERNMENT PUBLICATIONS

STATUTES
Canada. Statutes of Canada, 1957–1958. Broadcasting Act, Chap. 22.
────. 1967-1968. Broadcasting Act, Chap. 25

ROYAL COMMISSIONS AND COMMITTEES
Canada. Royal Commission on Broadcasting. *Report*. Ottawa: Queen's Printer, 1957.

Canada. Royal Commission on National Development in the Arts, Letters and Sciences. *Report*. Ottawa: Queen's Printer, 1951.

Canada. Royal Commission on Radio Broadcasting. *Report*. Ottawa: King's Printer, 1929.

Canada. Committee on Broadcasting, 1965. *Report*. Ottawa: Queen's Printer, 1965.

MONOGRAPHS
Economic Council of Canada. Robert E. Babe. *Canadian Television Broadcasting Structure, Performance and Regulation*. Ottawa: Ministry of Supply and Services Canada, 1979.

────. *Responsible Regulation*. Ottawa: Ministry of Supply and Services Canada, 1979.

────. *Reforming Regulation*. Ottawa: Ministry of Supply and Services Canada, 1981.

Law Reform Commission. *Independent Administrative Agencies*. Ottawa: Law Reform Commission of Canada, 1985.

Schultz, Richard. *The Cabinet as a Regulatory Body*. Ottawa: Economic Council of Canada, 1980.

Schultz, Richard and Alan Alexandroff. *Economic Regulation and the Federal System*. Ottawa: Ministry of Supply and Services Canada, 1985.

The Task Force on Program Review. *Regulatory Agencies*. Ottawa: Ministry of Supply and Services Canada, 1986.

———. *Regulatory Programs*. Ottawa: Ministry of Supply and Services Canada, 1986.

Trebilcock, M.J. et al. *The Choice of Governing Instruments*. Ottawa: Ministry of Supply and Services Canada, 1982.

Vandervort, Lucinda. *Political Control of Independent Administrative Agencies*. Ottawa: Ministry of Supply and Services Canada, 1979.

BOOKS, THESES AND JOURNAL ARTICLES

Adie, R.F. and P.G. Thomas. *Canadian Public Administration*. Scarborough: Prentice-Hall, 1982.

Alderson, Evan, et al., eds. *Reflections on Cultural Policy*. Waterloo: Wilfrid Laurier Press, 1993.

Atkinson, M.M., ed. *Governing Canada: Institutions and Public Policy*. Toronto: Harcourt, Brace, Jovanovich, 1993.

Babe, R.E. "Regulation of Private Television Broadcasting by the Canadian Radio-Television Commission: A Critique of Ends and Means." *Canadian Public Administration* 19 (Winter 1976): pp. 552–86.

Bartley, Allan. "Ottawa Ways: The State Bureaucracy and Broadcasting, 1955-1968." Unpublished thesis. McGill University, 1990.

Bernier, Ivan and Andrée Lajoie. *Regulations, Crown Corporations and Administrative Tribunals*. Toronto: University of Toronto Press, 1985.

Bernstein, M.H. *Regulation of Business by Independent Commission*. Princeton: Princeton University Press, 1955.

———. "The Government as Regulator." *The Annals of the American Academy of Political and Social Science* 400 (March 1972).

Brooks, Stephen. *Public Policy in Canada*. 2d ed. Toronto: McClelland and Stewart, 1993.

Brown-John, C.L. *Canadian Regulatory Agencies*. Toronto: Butterworths, 1981.

Campbell, A.E.H. "Regulations and the Orwellian State." *Canadian Public Administration* 28 (Spring 1985): pp. 150–55.

Coleman, W.D. "Canadian Business and the State." In *The State and Economic Interests*, ed. Keith Banting, pp. 245-89. Toronto: University of Toronto Press, 1986.

Dewar, K.C. "The Origins of Public Broadcasting in Comparative Perspective." *Canadian Journal of Communication* 8 (Jan. 1982): pp. 26–45.

Doern, G.B., ed. *The Regulatory Process in Canada*. Toronto: Macmillan, 1978.

Doern, G.B. and R.W. Phidd. *Canadian Public Policy. Ideas, Structure, Process*. 2d ed. Scarborough: Nelson Canada, 1992.

Franks, C.E.S. *Governance in a Mature Society: Essays in Honour of John Meisel*. Montreal and Kingston: McGill-Queen's University Press, forthcoming.

Foster, Frank. *Broadcasting Policy Development*. Ottawa: Franfost Communications Ltd., 1982.

Hartle, D.G. *Public Policy Decision Making and Regulation*. Toronto: Butterworths, 1979.

Hull, W.H.N. "Captive or Victim? The Board of Broadcast Governors and Berstein's Law, 1958–68." *Canadian Public Administration* 26 (Winter 1983): pp. 544–62.

Kernaghan, W.D.K. and D. Siegel. *Public Administration in Canada*. 2d. ed. Scarborough: Nelson Canada, 1991.

LaMarsh, Judy. *Memoirs of a Bird in a Gilded Cage*. Toronto: McClelland and Stewart, 1968.

Peers, F.W. *The Politics of Canadian Broadcasting, 1920–1951*. Toronto: University of Toronto Press, 1969.

———. *The Public Eye: Television and the Politics of Canadian Broadcasting, 1952–1968*. Toronto: University of Toronto Press, 1979.

Raboy, Marc. *Missed Opportunities: The Story of Canada's Broadcasting Policy*. Montreal and Kingston: McGill-Queen's University Press, 1990.

Sproule-Jones, Mark. *Governments at Work: Canadian Parliamentary Federalism and Its Public Policy Effects*. Toronto: University of Toronto Press, 1993.

Strick, J.C. *The Economics of Government Regulation*. Toronto: Thompson Educational Publishing, 1990.

Sutherland, S.L. and G.B. Doern. *Bureaucracy in Canada: Control and Reform*. Toronto: University of Toronto Press, 1985.

Strusberg, Peter. *Mr. Broadcasting: The Ernie Bushnell Story*. Toronto: Peter Martin Associates, 1971.

Tardi, Gregory. "The Appointment of Federal Regulatory Commissions: A Case Study of the CRTC." *Canadian Public Administration* 24 (Winter 1981): pp. 587–95.

University of Toronto Law Journal, Special Issue on Administrative Law, 40 (Summer 1990): pp. 305–688.

Vipond, Mary. *Listening In*. Montreal and Kingston: McGill-Queen's University Press, 1992.

Weir, E.A. *The Struggle for National Broadcasting in Canada*. Toronto: McClelland and Stewart, 1965.

Wilson, J.Q. *Bureaucracy*. New York: Basic Books, 1985.

INDEX

Aldred, Joel, 55, 68, 70, 86–87

Associated Television, 49, 53–54, 58–60

Balcer, Hon. Leon, 62, 68–71, 73

Bassett, John, 55, 66, 68, 70–71, 73–74, 78–79, 105–9, 326, 334 n 19

Baton, Aldred, Rogers, 14, 55–56, 60, 63, 66, 68, 203

Bernstein, Marver, 217, 259–63

Berton, Pierre, 301

Bill C-163, 197, 214, 277–78, 282, 344 n 5

Board of Broadcast Governors (BBG):

administration, 15–18, 239, 243–46, 252, 254–55, 263–72, 278–79

BBG/CBC relations, 22–24, 102–4, 109–12, 123–24, 129, 136–37, 162–63, 172, 221–22, 224, 243–44, 250–51, 264–69, 274–75, 330 n 16, 331 n 10

BBG/government relations, 103, 118–9, 127, 131, 136–37,

214, 229–31, 236, 244–46, 252–56, 262, 279–82

BBG/private sector relations, 254, 259–63, 264

Board solidarity/minority decisions, 72, 130–31, 244–45

consultative committees:

advertisers, 19, 21

private broadcasting, 19, 21, 81–83, 242, 255, 260, 264

public broadcasting, 19, 21–22, 98, 132, 136–37, 242, 256, 260, 264

financial affairs:

budgets, 16–17, 245, 270–72, 313

Chairman's attitudes, 254–55, 270–71

Grey Cup, 1962, 101–20, 221, 251, 253, 257, 285

membership:

appointing process, 9, 14, 214, 233, 247–48, 280, 283, 323 n 7, 340 n 17, 342 n 37 full-time:

Allison, Carlyle, 10–11, 81, 247–48, 321 n 3

Duhamel, Roger, 10, 248, 296

Goulet, Bernard, 11–12, 247–48

Juneau, Pierre, 12, 184–91, 247–48, 271, 321 n 4

Sim, David, 12, 159, 247–48, 271

Stewart, Andrew, 9–10, 24, 26, 40–43, 102–20, 160–62, 178–80, 218–19, 222, 226, 229, 239, 244, 248, 252, 254–55, 270–73, 281, 283, 289– 90, 320 n 2, 321 n 4, 325 n 12, 328 n 7, 332 n 16, 340 n 11, 341 n 35

part-time (see Appendix II for full list of part-time members):

Brown, Joseph, 12, 292, 299, 303–4, 323 n 5

Coyne, John, 13

Dunlop, Edward, 72, 87, 183, 293

Forsey, Eugene, 129–31, 293, 296–97

Gagnon, Claude, 12, 323 n 5

Hudon, Ivan, 129–31

Stott, Ian, 209, 212, 338 n 11

Sweatman, Lorraine, 160

Urquhart, George, 161

Woodfine, William, 209

political affiliations, 13–14, 66, 203, 244–45, 248, 280

representativeness, 13, 244, 247, 283

policy policies:

alternative service, 139–41, 147–51, 154–55, 160–62, 222–26, 250, 253, 261

cable television (CATV) 195–98, 227, 234, 275

canadian content, 29–43, 165, 221, 251, 259, 261, 270, 275, 279, 283

CBC "O & O" stations, 4, 23, 39, 93, 99, 121, 129, 133–37, 163, 224, 226

colour television, 193–94, 227, 251

educational television, 37, 175–91, 234, 242, 253, 275

networks, 75–99, 107, 242, 250, 261, 275

primary service, 172–73, 222–26, 234, 275

public hearings, 243–44, 260, 278, 296–99

public (national) interest, 87–88, 92, 106–7, 110, 115, 117, 165, 214, 219–20, 236, 257, 274, 278, 284–85, 290, 304

public/private sector relations, 79–80, 170–71

satellites, 193, 200–201, 227, 274, 275

single station policy, 122, 141, 203, 288

UHF band, 181, 186–90, 198–200, 227, 251, 253, 275

INDEX

Aldred, Joel, 55, 68, 70, 86–87
Associated Television, 49, 53–54, 58–60

Balcer, Hon. Leon, 62, 68–71, 73
Bassett, John, 55, 66, 68, 70–71, 73–74, 78–79, 105–9, 326, 334 n 19
Baton, Aldred, Rogers, 14, 55–56, 60, 63, 66, 68, 203
Bernstein, Marver, 217, 259–63
Berton, Pierre, 301
Bill C-163, 197, 214, 277–78, 282, 344 n 5
Board of Broadcast Governors (BBG):
    administration, 15–18, 239, 243–46, 252, 254–55, 263–72, 278–79
    BBG/CBC relations, 22–24, 102–4, 109–12, 123–24, 129, 136–37, 162–63, 172, 221–22, 224, 243–44, 250–51, 264–69, 274–75, 330 n 16, 331 n 10
    BBG/government relations, 103, 118–9, 127, 131, 136–37,
214, 229–31, 236, 244–46, 252–56, 262, 279–82
    BBG/private sector relations, 254, 259–63, 264
    Board solidarity/minority decisions, 72, 130–31, 244–45
    consultative committees:
        advertisers, 19, 21
        private broadcasting, 19, 21, 81–83, 242, 255, 260, 264
        public broadcasting, 19, 21–22, 98, 132, 136–37, 242, 256, 260, 264
    financial affairs:
        budgets, 16–17, 245, 270–72, 313
        Chairman's attitudes, 254–55, 270–71
    Grey Cup, 1962, 101–20, 221, 251, 253, 257, 285
    membership:
        appointing process, 9, 14, 214, 233, 247–48, 280, 283, 323 n 7, 340 n 17, 342 n 37

full-time:

Allison, Carlyle, 10–11, 81, 247–48, 321 n 3

Duhamel, Roger, 10, 248, 296

Goulet, Bernard, 11–12, 247–48

Juneau, Pierre, 12, 184–91, 247–48, 271, 321 n 4

Sim, David, 12, 159, 247–48, 271

Stewart, Andrew, 9–10, 24, 26, 40–43, 102–20, 160–62, 178–80, 218–19, 222, 226, 229, 239, 244, 248, 252, 254–55, 270–73, 281, 283, 289– 90, 320 n 2, 321 n 4, 325 n 12, 328 n 7, 332 n 16, 340 n 11, 341 n 35

part-time (see Appendix II for full list of part-time members):

Brown, Joseph, 12, 292, 299, 303–4, 323 n 5

Coyne, John, 13

Dunlop, Edward, 72, 87, 183, 293

Forsey, Eugene, 129–31, 293, 296–97

Gagnon, Claude, 12, 323 n 5

Hudon, Ivan, 129–31

Stott, Ian, 209, 212, 338 n 11

Sweatman, Lorraine, 160

Urquhart, George, 161

Woodfine, William, 209

political affiliations, 13–14, 66, 203, 244–45, 248, 280

representativeness, 13, 244, 247, 283

policy policies:

alternative service, 139–41, 147–51, 154–55, 160–62, 222–26, 250, 253, 261

cable television (CATV) 195–98, 227, 234, 275

canadian content, 29–43, 165, 221, 251, 259, 261, 270, 275, 279, 283

CBC "O & O" stations, 4, 23, 39, 93, 99, 121, 129, 133–37, 163, 224, 226

colour television, 193–94, 227, 251

educational television, 37, 175–91, 234, 242, 253, 275

networks, 75–99, 107, 242, 250, 261, 275

primary service, 172–73, 222–26, 234, 275

public hearings, 243–44, 260, 278, 296–99

public (national) interest, 87–88, 92, 106–7, 110, 115, 117, 165, 214, 219–20, 236, 257, 274, 278, 284–85, 290, 304

public/private sector relations, 79–80, 170–71

satellites, 193, 200–201, 227, 274, 275

single station policy, 122, 141, 203, 288

UHF band, 181, 186–90, 198–200, 227, 251, 253, 275

analyzed, 260–63, 342
defined, 259
Chercover, Murray, 158
colour television:
   BBG role in introduction of,
      193–94, 226–27
   CBC attitudes towards, 193–94,
      336
   CTV attitudes towards, 193
   Electronic Industry Association
      (EIA), 193, 284
   Expo '67, 194, 227
Committee on Broadcasting, 1965,
   15, 21, 147, 149–51, 165, 182,
   184, 194, 197, 214, 232–33,
   252, 259, 263–72, 276
Cooke, Jack Kent, 54, 62, 323 n 10
CTV Network, 75–99
   affiliation/disaffiliation of sta-
      tions, 169–70
   BBG's attitudes towards, 170,
      226
   CBC's attitudes towards, 226
   CBC's competitive activities,
      132–34
   cable's attitudes towards, 195
   Canadian content requirements,
      224
   equalization proposal, 166–69,
      219–20, 221, 243, 250, 254
   expansion, 121–46, 147–73,
      225, 231, 260–61
   financial matters, 87, 95–98,
      155, 158–59, 168, 225, 261,
      327 n 1
   Grey Cup, 1962, 105–19
   mutualization, 167, 255, 260,
      284
   national role of, 164, 220

network, definition of, 250
new licensees' attitudes towards,
   255–56
ownership, 20, 170
programming, 133
Toronto station, role of, 65, 75,
   150–51, 189, 285, 295

Davidson, George, 189
Davidson, Jack, 48, 86
Diefenbaker, Right Hon. John. G.,
   10, 66, 103, 307, 320 n 2
Dinsdale, Hon. Walter, 157, 161
Dunsmore, R.L., 11, 104, 110, 136

educational television,
   ban on provincial licensing or
      operation, 178, 181, 186
   BBG as co-ordinator for federal
      government, 189, 242, 253
   CBC's role: National Committee
      on School Broadcasting,
      179–80, 256
   Canadian content, 37
   federal ownership of facilities,
      183
   MEETA, 177, 184–185
   META, 56, 176–77, 180
   Province of Alberta, 175–76,
      181, 185, 257
   Province of Newfoundland, 188
   Province of Ontario, 175–76,
      181–85, 188, 257
   Province of Quebec, 177–78
   reservation of channels, 176–77
   role of federal government, 176,
      181, 183–84
   role of provinces, 176–78, 191,
      234, 257

Standing Committee of Ministers, 178, 180
UHF channels, 181, 186–90
extension of television service:
  local issues:
    Brandon, 147–62, 200, 244
    Charlottetown, 160
    Lethbridge, 147–60
    Moncton, 96, 99, 147–70, 222, 244
    Quebec City, 93, 121–42, 178, 198, 229, 231, 245
    Regina-Moose Jaw, 153, 159, 168, 188
    St. John, 138–40, 149, 151, 159, 160, 170
    St. John's, 53, 121–47, 151, 159, 169, 198, 229, 231, 234, 242
    Saskatoon, 139, 149, 151–53, 160, 170, 188, 234
    Sudbury, 140, 149, 159, 160, 170
    Victoria, 149, 204
  under the Conservatives, 121–46
  under the Liberals, 147–73

factors influencing agency behaviour on a day to day basis:
  agency goals, 249–51
  agency leaders and senior staff, 254–55
  clientele pressure, 255–57
  dependence on clientele, 253–54
  ministerial intervention, 252–53, 287
  multi-functionality of agency, 240–46, 251–52
Famous Players, 53, 128

Flynn, Hon. Jacques, 131
Fowler Commission. See Royal Commission on Broadcasting, 1957
Fowler Committee. See Committee on Broadcasting, 1965
Fowler, R.M., 272, 274, 340 n 16
Fraser, Ronald, 158

Granada Television, 53–54, 59–60, 71, 228
Grey Cup, 1962, 101–19, 331 n 26

Hallman, Eugene, 189
Halpenny, Hon. G.E., 118–19, 143, 307, 321 n 2, 332 n 16
Henderson, Maxwell, 136, 271

Independent Television Organization (ITO), 75, 81, 84–87, 93
interest groups:
  Alberta Federation of Labour, 125
  Associated Chambers of Commerce of the Peace River District, 125
  Association of Canadian Television and Radio Artists (ACTRA), 56, 99, 257
  British Columbia Federation of Labour, 50
  Canadian Association for Adult Education, 189, 257
  Canadian Association of Advertising Agencies, 115
  Canadian Association of Consumers, 125
  Canadian Education Association, 178–79

Canadian Federation of Agriculture, 103, 257, 262
Canadian Football League, 115
Electronic Industry Association, 193, 227, 244, 256
French-Canadian Association of Alberta, 125
Grand Prairie Chamber of Commerce, 125
Halifax Board of Trade, 58
Halifax-Dartmouth and District Labour Council, 58
Retail Merchants Association of Canada, 50

Jamieson, Donald, 21, 53, 141–45, 262, 266, 293

Keeble, Gordon, 55, 65, 87, 158

LaMarsh, Hon. Judy, 21, 152–53, 158–59, 168, 183–85, 190–91, 194–95, 205, 209–10, 211–14, 252, 264–65, 269, 307, 321 n 2, 333 n 2, 342 n 39, 343 n 12
Lamontagne, Hon. Maurice, 11, 181–82, 307, 321 n 2, 335 n 22
Liberal Party:
    acts of creation, 3–7, 262–63
    alternative service, 121, 147–73
    appointments to the Board, 10–14, 247–48, 308–10, 320 n 2, 321 n 3, 321 n 4
    BBG, relations with, 231–32, 236–37, 251, 252, 262–63
    cable, 196–97
    CBC, relations with, 265, 268–69
    ministerial actions, 145–46,

148–49, 152–55, 158–60, 172, 186, 188–89, 194, 196–97, 205, 209, 211–13, 231–34, 239, 243, 245, 252–53, 262, 268, 276
    partisan activities, 141, 204, 208–14, 230, 244–45, 250–51, 290, 337 n 2, 337 n 3, 338 n 11, 338 n 15, 338 n 17, 340 n 10
    single station policy, 3, 101, 121–22, 238, 285, 288
licensing:
    BBG powers, 62, 90–91, 229–30, 325 n 12, 339 n 11
    charges of political favouritism, 13–14, 66, 280, 290, 327 n 17, 344 n 10
    government reactions, 229–30

MacDonald, Finlay, 58, 157, 298, 334 n 19
Maclean-Hunter, 53, 54, 155
Massey Commission. See Royal Commission on National Development in the Arts, Letters and Sciences, 1951
McIlraith, Hon. George, 145, 149
Mills, W.D., 294–95, 311
Misener, R.S., 48–49

networks:
    cross-programming, 85, 87, 91, 93
    definition, 88, 92–93, 250
    equalization in CTV, 166–69, 221, 243, 250
    financing of, 86

newspapers:

FP Publications, 59, 63

Le Droit, 213

Ottawa *Citizen*, 58

Ottawa *Journal*, 59

Southam Press, 49, 53–54, 58, 61, 63, 69

Thomson Newspapers, 69, 71

Toronto *Globe and Mail*, 53, 54–55, 61, 203–4, 338, 342

Toronto *Star*, 53–54, 61, 204, 212

Toronto *Telegram*, 53, 55, 61, 66–69, 203, 326

Vancouver *Province*, 49, 60

Vancouver *Sun*, 49, 60

Winnipeg *Free Press*, 48, 326

Winnipeg *Tribune*, 10

Niagara Television, 200

Nowlan, Hon. George, 9, 20, 29–30, 40, 122–23, 204, 219, 304, 307, 321 n 2, 323 n 7, 337 n 5, 340 n 15

Ouimet, J.A., 12, 21, 83, 85, 88, 94, 101–19, 126–27, 136, 145, 206, 269, 293, 303, 330 n 16, 331 n 10, 332 n 16, 343 n 12

Pearson, Right Hon. L.B., 11–12, 148, 150, 158–59, 168, 185, 198–199, 210, 226, 307, 320 n 2, 321 n 3, 321 n 4, 337 n 3, 338 n 7, 340 n 16, 340 n 17, 343 n 12

Pearson, William, 294, 311

Pickersgill, Hon. J.W., 10, 20, 145–48, 153, 158–59, 196–99, 204, 211–13, 251, 276, 307, 321 n 4, 336 n 10, 337 n 3

primary service, 172, 223, 234

Progressive Conservative Party:

acts of creation, 3–7, 262–63, 281

alternative service, 77, 121–46

appointments to the Board, 9–14, 247–48, 308–10, 320 n 2, 323 n 7

BBG, relations with, 231–32, 236–37, 251, 262–63

CBC, relations with, 137, 236–37, 265, 268–69,

Canadian content, 281

ministerial actions, 29–30, 40, 111, 118–19, 123, 128, 131, 143–44, 172, 195, 219, 232–34, 243, 245, 253, 262, 268, 276, 304

partisan activities, 66, 127, 203, 230, 244–45, 250–51, 290

single station policy, 77, 122–23

public policy. See Broad of Broadcast Governors, public policy

Rank, J. Arthur, 54, 60, 295

regulatory environment:

philosophical underpinnings:

corporatism, 218, 221–22

liberalism, 218, 219–20

pluralism, 218, 220–21

economics of regulation:

access to industry, 222–23

ownership, 228

price, 224

rate of return, 224–26

technology, 226–28, 274

Cabinet-parliamentary government:

board independence, 229, 230–31

federalism, 228–229

licensing, 229

ministerial directives, 229–30, 236, 287

parliamentary reviews, 233

support from other departments, 231–34

legal and procedural determinants, 246

policy, organizational forms and administration, 239–46

the regulators:

board members, 246–48

senior staff, 248–49, 254

Rideout, Margaret, 157

Royal Commission of Broadcasting, 1957, 5–7, 13, 123, 262, 276

Royal Commission on National Development in the Arts, Letters and Sciences, 1951, 5, 262

Royal Commission of Radio Broadcasting, 1929 (Aird), 55, 281

satellites, 193, 200–201

Saturday Night, 53

second station applications, 45–66

announcement of, 45

applications compared, 59–66

CBC applications, 56

Canadian content, 64–65

Cabinet and ministerial involvement, 45–46, 62

charges of political favouritism, 66

cross-media involvement, 60, 66, 225

non-Canadian interests, 58–59, 228

possibility of forming network, 65–66

procedures for hearings, 45–47

public hearings and decisions:

Calgary, 45, 47, 56–57, 59–66, 76, 121, 123, 124, 126, 155–57, 187, 228

Edmonton, 45–56, 86, 121, 123, 124–28, 229

Halifax, 45, 47, 57–58, 59–66, 153, 157, 159, 169, 223, 228

Ottawa, 45, 47, 51, 58–59, 60–63, 66, 78, 86–87, 169, 228

Montreal, 45, 47, 51–53, 60, 62, 170

Toronto, 13, 45, 47, 53–56, 59–66, 68, 78, 82–87, 169, 204–14, 225, 228

Vancouver, 45–47, 49–51, 59–66, 87

Winnipeg, 30, 45–49, 59–66, 86, 228

Selkirk Holdings, 63, 125, 155–56

Sinclair, Gordon, 301

Soble, Ken, 58, 99, 200, 227

Spry, Graham, 87

stations:

radio:

CFAM-Altona, 48

CFCF-Montreal, 52

CFCN-Calgary, 56, 155

CFRA-Ottawa, 58, 62

CFRB-Toronto, 53, 55, 60, 205–11

CFRN-Edmonton, 10, 56

CFUN-Vancouver, 50

CHED-Edmonton, 125

CHML-Hamilton, 58

CHUM-Toronto, 157, 293

CJCA-Edmonton, 125
CJOB-Winnipeg, 48
CJON-St John's, 53
CJOR-Vancouver, 49, 252, 301
CKCK-Regina, 48
CKEY-Toronto, 53–54, 60
CKGM-Montreal, 53
CKNW-New Westminster, 49, 300
CKVL-Verdun, 52, 198, 213
CKY-Winnipeg, 48
XWA-Montreal, 52
television:
CFCF-TV, Montreal, 53, 105–6
CFCN-TV, Calgary, 56–57, 155–157
CFRN-TV, Edmonton, 56, 86, 125–26
CFTM-TV, Montreal, 86, 105, 165–66
CFTO-TV, Toronto, 67–74, 86, 105–7, 164–65, 168–69, 228, 242, 256, 325 n 7, 327 n 17
CHAB-TV, Moose Jaw, 152–53, 165, 168, 169
CHCA-TV, Red Deer, 125
CHCH-TV, Hamilton, 70, 203
CHCT-TV, Calgary, 57, 156
CHEK-TV, Victoria, 204, 337 n 5
CHLT-TV, Sherbrooke, 210
CHSA-TV, Lloydminster, 125
CJAY-TV, Winnipeg, 10, 86, 153, 156–58, 160

CJCH-TV, Halifax, 58, 153, 157–58, 160
CJLH-TV, Lethbridge, 155–56
CJOH-TV, Ottawa, 86, 105–6, 109
CJON-TV, St. John's, 141–46, 165, 242, 337 n 3
CKCK-TV, Regina, 152–53
CKCW-TV, Moncton, 99
CKVR-TV, Barrie, 14, 56, 164, 169, 199, 204–14, 225, 230, 254, 338 n 15
CKX-TV, Brandon, 156, 159
Steele, G.G.E., 155, 189, 201
Stirling, Geoffery, 53, 141, 203–14, 253, 337 n 3, 338 n 16

Thomas, Alan, 50, 189
Tory, J.S.D., 55, 298
Transport, Department of, role of, 15, 17–18, 45–46, 62, 145, 185–87, 196, 205, 225, 236, 246, 249, 255, 272, 279
Troika, 15, 20–24, 145, 147, 151, 232, 252, 266, 276, 284, 293, 304, 333 n 5

UHF channels, 187, 198–201, 203, 205, 211, 227, 242, 243, 251–53, 257

Waters, Alan, 157, 204, 208, 293
White Paper on Broadcasting, 1966, 15, 21, 25, 147–51, 164–65, 168, 175, 184–85, 188–89, 191, 197, 214, 225, 232, 241, 243, 252, 276, 282, 321 n 4